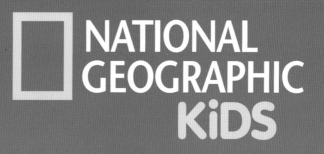

NATIONAL GEOGRAPHIC
KiDS

WORLD ATLAS

SIXTH EDITION

NATIONAL GEOGRAPHIC
WASHINGTON, D.C.

TABLE OF CONTENTS

North America: Mexican boy, page 60

South America: Llama, page 77

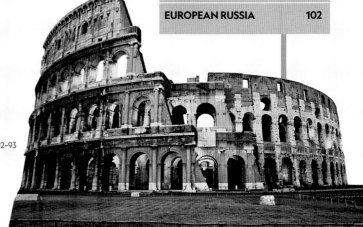

Europe: Colosseum, pages 92–93

Title page (left to right): tarsier, Philippines; Lower Yellowstone Falls, Wyoming, U.S.A; young boy, Brazil; Montreal skyline, Quebec, Canada; lion, African savanna; Guggenheim Museum, Bilbao, Spain; young girl, Gambia, Africa; fall foliage, U.S.A.

Antarctica: Penguins, page 160

Australia, New Zealand & Oceania: Maori man, page 150

Africa: Mother and child, page 133

Asia: Panda, page 108

How to Use This Atlas

This atlas is a window for exploring the world. To learn about maps, use the first section, Understanding Maps. Basic facts about Earth as a planet are presented in the section called Planet Earth. Maps in the Physical World section focus on different aspects of nature and the environment. The Political World section contains world maps about how humans live on the planet. In the pages that follow, the maps, photographs, and essays are arranged by continent and region. You can find details about specific countries in the Flags & Facts section beginning on page 176.

"YOU ARE HERE"
Locator globes help you see where one area is in relation to others. On regional pages (as shown here), the area covered by the main map is yellow on the globe, and its continent is green. On pages with continent maps, the locator globe shows the whole continent in yellow. The surrounding land is gray.

NORTHEASTERN SOUTH AMERICA

THE CONTINENT:
SOUTH AMERICA

Northeastern South America

THE BASICS
STATS
Largest country
Brazil
3,287,611 sq mi (8,514,877 sq km)
Smallest country
Suriname
63,251 sq mi (163,820 sq km)
Most populous country
Brazil 208,847,000
Least populous country
Suriname 598,000
Predominant languages
Portuguese, English, Dutch, Hindi
Predominant religions
Christianity, Hinduism, Islam
Highest GDP per capita
Brazil $15,600
Lowest GDP per capita
Guyana $8,200
Highest life expectancy
Brazil 74 years
Lowest life expectancy
Guyana 68 years

GEO WHIZ
Guyana's roughly 300 species of catfish are hunted for the international aquarium trade.

Brazil's Pantanal is the world's largest freshwater wetland.

Paramaribo, Suriname's capital, is a mix of Dutch, Hindu, Chinese, East Indian, and Javanese cultures. Dutch is the only official language.

⚽ GOAL! Fans of soccer cheer on the women from Brazil and Jamaica in the 2019 FIFA Women's World Cup in Grenoble, France.

Brazil dominates the region as well as the continent in size and population. It is the world's fifth largest country in area, and it is home to about half of South America's 430 million people. São Paulo and Rio de Janeiro are among the world's largest cities, and the country's vast agricultural lands make it a top global exporter of coffee, soybeans, beef, orange juice, and sugar. The Amazon rainforest, once a dense wilderness of unmatched biodiversity, is now threatened farmers, loggers, and miners. Lands colonized by the British, Dutch, and French make up sparsely settled Guyana and Suriname as well as French Guiana, a French overseas department. Formerly known as the Guianas, these lands are populated by people of African, South Asian, and European heritage.

VAST WATERSHED
The United States and South America are shown at the same scale.
Amazon Basin
SOUTH AMERICA
The Amazon River basin includes 2.4 million square miles (6.1 million sq km). It would cover much of the contiguous, or lower 48, U.S. states.

◐ NATIONAL RHYTHM. Samba, often called Brazil's national music, combines the music traditions of the country's populations—Amerindian, Portuguese, and African. Here, a samba band practices on Rio de Janeiro's Ipanema Beach.

STATS & FACTS
At the left-hand edge of each continent opener and regional page is a bar that includes basic information about the subject. This feature is a great first stop if you're writing a report.

CHARTS & GRAPHS
Each region includes a chart or graph that shows information visually.

ABOUT THE CONTINENT 92
more about
EUROPE
Europe

ABOUT THE CONTINENT 93
EUROPE

WHERE THE PICTURES ARE

WHERE ARE THE PICTURES?
If you want to know where a picture in a regional section of this atlas was taken, look for the map in the photo essay. Find the label that describes the picture you're curious about, and follow the line to its location.

Maps use symbols to represent political and physical features. At right is the key to the symbols used in this atlas. If you are wondering what you're looking at on a map, check here.

INDEX AND GRID

Look through the index for the place-name you want. Next to it is a page number in bold, a letter, and another number. Go to the page. Draw imaginary lines from the letter along the side of the map and the number along the top. Your place will be close to where the lines meet.

Boulia, Australia **155** C6
Bourke, Australia **155** E7
Boyoma Falls, Dem. Rep. of the
    Congo **143** E5
Brahmaputra (river), Asia **123** C7
Brăila, Romania **101** B7
Brasília, Brazil **83** E5

COLOR BARS

Every section of this atlas has its own color. Look for the color on the Table of Contents pages and across the top of every page in the atlas. Within that color bar, you'll see the name of the section and the title for each topic or map. These color bars are a handy way to find the section you want.

NORTHEASTERN SOUTH AMERICA

THE CONTINENT:
SOUTH AMERICA

❶ THE SIX-BANDED ARMADILLO, found throughout the dry grassland areas of the region, lives on plants and insects. Unlike others of its species, it remains active during the day.

Map Key
⊛ Country capital
•• City or town
····· Boundary
···· Claimed boundary

0   400 miles
0   400 kilometers
Azimuthal Equidistant Projection

VENEZUELA · Georgetown · Paramaribo
GUYANA · SURINAME · French Guiana (France) · Cayenne
COLOMBIA · Boa Vista
ATLANTIC OCEAN
Boundary claimed by Venezuela · Boundary claimed by Suriname · Macapá
EQUATOR · Pico da Neblina 9,820 ft 2,995 m
AMAZON BASIN · Manaus · Tefé · Coari · Marajó Island · Belém · São Luís · Parnaíba · Altamira · Paragominas · Tucuruí · Codó · Caxias · Sobral · Fortaleza
Cruzeiro do Sul · Porto Velho · Ariquemes · Ji-Paraná · Marabá · Imperatriz · Teresina · Crato · Natal
Rio Branco · BRAZIL · Araguaína · Palmas · Petrolina · Olinda · João Pessoa · Recife · Jaboatão
PERU · BOLIVIA · Gurupi · Alvorado · Barreiras · Feira de Santana · Arapiraca · Maceió · Aracaju · Alagoinhas
Várzea Grande · Cuiabá · Rondonópolis · Brasília · Vitória da Conquista · Ilhéus · Salvador (Bahia)
BRAZILIAN HIGHLANDS · Goiânia · Anápolis · Teófilo Otoni · Governador Valadares · Linhares
CHILE · Campo Grande · São José do Rio Preto · Uberlândia · Belo Horizonte · Ribeirão Preto · Juiz de Fora · Vitória · Vila Velha · Niterói
PARAGUAY · São José dos Campos · Nova Iguaçu · Duque de Caxias · Rio de Janeiro · Guaratinguetá
TROPIC OF CAPRICORN · Londrina · São Paulo · Santo André · Santos · Paranaguá
ARGENTINA · Curitiba · Joinville · Florianópolis
Caxias do Sul · Santa Maria · Criciúma · Canoas · Novo Hamburgo · Porto Alegre · Pelotas
URUGUAY

❶ BAUXITE TO ALUMINUM. By exploiting rich deposits of bauxite, the ore from which aluminum is made, and inexpensive hydropower, Suriname produces aluminum ingots, such as these headed for global markets.

North America
South America
Europe
Asia
Africa
Australia, New Zealand & Oceania
Antarctica

BAR SCALE

To find out how far on Earth's surface it is from one place on a map to another, use the scale. A bar scale appears on every map. It shows how distance on paper relates to distance in the real world.

MAP KEY

••• City or town	★ Pole	⟋⟍ Waterfall	Dry salt lake
⊛ Country capital	791 ft 241 m + Mountain peak with elevation above sea level	⟋ Dam	Glacier
⊚ Dependency, state, provincial or territorial capital	-282 ft -86 m • Low point with elevation below sea level	Canal	Swamp
⊛ Capital of Northern Ireland, Scotland, or Wales		⟋⟍ Ice shelf	Sand
◎ Other capital	····· Defined boundary	Reef	Tundra
◆ Small country	··· ·· Disputed or undefined boundary	Lake	Lava
∴ Ruin	····· Claimed boundary	Intermittent lake	Below sea level
■ Point of interest	⟋ River		

Exploring Your World

Earth is a big place. Even from space you can't see it all at one time. But with a map you can see the whole world—or just a part of it. Thanks to the internet, you can experience Earth from space, pick a place you want to explore, and zoom closer and closer until you are "standing" right there! These screenshots (right) take you from London to space at the click of a mouse. You can even find a satellite view of your neighborhood (box below).

Compare the computer-enhanced satellite images with the maps on the opposite page. You will see how the same places can be shown in very different ways.

FIND YOUR HOUSE

This image shows the offices of National Geographic in Washington, D.C. To see where you live, go to **showmystreet.com,** one of several websites that allow you to view satellite imagery of the world.

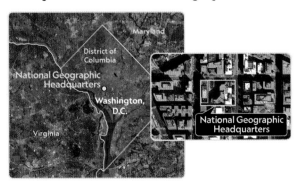

COMPUTER ENHANCED VIEWS OF ...

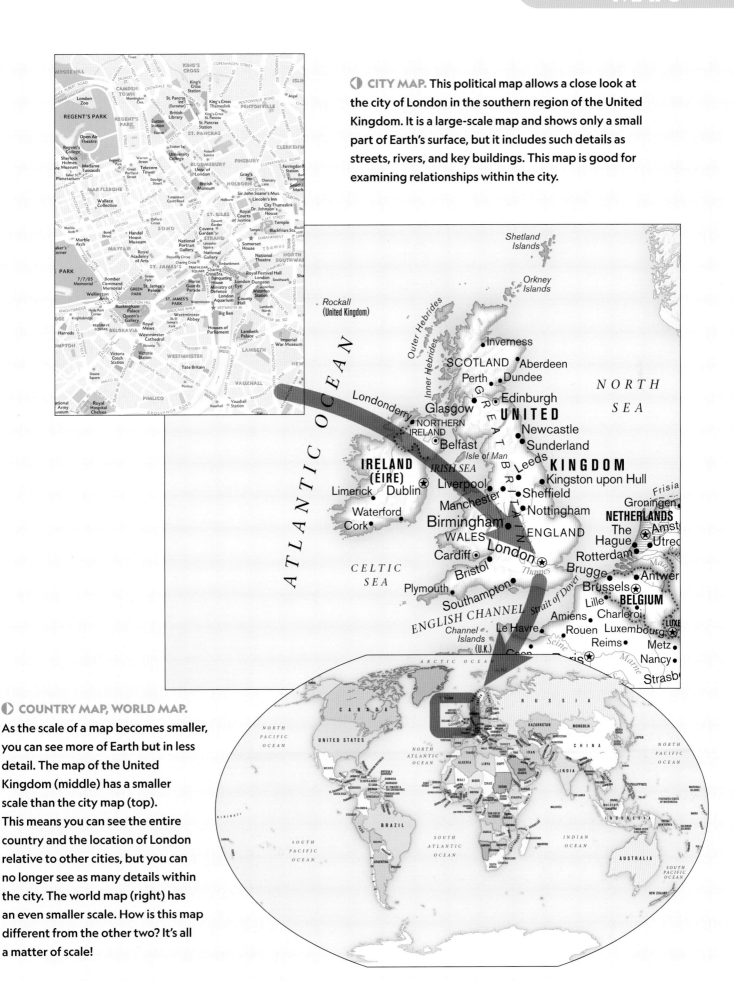

◗ **CITY MAP.** This political map allows a close look at the city of London in the southern region of the United Kingdom. It is a large-scale map and shows only a small part of Earth's surface, but it includes such details as streets, rivers, and key buildings. This map is good for examining relationships within the city.

◗ **COUNTRY MAP, WORLD MAP.**

As the scale of a map becomes smaller, you can see more of Earth but in less detail. The map of the United Kingdom (middle) has a smaller scale than the city map (top). This means you can see the entire country and the location of London relative to other cities, but you can no longer see as many details within the city. The world map (right) has an even smaller scale. How is this map different from the other two? It's all a matter of scale!

UNDERSTANDING MAPS

Kinds of Maps

Maps are special tools that tell a story about Earth. Some maps show physical features, such as mountains or vegetation. Other maps illustrate different human features on Earth—political boundaries, urban centers, and economic systems.

Maps are not perfect. A globe is a scale model of Earth with accurate relative sizes and locations. Because maps are flat, they involve distortions of size, shape, and direction. Also, cartographers—people who create maps—make choices about what information to include. Because of this, it is important to study many different types of maps to learn the complete story of Earth.

PHYSICAL MAPS. Earth's natural features—landforms, water bodies, and vegetation—are shown on physical maps. The map above uses color and shading to illustrate mountains, lakes, rivers, and deserts in western Africa. Country names and borders are added for reference, but they are not natural features.

MAP PROJECTIONS. To create a map, cartographers transfer an image of the round Earth onto a flat surface, a process called projection. Some types of projection include cylindrical, conic, azimuthal, and interrupted. Each has certain advantages, but all have some distortions. The world maps in the thematic section of this atlas are a projection called Winkel Tripel (shown above), a compromise projection that moderates size and shape distortions. As you use this atlas, look for different map projections on the regional maps, identified below the scale bar.

MAKING MAPS

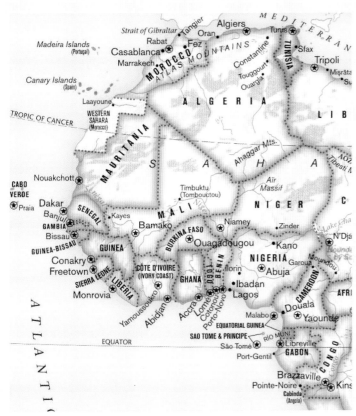

◯ **POLITICAL MAPS.** These maps represent human characteristics of the landscape, such as boundaries, cities, and other place-names. Natural features are added only for reference. On the map above, capital cities are represented with a star inside a circle, while other cities are shown as black dots.

◯ **THEMATIC MAPS.** Patterns related to a particular topic, or theme, such as population distribution, appear on these maps. The map above displays a region's climate zones, which range from tropical wet (bright green) to tropical wet and dry (light green) to semiarid (dark yellow) to arid (light yellow).

Long ago, cartographers worked with pen and ink, carefully handcrafting maps based on explorers' observations and diaries. Today, mapmaking is a high-tech business. Cartographers use Earth data stored in "layers" in a geographic information system (GIS) and special computer programs to create maps that can be easily updated as new information becomes available. These cartographers are making changes to a map in another National Geographic Kids atlas.

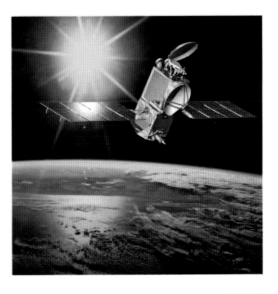

Satellites in orbit around Earth act as eyes in the sky, recording data about the planet's land and ocean areas. The data are converted to numbers that are transmitted back to computers that are specially programmed to interpret the data. They record the data in a form that cartographers can use to create maps.

UNDERSTANDING MAPS

How to Read a Map

Every map has a story to tell, but first you have to know how to read the map.

Maps are useful for finding places because every place on Earth has a special address called its absolute location. Imaginary lines, called latitude and longitude, create a grid that makes finding places easy because every spot on Earth has a unique latitude and longitude. In addition, special tools, making use of the Global Positioning System (GPS), communicate with orbiting satellites to determine absolute location.

Maps are also useful for determining distance and direction. The map scale shows the relationship between distance on the map and actual distance on Earth. Since north is not always at the top of every map, a compass rose or arrow is used to indicate direction.

Maps represent other information by using a language of symbols. To find out what each symbol means, you must use the map key. Think of this key as your secret decoder, identifying information represented by each symbol on the map.

◗ **LATITUDE AND LONGITUDE.** Lines of latitude run west to east parallel to the Equator. They measure distance in degrees from 0° latitude (Equator) to 90°N (North Pole) or to 90°S (South Pole). Lines of longitude run north to south and measure distance in degrees east or west from 0° longitude (prime meridian) to 180° longitude. The prime meridian runs through Greenwich, England.

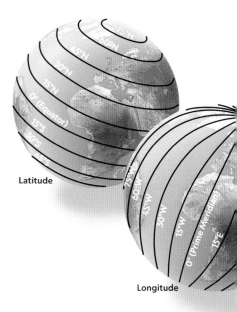

Latitude

Longitude

◗ **ABSOLUTE LOCATION.** The imaginary grid composed of lines of latitude and longitude helps us locate places on a map. Suppose you are playing a game of global scavenger hunt. The prize is hidden at absolute location 30°S, 60°W. On the map at right, look south of the Equator to find the line of latitude labeled 30°S and west of 0° longitude to find the line of longitude labeled 60°W. Trace these lines with your fingers until they meet (arrow at right). The prize must be located in central Argentina.

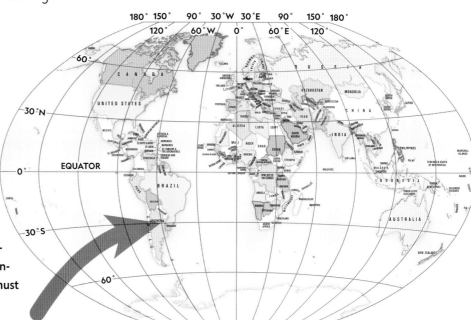

UNDERSTANDING MAPS

90°N (North Pole)

SYMBOLS

Points, lines, and areas are the three main types of map symbols. Points, which can be either dots or small icons, represent the location or the number of things, such as cities or landmarks. Lines are used to show boundaries, roads, or rivers and can vary in color and thickness. Area symbols use patterns or color to show regions, such as a sandy area or a neighborhood.

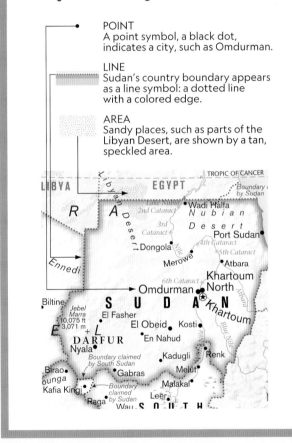

POINT
A point symbol, a black dot, indicates a city, such as Omdurman.

LINE
Sudan's country boundary appears as a line symbol: a dotted line with a colored edge.

AREA
Sandy places, such as parts of the Libyan Desert, are shown by a tan, speckled area.

SCALE & DIRECTION

The scale on a map can be shown as a fraction, as words, or as a line or bar. It relates distance on the map to distance in the real world. Sometimes the type of map projection is named below the scale. A map may include an arrow or compass rose to indicate north on the map. Maps in this atlas are oriented north, so they do not use a north indicator.

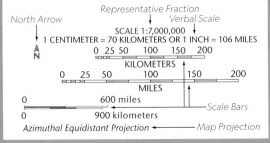

Representative Fraction
North Arrow   *Verbal Scale*
SCALE 1:7,000,000
1 CENTIMETER = 70 KILOMETERS OR 1 INCH = 106 MILES
0 25 50 100 150 200
KILOMETERS
0 25 50 100 150 200
MILES
0   600 miles
0   900 kilometers   *Scale Bars*
Azimuthal Equidistant Projection ←   *Map Projection*

◐ APPLYING WHAT YOU'VE LEARNED. Now that you know how to read a map, can you find Sapporo in the eastern Asian country of Japan? The index for this atlas says Sapporo is on page 117 B10. Go to page 117, place one finger on the B at the side of the map and another finger on the 10 at the top. Now trace straight across from the B and down from the 10. Sapporo is near where your fingers meet!

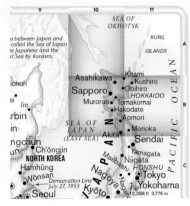

PLANET EARTH

Earth in Space

Earth is part of a cosmic family called the solar system. It is one of the planets that revolves around a giant solar nuclear reactor that we call the sun.

The extreme heat and pressure on the sun cause atoms of hydrogen to combine in a process called fusion, producing new atoms of helium and releasing tremendous amounts of energy. This energy makes life on Earth possible.

Time on Earth is defined by our relationship to the sun. It takes Earth, following a path called an orbit, approximately 365 days—one year—to make one full revolution around the sun. As Earth makes its way around the sun, it also turns on its axis, an imaginary line that passes between the North and South Poles. This motion, called rotation, occurs once every 24 hours and results in day and night.

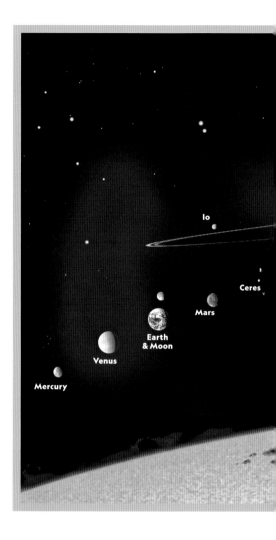

◖ TIME ZONES. Long ago, when people lived in relative isolation, they measured time by the position of the sun. That meant that noon in one place was not the same as noon in a place 100 miles (160 km) to the west. Later, with the development of long-distance railroads, people needed to coordinate time. In 1884, a system of 24 standard time zones was adopted. Each time zone reflects the fact that Earth rotates west to east 15 degrees each hour. Time is counted from the prime meridian (0° longitude).

Callisto

Titan

Triton

Jupiter

Saturn

Uranus

Charon

Haumea

Neptune

Pluto

Makemake

Eris

Note: Art shows relative sizes of the sun and planets, but distances are not to scale.

SOLAR SYSTEM. The sun and its family of planets are located near the outer edge of the Milky Way, a giant spiral galaxy. Earth is the third planet from the sun and one of the four "terrestrial" planets. These planets—Mercury, Venus, Earth, and Mars—are made up of solid rocky material. Beyond these inner planets are the two gas giants, Jupiter and Saturn, and the two ice giants, Uranus and Neptune. Astronomers— scientists who study space—created a category called "dwarf" planets that includes Pluto, Ceres, Eris, Haumea, and Makemake. Astronomers continue to find more possible dwarf planets. Many planets, including Earth, have one or more moons orbiting them. The art above names a few: Io, Callisto, Titan, Triton, and Charon.

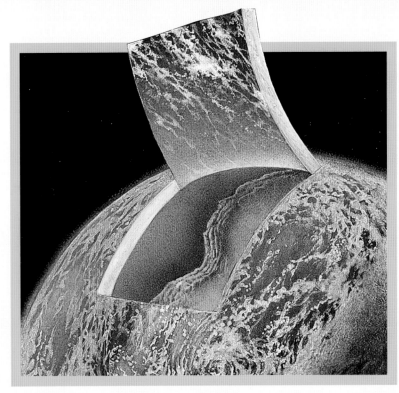

ENVELOPE OF AIR. Earth is enclosed within a thick layer of air called the atmosphere. Made up of a mixture of nitrogen, oxygen, and other gases, the atmosphere provides us with the life-giving air that we breathe. It also protects us from dangerous radiation from the sun. Weather systems move through the atmosphere, redistributing heat and moisture and creating Earth's climates.

PLANET EARTH

Earth in Motion

If we could step into a time machine and travel 240 million years into the past, we probably would not recognize Earth. Back then, most of the landmasses we call continents were joined together in a single giant landmass called Pangaea (below). So how did the continents break away from Pangaea and move to their current positions? The answer lies in a process called plate tectonics. These maps and diagrams tell the story.

🌀 **A LOOK WITHIN.** Earth's crust is a thin shell of solid rock that covers the partially molten rock of the mantle (upper and lower). Currents of heat rising and falling within the mantle break the crust into large pieces called plates. As plates creep across Earth's surface, they reshape its features. Major plates appear on the map at right. Earthquakes and volcanoes are most frequent where plates collide or grind past each other.

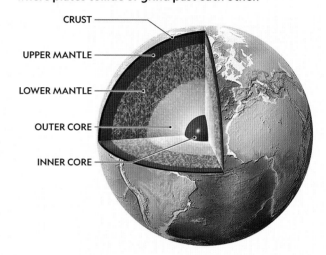

CRUST
UPPER MANTLE
LOWER MANTLE
OUTER CORE
INNER CORE

CONTINENTS ON THE MOVE

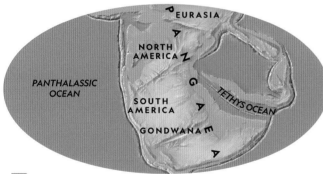

1 PANGAEA. About 240 million years ago, Earth's landmasses were joined together in one supercontinent—Pangaea—that extended from pole to pole.

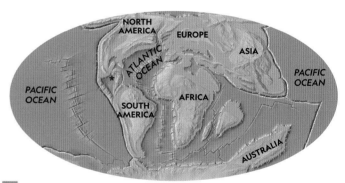

3 EXTINCTION. About 66 million years ago, an asteroid smashed into Earth (red * on map), leading to the extinction of half of all species, including the dinosaurs—one of several major extinctions.

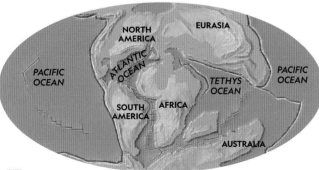

2 BREAKUP. By 94 million years ago, Pangaea had broken into what would become today's continents. Dinosaurs roamed Earth during this period of warmer climates.

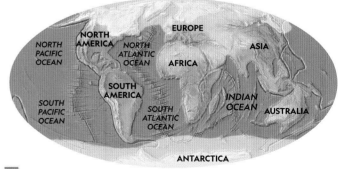

4 ICE AGE. By 18,000 years ago, the continents had drifted close to their present positions, but most far northern and far southern lands were buried beneath huge glaciers.

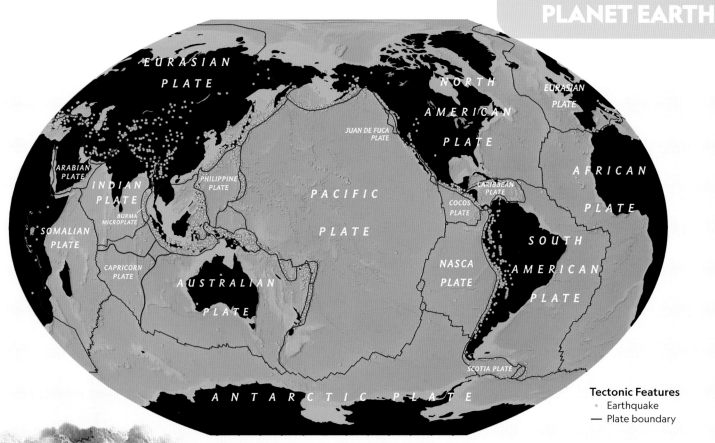

Tectonic Features
- Earthquake
— Plate boundary

Earth Shapers

Earth's features are constantly undergoing change—being built up, destroyed, or just rearranged. Plates are in constant, very slow motion. Some plates collide, others pull apart, and still others slowly grind past each other. As the plates move, mountains are uplifted, volcanoes erupt, and new land is created.

◯ VOLCANOES form when molten rock, called magma, rises to Earth's surface. Some volcanoes occur as one plate pushes beneath another plate. Other volcanoes result when a plate passes over a column of magma, called a hot spot, rising from the mantle.

◯ SUBDUCTION occurs when an oceanic plate dives under a continental plate. This often results in volcanoes and earthquakes, as well as mountain building.

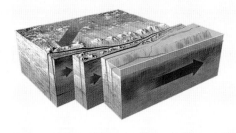

◯ FAULTING happens when two plates grind past each other, creating large cracks along the edges of the plates. A famous fault is the San Andreas, in California, U.S.A., where the Pacific and North American plates meet, causing damaging earthquakes.

◯ SPREADING results when oceanic plates move apart. The ocean floor cracks, magma rises, and new crust is created. The Mid-Atlantic Ridge spreads a few centimeters—about an inch—a year, pushing Europe and North America farther apart.

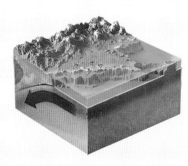

◯ COLLISION of two continental plates causes plate edges to break and fold, creating mountains, Earth's highest landforms. The Himalaya are the result of the Indian plate colliding with the Eurasian plate, an ongoing process that began 50 million years ago.

The Physical World

Earth is dominated by large landmasses called continents—seven in all—and by an interconnected global ocean that is divided into four parts by the continents. More than 70 percent of Earth's surface is covered by water. Land areas cover the remaining 30 percent.

Different landforms give variety to the surface of the continents. The Rockies and Andes mark the western edge of North and South America, and the Himalaya tower above southern Asia. The Plateau of Tibet forms the rugged core of Asia, while the Northern European Plain extends from the North Sea to the Ural Mountains. Much of Africa is a plateau, and dry plains cover large areas of Australia. In Antarctica, mountains rise more than 16,000 feet (4,877 m) beneath massive ice sheets.

Mountains and trenches make the ocean floors as varied as the surface of any continent (see page 166). The Mid-Atlantic Ridge runs the length of the Atlantic Ocean. In the western Pacific Ocean, trenches drop to depths greater than 36,000 feet (10,972 m).

○ **LAND AND WATER.** This world physical map shows Earth's seven continents—North America, South America, Europe, Africa, Asia, Australia, and Antarctica—as well as the four oceans: Pacific, Atlantic, Indian, and Arctic. Some people regard the area from Antarctica to 60°S, where the oceans merge, as a fifth ocean called the Southern Ocean.

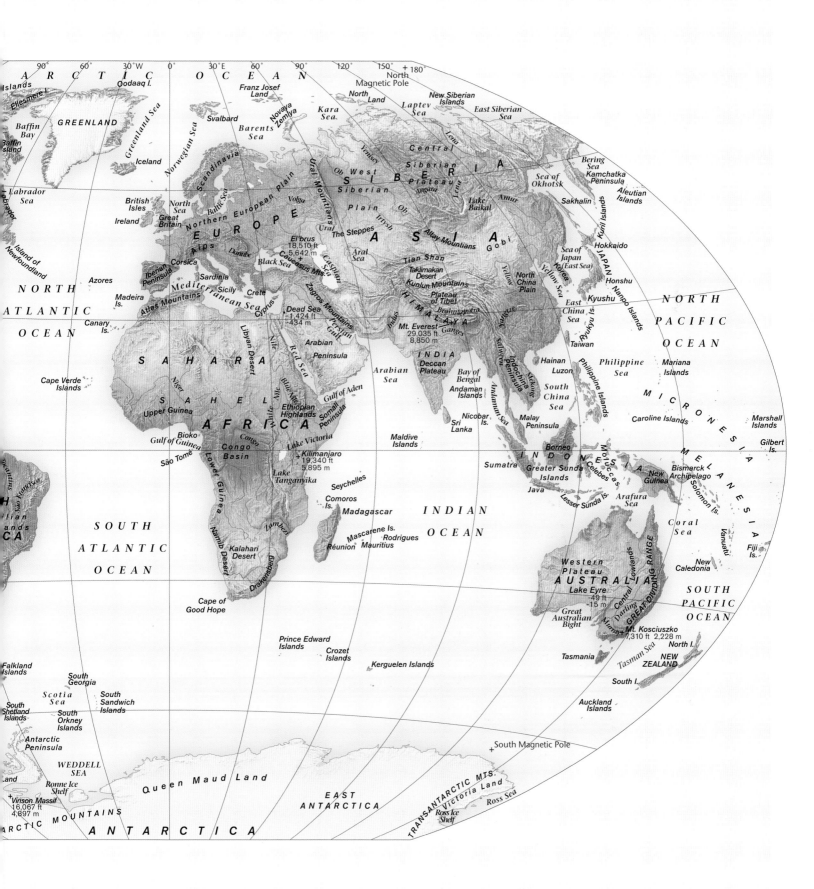

ARCTIC OCEAN

Islands
Ellesmere I.
Oodaaq I.
Franz Josef Land
North Land
North Magnetic Pole
New Siberian Islands
East Siberian Sea

GREENLAND
Baffin Bay
Baffin Island
Iceland
Greenland Sea
Norwegian Sea
Svalbard
Novaya Zemlya
Barents Sea
Kara Sea
Laptev Sea
Bering Sea
Kamchatka Peninsula
Aleutian Islands

Labrador Sea
Labrador
British Isles
Ireland
Great Britain
North Sea
Baltic Sea
Scandinavia
Northern European Plain
Ural Mountains
Ob
West Siberian Plateau
Lena
Central Siberian
SIBERIA
Angara
Ob
Yenisey
ASIA
Lake Baikal
Amur
Sea of Okhotsk
Sakhalin
Kuril Islands
Hokkaido
JAPAN
Honshu

Island of Newfoundland

NORTH ATLANTIC OCEAN

EUROPE
Alps
Iberian Peninsula
Corsica
Sardinia
Sicily
Crete
Cyprus
Danube
Black Sea
Volga
El'brus 18,510 ft 5,642 m
Caucasus Mts.
Caspian Sea
Aral Sea
Ural
The Steppes
Irtysh
West Siberian Plain
Ob
Altay Mountains
Gobi
Tian Shan
Taklimakan Desert
Kunlun Mountains
Plateau of Tibet
Yellow
North China Plain
Yellow Sea
East China Sea
Sea of Japan (East Sea)
Korea
Kyushu
Nampo Islands
Ryukyu Is.
Taiwan

Azores
Madeira Is.
Canary Is.
Cape Verde Islands
Atlas Mountains
Mediterranean Sea
Libyan Desert
Nile
Red Sea
Arabian Peninsula
Dead Sea -1,424 ft -434 m
Zagros Mountains
Persian Gulf
Gulf of Aden
Indus
Mt. Everest 29,035 ft 8,850 m
HIMALAYA
Ganges
Brahmaputra
Salween
Mekong
Indochina Peninsula
Hainan
Luzon
South China Sea
Philippine Islands
Philippine Sea
Mariana Islands

NORTH PACIFIC OCEAN

MICRONESIA

SAHARA
SAHEL
Upper Guinea
AFRICA
Niger
Bioko
Gulf of Guinea
São Tomé
Congo
Congo Basin
Lower Guinea
Blue Nile
White Nile
Ethiopian Highlands
Somali Peninsula
Lake Victoria
Kilimanjaro 19,340 ft 5,895 m
Lake Tanganyika
Arabian Sea
INDIA
Deccan Plateau
Bay of Bengal
Andaman Islands
Sri Lanka
Nicobar Is.
Andaman Sea
Malay Peninsula
Maldive Islands
Sumatra
Greater Sunda Islands
Java
INDONESIA
Celebes
Moluccas
Lesser Sunda Is.
Borneo
New Guinea
Arafura Sea
Bismarck Archipelago
Solomon Is.
MELANESIA
Caroline Islands
Marshall Islands
Gilbert Is.

SOUTH ATLANTIC OCEAN

SOUTH AMERICA
Brazilian Highlands

Zambezi
Namib Desert
Kalahari Desert
Drakensberg
Cape of Good Hope
Madagascar
Comoros Is.
Seychelles
Mascarene Is.
Rodrigues
Réunion
Mauritius
INDIAN OCEAN

Western Plateau
AUSTRALIA
Lake Eyre -49 ft -15 m
Central Lowlands
Darling
Murray
GREAT DIVIDING RANGE
Great Australian Bight
Mt. Kosciuszko 7,310 ft 2,228 m
North I.
NEW ZEALAND
Tasmania
Tasman Sea
South I.
Coral Sea
New Caledonia
Vanuatu
Fiji Is.

SOUTH PACIFIC OCEAN

Falkland Islands
South Georgia
Scotia Sea
South Sandwich Islands
South Shetland Islands
South Orkney Islands
Antarctic Peninsula
Prince Edward Islands
Crozet Islands
Kerguelen Islands
Auckland Islands

WEDDELL SEA
Ronne Ice Shelf
Vinson Massif 16,067 ft 4,897 m
ANTARCTIC MOUNTAINS
ANTARCTICA
Queen Maud Land
EAST ANTARCTICA
South Magnetic Pole
TRANSANTARCTIC MTS.
Victoria Land
Ross Ice Shelf
Ross Sea

The Land

A closer look at Earth's surface reveals many varied forms and features that make each place unique. This drawing of an imaginary landscape captures 41 natural and human-made features and shows how they relate to each other. For example, a large moving "river" of ice (called a glacier) descends from a high mountain range, and a harbor, built by people, creates safe anchorage for ships.

Such features can be found all over the world because the same forces are at work around the globe. Volcanoes and movement of the plates of Earth's crust are constantly creating and building up new landforms, while external forces such as wind, water, and ice continuously wear down surface features.

Earth is dynamic—constantly changing, never the same.

ARCHIPELAGO

Groupings of islands are known as archipelagos. Above, the tropical islands in Ang Thong National Marine Park create an archipelago in Thailand.

CANYON

Steep-sided valleys called canyons are created mainly by running water. Buckskin Gulch (above) is the deepest slot canyon in the American Southwest.

ICEBERG

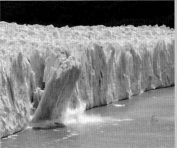

Icebergs are formed by chunks of ice that break from glaciers into a body of water. Above, a large piece of ice breaks from the Perito Moreno Glacier in Argentina.

OASIS

Occasionally, water rises from deep below a desert, creating an oasis—a fertile area that supports trees and sometimes crops—such as this one in the Sahara desert in Africa.

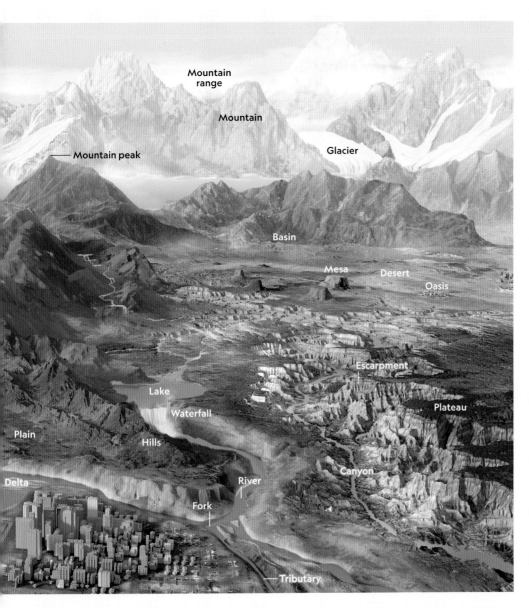

Mountain range

Mountain

Mountain peak

Glacier

Basin

Mesa

Desert

Oasis

Escarpment

Lake

Waterfall

Plateau

Plain

Hills

Delta

Canyon

River

Fork

Tributary

A NAME FOR EVERY FEATURE.

Land has a vocabulary all its own, each name identifying a specific feature of the landscape. A cape, for example, is a broad chunk of land extending out into the sea. It is not pointed, however, because then it would be a point. Nor does it have a narrow neck. A sizable cape or point with a narrow neck is a peninsula. The narrow neck is an isthmus. Such specific identifiers have proven useful over the centuries. In the early days of exploration, even the simplest maps showed peninsulas, bays, and straits. Sailors used these landmarks to reach safe harbor or to avoid disasters, such as breaking up on a reef.

◑ **EXPLORING THE LANDSCAPE.**

How many of these landscape features have you seen where you live or in your travels to other places?

ISTHMUS

An isthmus, like the one above in Costa Rica, is a narrow piece of land connecting two larger pieces of land. The isthmus at San Juanillo Beach combines two beaches.

GLACIER

Glaciers, such as the Kaskawulsh Glacier in Yukon, Canada (above), move slowly from mountains to the sea. Climate change is causing them to melt.

MESA

A mesa is a flat-topped hill or mountain. The word "mesa" comes from the Spanish word for table. This is a mesa in the Table Mountains in Namibia, Africa.

STRAIT

The coast of the island of Lošinj, Croatia, creates a strait. A strait is a narrow area of water that connects two larger bodies of water.

PHYSICAL WORLD

World Climate

Weather is the condition of the atmosphere—temperature, precipitation, humidity, wind—at a given place at a given time. Climate, however, is the average weather for a particular place over a long period of time. Climate is not a random occurrence. It is a pattern that is controlled by factors such as latitude, elevation, prevailing winds, temperature of ocean currents, and location on land relative to water. Climate is generally constant, but many people are concerned that human activity is causing a change in climate patterns.

THE BASICS

According to the National Oceanic and Atmospheric Administration (NOAA), 2020 was the second warmest year on record over the last 141 years. The 2020 global annual temperature for combined land and ocean surfaces was 1.8°F (.98°C) warmer than the 20th-century average.

Ice cores taken from Antarctica and Greenland allow scientists to gain detailed information about the history of Earth's climate and its atmosphere—especially the presence of greenhouse gases—dating back thousands of years.

According to climatologists—people who study climate—Earth experienced what is called the Little Ice Age, which lasted from the 17th century to the late 19th century. During that time, temperatures were cold enough to cause glaciers to advance.

CLIMATE GRAPHS. Temperature and precipitation data provide a snapshot of the climate of a particular place. This information can be shown in a climate graph, or climograph (below). Average monthly temperatures (scale on the left side of the graphs) are represented by the lines at the tops of the colored areas, while average monthly precipitation totals (scale on the right side of the graphs) are reflected in the bars. For example, the graph for Belém, Brazil, shows a constant warm temperature of about 80°F (27°C) with abundant rainfall year-round. In contrast, the graph for Fairbanks, Alaska, shows a cool, variable temperature with only limited precipitation.

Map labels: Fairbanks, ROCKY MOUNTAINS, NORTH AMERICA, Des Moines, Subarctic Current, North Pacific Drift, California Current, Gulf Stream, North Pacific Drift, Hawaiian Islands, Monterrey, Gulf of Mexico, North, North Equatorial Current, PACIFIC OCEAN, Equatorial Countercurrent, EQUATOR, AMAZONIA, South Equatorial Current, Peru Current, ANDES, SO AME

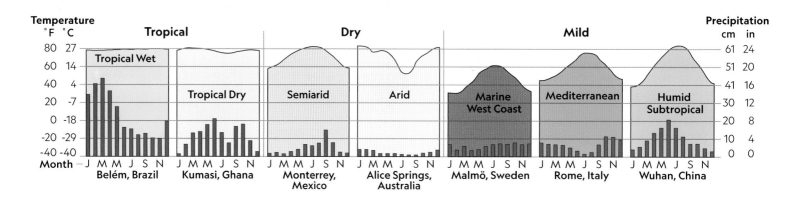

Climographs: Temperature °F °C (left axis: 80/27, 60/14, 40/4, 20/-7, 0/-18, -20/-29, -40/-40); Precipitation cm in (right axis: 61/24, 51/20, 41/16, 30/12, 20/8, 10/4, 0/0); Month (J M M J S N)

Tropical — Tropical Wet (Belém, Brazil); Tropical Dry (Kumasi, Ghana)

Dry — Semiarid (Monterrey, Mexico); Arid (Alice Springs, Australia)

Mild — Marine West Coast (Malmö, Sweden); Mediterranean (Rome, Italy); Humid Subtropical (Wuhan, China)

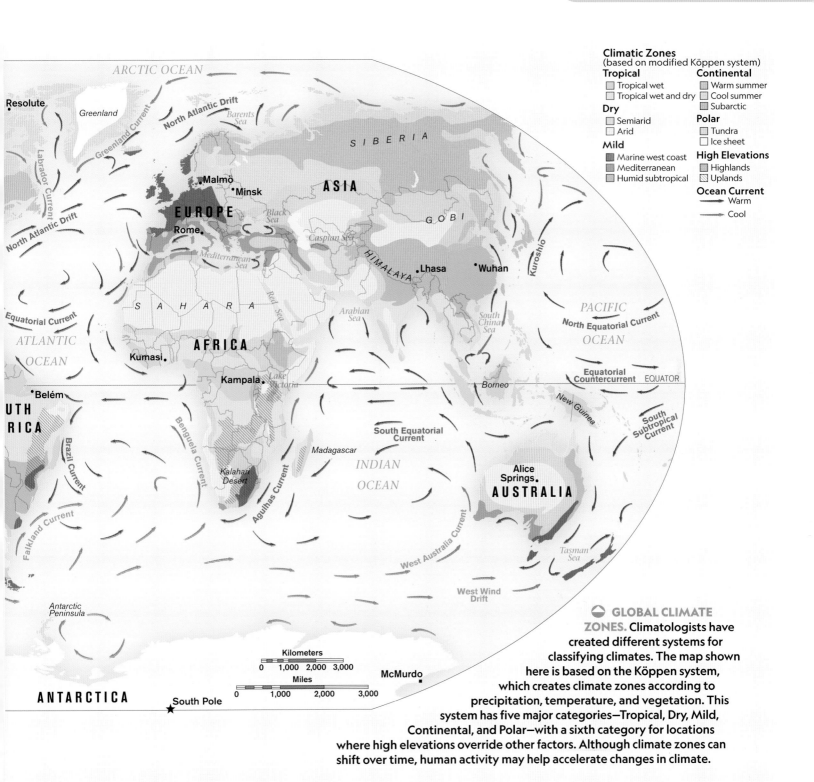

Climatic Zones
(based on modified Köppen system)

Tropical
- Tropical wet
- Tropical wet and dry

Dry
- Semiarid
- Arid

Mild
- Marine west coast
- Mediterranean
- Humid subtropical

Continental
- Warm summer
- Cool summer
- Subarctic

Polar
- Tundra
- Ice sheet

High Elevations
- Highlands
- Uplands

Ocean Current
→ Warm
→ Cool

GLOBAL CLIMATE ZONES. Climatologists have created different systems for classifying climates. The map shown here is based on the Köppen system, which creates climate zones according to precipitation, temperature, and vegetation. This system has five major categories—Tropical, Dry, Mild, Continental, and Polar—with a sixth category for locations where high elevations override other factors. Although climate zones can shift over time, human activity may help accelerate changes in climate.

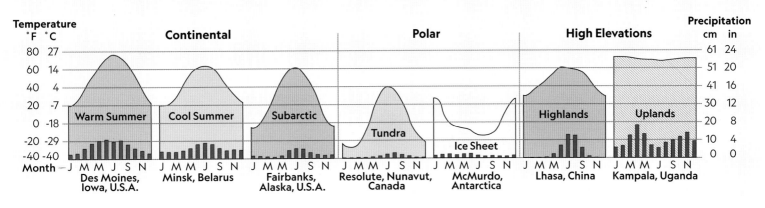

Temperature °F °C — Continental — Polar — High Elevations — Precipitation cm in

Warm Summer	Cool Summer	Subarctic	Tundra	Ice Sheet	Highlands	Uplands
Des Moines, Iowa, U.S.A.	Minsk, Belarus	Fairbanks, Alaska, U.S.A.	Resolute, Nunavut, Canada	McMurdo, Antarctica	Lhasa, China	Kampala, Uganda

Month — J M M J S N

Temperature scale: 80/27, 60/14, 40/4, 20/-7, 0/-18, -20/-29, -40/-40

Precipitation scale: 61/24, 51/20, 41/16, 30/12, 20/8, 10/4, 0/0

PHYSICAL WORLD

Factors Influencing Climate

Earth's climate is a bit like a big jigsaw puzzle. To understand it, you need to fit all the pieces together, because climate is influenced by a number of different, but interrelated factors. These include latitude, topography (shape of the land), elevation above sea level, wind systems, ocean currents, and distance from large bodies of water. Climate has always affected the way we live, but pollution from industries and motor vehicles is changing Earth's climate.

TOPOGRAPHY. Mountain ranges are natural barriers to the movement of air. In North America, prevailing westerly winds carry air full of moisture from the Pacific Ocean to the West Coast. As air rises over the Coast Ranges, light precipitation falls. Farther inland, the much taller Sierra Nevada range triggers heavy precipitation as air rises higher. On the leeward side of the Sierra Nevada, sinking air warms, water evaporates, and dry "rain shadow" conditions prevail. As winds continue across the interior plateau, the air remains dry because there is no significant source of moisture.

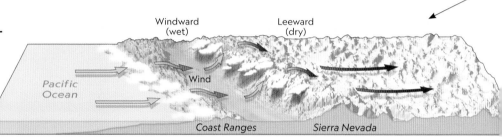

Temperature changes as air moves over mountains

PROXIMITY TO WATER. The distance a location is from water can affect the climate in that location. Using Australia as an example, look at the climographs on the left of the map below. The line graph represents temperature and the bar graph represents precipitation. Gladstone, which is near the coast, receives more precipitation than Alice Springs. Notice that Alice Springs and Longreach are farther from the coast, and both locations have larger differences between the winter and summer temperatures. Locations near large bodies of water tend to be more moderate in their temperature differences between seasons.

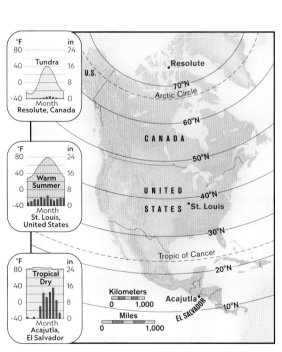

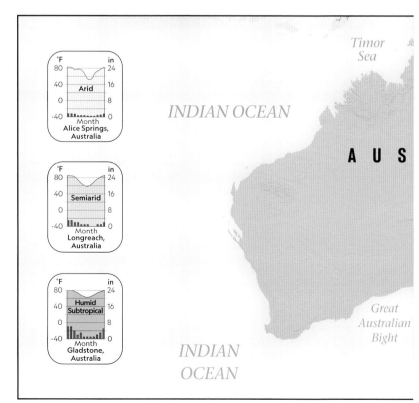

LATITUDE. Energy from the sun drives global climates. Latitude—distance north or south of the Equator—affects the amount of solar energy received. Places near the Equator (e.g., Acajutla, El Salvador, above) have warm temperatures year-round. As distance from the Equator increases (St. Louis, U.S.A., and Resolute, Canada, above), average temperatures decline, and cold winters become more pronounced.

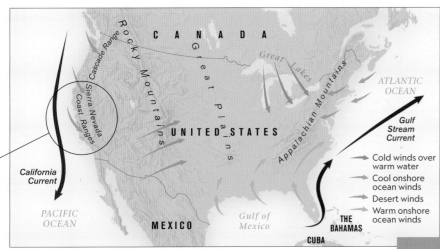

⬤ DIGGING OUT. Arctic winds roar across Canada, picking up moisture from the Great Lakes (purple arrows on map, left). As the moist air crosses over the frozen land, temperatures fall and heavy precipitation—called lake effect snow—occurs, burying cars and roads, as shown here in Oswego, New York, U.S.A.

⬤ WARM CURRENT.
The Gulf Stream, a warm ocean current averaging 50–93 miles (80–150 km) wide, sweeps up the East Coast of North America (red arrow on map above). One branch continues across the North Atlantic Ocean and above the Arctic Circle (map, page 23). In the color-enhanced satellite image (left), the Gulf Stream looks like a dark red river moving up the coast. This "river" of warm water influences climate along its path, bringing moisture and mild temperatures to the East Coast of the United States and causing ice-free ports above the Arctic Circle in Europe.

CLIMATE CHANGE

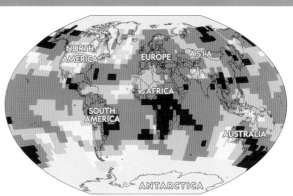

Land & Ocean Temperature Averages (January–July 2019)

No data | Cooler than average | Near average | Warmer than average | Much warmer than average | Record warmest

Earth's climate history is a story of change, with warm periods followed by periods of bitter cold. The early part of the 21st century has seen some of the warmest temperatures ever recorded (map, above). This warming trend is related to human activity and poses many risks to people, including rising sea levels. As average temperatures rise, glaciers melt and ocean waters expand, causing sea levels to rise and flood coastal areas, indicated by the red areas in Florida (below, right).

Current

By 2100

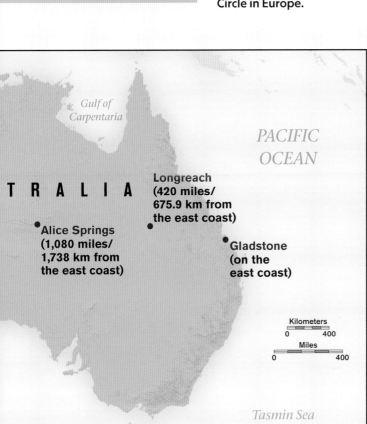

Gulf of Carpentaria

PACIFIC OCEAN

T R A L I A

Longreach (420 miles/ 675.9 km from the east coast)

●Alice Springs (1,080 miles/ 1,738 km from the east coast)

●Gladstone (on the east coast)

Kilometers
0   400

Miles
0   400

Tasmin Sea

World Vegetation

Natural vegetation—plants that would grow under ideal conditions at a particular place—depends on several factors. The quality and type of soil and climate are key. In fact, vegetation often reflects patterns of climate. (Compare the vegetation map at right with the world climate map on pages 22–23.) Forests thrive in places with ample precipitation; grasses are found where there is less precipitation or only seasonal rainfall; and xerophytes—plants able to survive lengthy periods with little or no water—are found in arid areas that receive very little annual precipitation.

NORTH AMERICA

ATLANTIC OCEAN

PACIFIC OCEAN

SOUTH AMERICA

Kilometers
0   1,000 2,000 3,000

Miles
0   1,000   2,000   3,000

TUNDRA

With only two to three months of above-freezing temperatures, tundra plants are mostly dwarf shrubs, short grasses, mosses, and lichens (above). Much of Russia's Arctic Circle region has tundra vegetation, which turns red as winter approaches.

TEMPERATE CONIFEROUS

Needleleaf trees with cones to protect their seeds from bitter winters grow in cold climates with short summers, such as those in British Columbia, Canada (above). These trees are important in the lumber and papermaking industries.

TEMPERATE GRASSLAND

Grasslands are found in areas where precipitation is too low to support forests. Much of the Pampas grasslands in Patagonia, Chile, is used for ranching. Winds from the Andes mountain range sweep across this region.

DESERT SHRUB

Deserts, areas that receive less than 10 inches (25 cm) of rainfall a year, have vegetation that is specially adapted to survive under dry conditions, such as these dry shrubs growing in South Australia.

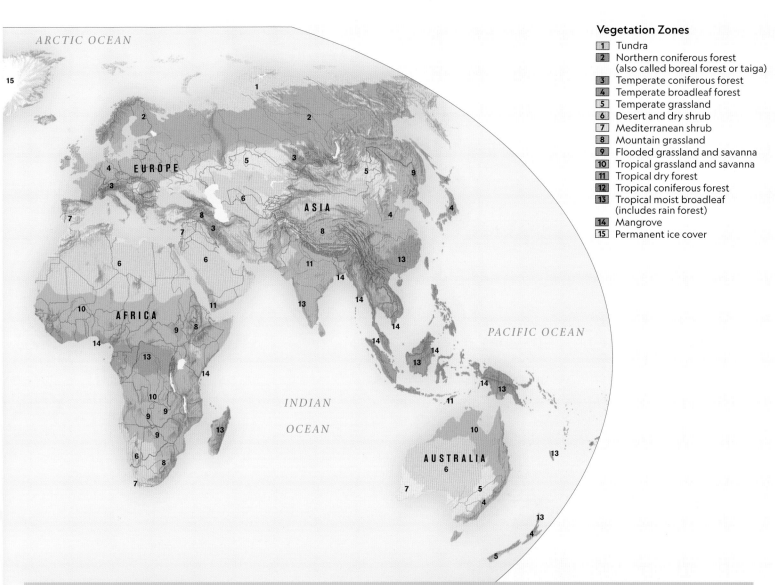

ARCTIC OCEAN

EUROPE

ASIA

AFRICA

PACIFIC OCEAN

INDIAN

OCEAN

AUSTRALIA

Vegetation Zones

1. Tundra
2. Northern coniferous forest (also called boreal forest or taiga)
3. Temperate coniferous forest
4. Temperate broadleaf forest
5. Temperate grassland
6. Desert and dry shrub
7. Mediterranean shrub
8. Mountain grassland
9. Flooded grassland and savanna
10. Tropical grassland and savanna
11. Tropical dry forest
12. Tropical coniferous forest
13. Tropical moist broadleaf (includes rain forest)
14. Mangrove
15. Permanent ice cover

7

MEDITERRANEAN SHRUB

The warm, dry summers and mild winters of Greece create an area with plants that can survive low precipitation. The region is known for growing citrus fruits, grapes, figs, and olives.

11

TROPICAL DRY FOREST

Although the tropical dry forest is warm year-round and receives substantial rainfall, such forests must survive long periods of dry conditions. The Guanacaste region of Costa Rica contains trees that shed their leaves during the dry season.

14

MANGROVE

Mangroves are found in tidal areas such as in the Caribbean region of Belize. Many species, like sea stars, make their home within the underwater root systems. Mangrove trees prevent erosion in warmer areas that have hurricanes.

CROPLAND

People remove natural vegetation in many places to create fields to grow crops to feed both people and animals. Here, a farmer in the Catskill Mountains of New York, U.S.A., cultivates land that was likely once a temperate forest.

Environmental Hot Spots

People are putting more and more pressure on the environment by dumping pollutants into the air and water and by removing natural vegetation to extract mineral resources or to create cropland for farming. In higher-income countries, industries create waste and pollution; farmers use fertilizers and pesticides that run off into water supplies; and motor vehicles release exhaust fumes into the air. In lower-income countries, forests are cut down for fuel or to clear land for farming; grasslands are turned into deserts as farmers and herders overuse the land; and expanding urban areas face problems of water quality and sanitation.

Environmental Stresses
- Megacity with more than 10 million people
- Deforestation
- Desertification
- Major air pollution
- Major human impact to the oceans

HUMAN FOOTPRINT. This map uses population density, land use, transportation, and energy production and use to identify environmental hot spots—areas of Earth where human impact is greatest.

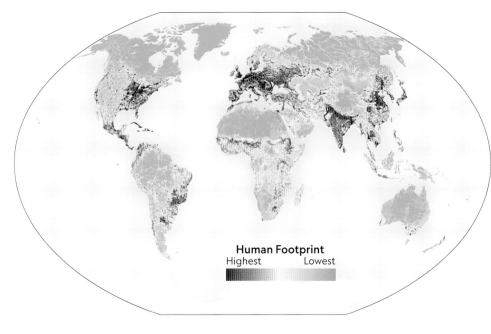

Human Footprint
Highest   Lowest

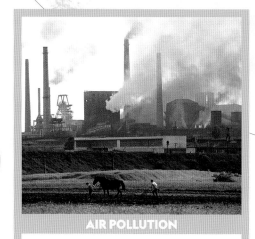

AIR POLLUTION

Poor air quality is a serious environmental problem. Industrial plants are a major source of pollution. Smoke, which contains particles that combine with moisture in the air to create acid rain, is released from a factory in Poland (above).

EUROPE

Moscow

Paris

ASIA

Istanbul

Beijing Tianjin

Tokyo

Osaka

Lahore

Chongqing

Shanghai

Cairo

Delhi

Dhaka

Guangzhou

Karachi

Kolkata

Shenzhen

AFRICA

Mumbai

Hyderabad

Chennai

Bangkok

Manila

Bengalore

Lagos

Kinshasa

Jakarta

Rio de Janeiro

São Paulo

AUSTRALIA

Buenos Aires

Kilometers

0   1,000   2,000   3,000

Miles

0   1,000   2,000   3,000

DEFORESTATION

Loss of forest cover, such as on this hillside in Malaysia, contributes to a buildup of carbon dioxide in the atmosphere, as well as to a loss of biodiversity, or variety of species. These are common problems in the tropics.

DESERTIFICATION

Villagers in Mauritania (above) shovel sand away from their schoolhouse. In semiarid areas, which receive limited and often unreliable rainfall, land that is overgrazed or overcultivated can become desertlike.

OCEAN POLLUTION

Plastic trash, ranging from bottles and bags to microscopic bits, is a serious threat to sea birds and other marine life. Scientists estimate 8.8 million tons (8 million t) of plastic, including this trash off Dakar, Senegal, end up in the oceans every year.

Endangered Species

Earth's environment is made up of a complex system of life-forms ranging from microscopic organisms to giant blue whales. Throughout Earth's history, species such as the dinosaurs have become extinct. Scientists have concluded that in recent years many species are becoming endangered at an increasing rate as humans spread into natural areas for agricultural and urban use and contribute to climate change by using fossil fuels. Loss of species could mean fewer medical discoveries to fight disease and loss of plants and animals that enrich our lives each day.

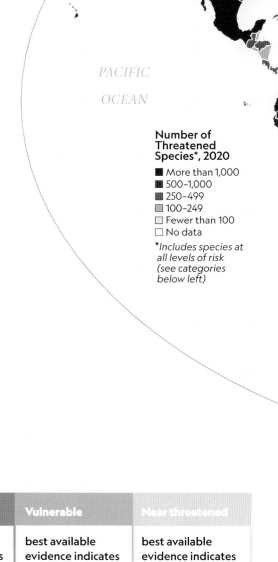

PACIFIC

OCEAN

NORTH AMERICA

Number of Threatened Species*, 2020

- ■ More than 1,000
- ▨ 500–1,000
- ▨ 250–499
- ▨ 100–249
- ☐ Fewer than 100
- ☐ No data

*Includes species at all levels of risk (see categories below left)

SPECIES AT RISK

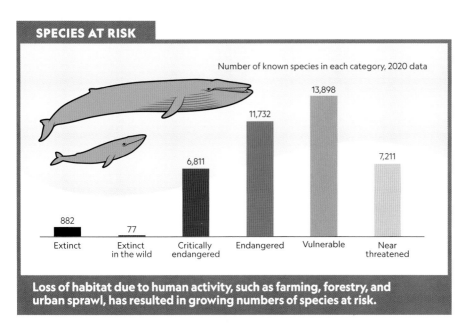

Number of known species in each category, 2020 data

882	77	6,811	11,732	13,898	7,211
Extinct	Extinct in the wild	Critically endangered	Endangered	Vulnerable	Near threatened

Loss of habitat due to human activity, such as farming, forestry, and urban sprawl, has resulted in growing numbers of species at risk.

Extinct*	Extinct in the wild	Critically endangered	Endangered	Vulnerable	Near threatened
no reasonable doubt that the last example of the species has died	best available evidence indicates the species is extinct in its natural habitat, surviving only in captivity	best available evidence indicates the species faces extremely high risk of extinction in the wild	best available evidence indicates the species faces very high risk of extinction in the wild	best available evidence indicates the species faces high risk of becoming endangered in the wild	best available evidence indicates the species is not yet vulnerable, but is likely to be without ongoing conservation action

*Categories and definitions are based on IUCN Red List.

PHYSICAL WORLD

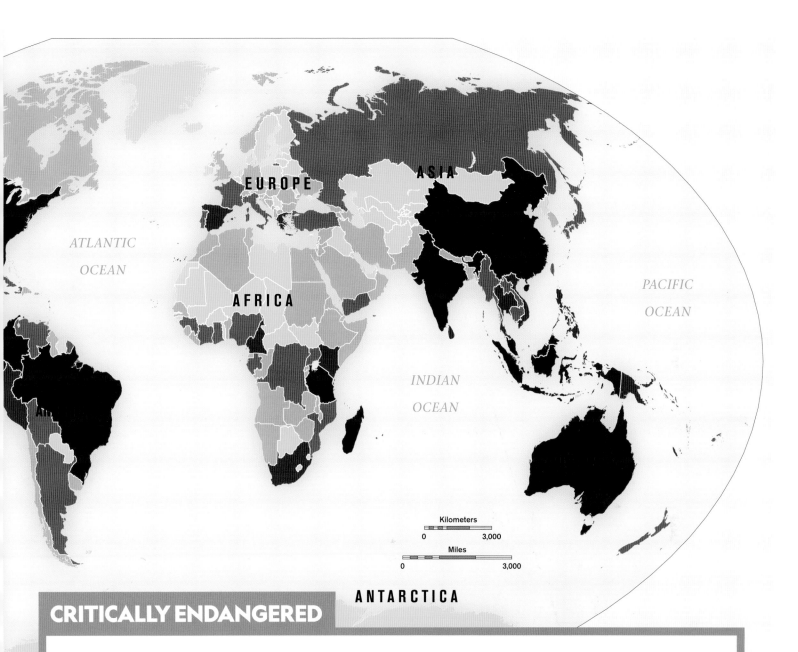

ATLANTIC OCEAN

EUROPE

ASIA

PACIFIC OCEAN

AFRICA

INDIAN OCEAN

Kilometers
0   3,000

Miles
0   3,000

ANTARCTICA

CRITICALLY ENDANGERED

Human activity poses the greatest threat to Earth's rich variety of species. Climate change and loss of habitat put many species at great risk. Experts estimate that species are facing extinction at a greater rate than at any other time in human history. The species shown here were critically endangered as of 2019.

Diademed Sifaka

Eastern Gorilla

Chinese Pangolin

Swift Parrot

Canterbury Knobbled Weevil

Geometric Tortoise

Torrey Pine

Gentiana kurroo

Natural Disasters

Every world region has its share of natural disasters. The Ring of Fire—grinding tectonic plate boundaries that follow the coasts of the Pacific Ocean—shakes with volcanic eruptions and earthquakes (page 17). Coastal areas can be swept away by quake-caused tsunamis. The U.S. heartland endures blizzards in winter and dangerous tornadoes that can strike in spring, summer, or fall. Tropical cyclones batter many coastal areas with ripping winds, torrents of rain, and huge storm surges along their deadly paths.

Natural Disasters
(1900–2019)

← Typical storm track of hurricane, typhoon, or cyclone

☐ "Tornado Alley" (highest concentration of tornadoes worldwide)

· Earthquake greater than 6.5 magnitude

· Tsunami quake epicenter

⊙ Notable tornado

● Notable hurricane, typhoon, or cyclone

▲ Notable volcanic eruption

⬙ **TORNADO.** A funnel cloud moves across open country near Campo, Colorado, U.S.A. More of these storms occur in "Tornado Alley" (see map) than anywhere else on Earth.

◗ **RAGING HURRICANE.**
In November 2019, Hurricane Dorian roared through Great Abaco Island in the Bahamas (right). With peak sustained winds of 185 miles an hour (298 km/h), the storm destroyed most structures and became one of the most intense hurricanes on record.

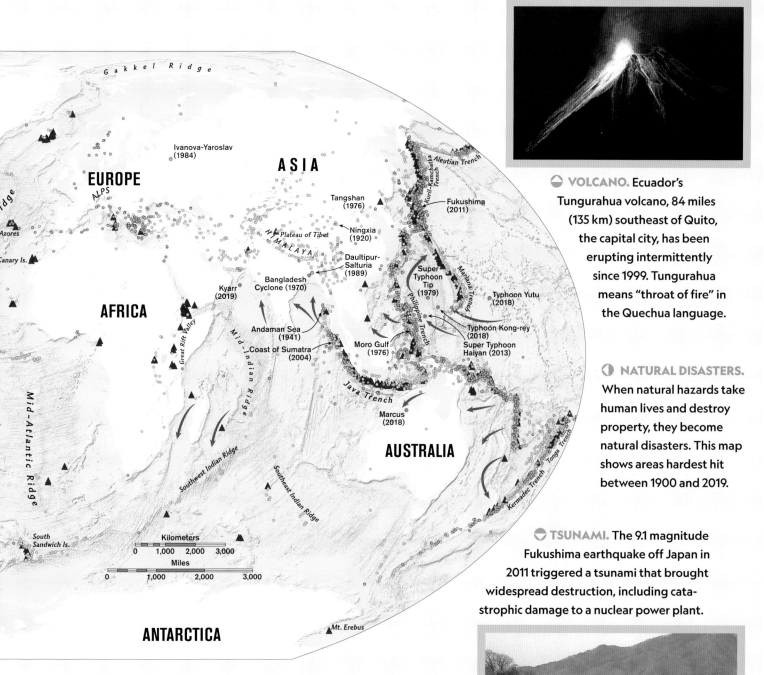

Gakkel Ridge

EUROPE
ALPS
Azores
Canary Is.
AFRICA
Great Rift Valley
Mid-Indian Ridge
Mid-Atlantic Ridge
Southwest Indian Ridge
Southeast Indian Ridge
South Sandwich Is.
ANTARCTICA

ASIA
Ivanova-Yaroslav (1984)
Tangshan (1976)
Plateau of Tibet
Ningxia (1920)
HIMALAYA
Daultipur-Salturia (1989)
Bangladesh Cyclone (1970)
Kyarr (2019)
Andaman Sea (1941)
Coast of Sumatra (2004)
Moro Gulf (1976)
Java Trench
Marcus (2018)

Aleutian Trench
Kuril-Kamchatka Trench
Fukushima (2011)
Super Typhoon Tip (1979)
Mariana Trench
Typhoon Yutu (2018)
Philippine Trench
Typhoon Kong-rey (2018)
Super Typhoon Haiyan (2013)

AUSTRALIA
Kermadec Trench
Tonga Trench

Mt. Erebus

Kilometers
0 1,000 2,000 3,000
Miles
0 1,000 2,000 3,000

VOLCANO. Ecuador's Tungurahua volcano, 84 miles (135 km) southeast of Quito, the capital city, has been erupting intermittently since 1999. Tungurahua means "throat of fire" in the Quechua language.

NATURAL DISASTERS. When natural hazards take human lives and destroy property, they become natural disasters. This map shows areas hardest hit between 1900 and 2019.

TSUNAMI. The 9.1 magnitude Fukushima earthquake off Japan in 2011 triggered a tsunami that brought widespread destruction, including catastrophic damage to a nuclear power plant.

MEASURING QUAKES. Scientists, like this one, use an instrument called a seismograph to measure and record the strength of tremors caused by shifts in Earth's crust.

The Political World

Earth's land area is mainly made up of seven giant continents that people have divided into smaller political units called countries—with two exceptions. Australia is a continent with a single country, and Antarctica is set aside for scientific research. But the other five continents include almost 200 independent countries. This political map shows boundaries—imaginary lines agreed to by treaties—that separate countries. Some boundaries are very stable and have been recognized for many years. Other boundaries are relatively new and are still disputed. Countries come in all shapes and sizes. Russia and Canada are giants. Other countries, such as Luxembourg in western Europe, are small. Some countries are long and skinny—look at Chile in South America! Still other countries, such as Indonesia and Japan in Asia, are made up of groups of islands.

◖ **COUNTRIES AND CAPITALS.** The world political map looks a bit like a patchwork quilt. Each country's boundary is outlined in one color. Some countries also include territory beyond the main land area. For example, the United States is shaded bright green, but so are Alaska and Hawai'i, which are also U.S. states. Most countries have one city—called the capital— that is the center of political decision-making. For example, Beijing is the capital of China. But a few countries have more than one capital, such as La Paz and Sucre in Bolivia. The capital of each country is marked with a star inside a circle.

90° 60° 30°W 0° 30°E 60° 90° 120° 150° 180°

ARCTIC OCEAN

Greenland

Svalbard

Reykjavik ⊛ ICELAND

R U S S I A

NORWAY
SWEDEN
FINLAND

Oslo ⊛ ⊛ Helsinki
Stockholm ⊛ ⊛ Moscow

UNITED KINGDOM
Copenhagen ⊛ DENMARK
Dublin ⊛
IRELAND
London ⊛ NETH. BELG. GERMANY POLAND Berlin
Paris ⊛ LUX. CZECHIA Warsaw
FRANCE SWITZ. SLOVENIA AUSTRIA HUNGARY MOLDOVA
SLOVAKIA
CROATIA ROMANIA
BOSN. & HERZ. SERBIA BULGARIA
Rome ⊛ ITALY MONT. KOSOVO
PORTUGAL Madrid ⊛ ALBANIA N. MACEDONIA
Lisbon ⊛ SPAIN GREECE
Algiers ⊛ MALTA Athens
Rabat ⊛ Tunis ⊛ CYPRUS
TUNISIA
MOROCCO
Tripoli ⊛

ESTONIA
LATVIA
LITHUANIA
Minsk ⊛ BELARUS
Kyiv ⊛
UKRAINE
CRIMEA
GEORGIA
TURKEY Ankara ⊛ ARMENIA AZERBAIJAN
LEBANON SYRIA
ISRAEL IRAQ
JORDAN Baghdad ⊛
Tehran ⊛

KAZAKHSTAN
Nur-Sultan (Astana)
Tashkent ⊛ Bishkek ⊛
UZBEKISTAN KYRGYZSTAN
TURKMENISTAN Dushanbe ⊛
Ashgabat ⊛ TAJIKISTAN
Kabul ⊛
IRAN AFGHANISTAN Islamabad ⊛
PAKISTAN

MONGOLIA
Ulaanbaatar ⊛

Beijing ⊛
C H I N A

NORTH KOREA
Pyongyang ⊛ Seoul ⊛ JAPAN
SOUTH KOREA Tokyo ⊛

NORTH PACIFIC OCEAN

NORTH ATLANTIC OCEAN

WESTERN SAHARA (Morocco)
Nouakchott ⊛
MAURITANIA
CABO VERDE
SENEGAL
Dakar ⊛
THE GAMBIA
Bissau ⊛ GUINEA-BISSAU
Conakry ⊛ GUINEA
Freetown ⊛
SIERRA LEONE
Monrovia ⊛
LIBERIA
Yamoussoukro ⊛
Abidjan ⊛

ALGERIA
LIBYA
EGYPT Cairo ⊛
Riyadh ⊛
SAUDI ARABIA

MALI
NIGER
CHAD
Niamey ⊛
Bamako ⊛ BURKINA FASO
Ouagadougou ⊛
NIGERIA
Abuja ⊛
CÔTE BENIN
D'IVOIRE GHANA TOGO
Accra ⊛ Lomé
Khartoum ⊛
SUDAN
Asmara ⊛ ERITREA
SOUTH SUDAN
CENTRAL AFRICAN REPUBLIC
Yaoundé ⊛
Bangui ⊛ Juba ⊛
Sanaa ⊛ YEMEN
Addis Ababa ⊛
ETHIOPIA
SOMALILAND
DJIBOUTI

BAHRAIN
KUWAIT
QATAR
U.A.E.
OMAN Muscat ⊛

New Delhi ⊛
NEPAL Kathmandu ⊛
Thimphu ⊛ BHUTAN
BANGLADESH
Dhaka ⊛
I N D I A
MYANMAR (BURMA)
Nay Pyi Taw ⊛

TAIWAN

Hanoi ⊛
Vientiane ⊛ LAOS
VIETNAM
THAILAND
Bangkok ⊛ CAMBODIA
Phnom Penh ⊛

Manila ⊛
PHILIPPINES

MARSHALL ISLANDS
Ngerulmud ⊛ Palikir ⊛
PALAU
FEDERATED STATES OF MICRONESIA
Majuro ⊛
Tarawa ⊛
KIRIBATI
NAURU

EQUATORIAL GUINEA
SAO TOME & PRINCIPE
Libreville ⊛ GABON
CAMEROON
Brazzaville ⊛ CONGO
Kinshasa ⊛
DEM. REP. OF THE CONGO
Luanda ⊛
Kampala ⊛ UGANDA
RWANDA Kigali ⊛
Gitega ⊛ KENYA
BURUNDI
Bujumbura ⊛ Dodoma ⊛
TANZANIA
Nairobi ⊛
Dar es Salaam ⊛
Mogadishu ⊛
SOMALIA
Victoria ⊛
SEYCHELLES

SRI LANKA
Colombo ⊛ Sri Jayewardenepura Kotte
Male ⊛
MALDIVES

BRUNEI
Bandar Seri Begawan
Kuala Lumpur ⊛ MALAYSIA
SINGAPORE ⊛

I N D O N E S I A

Jakarta ⊛
Dili ⊛ TIMOR-LESTE (EAST TIMOR)

PAPUA NEW GUINEA
Port Moresby ⊛

SOLOMON ISLANDS
Honiara ⊛
Funafuti ⊛ TUVALU
VANUATU
Port-Vila ⊛ FIJI
Suva ⊛

SOUTH ATLANTIC OCEAN

ANGOLA
ZAMBIA
Lusaka ⊛
Harare ⊛
ZIMBABWE
NAMIBIA
Windhoek ⊛ BOTSWANA
Gaborone ⊛
(Tshwane) Pretoria ⊛
Bloemfontein ⊛
SOUTH AFRICA
Cape Town ⊛
LESOTHO
ESWATINI (SWAZILAND)
Maputo ⊛
MALAWI Lilongwe ⊛
MOZAMBIQUE
COMOROS Moroni ⊛
MADAGASCAR
Antananarivo ⊛
MAURITIUS
Port Louis ⊛

INDIAN OCEAN

AUSTRALIA

Canberra, A.C.T. ⊛

SOUTH PACIFIC OCEAN

NEW ZEALAND
Wellington ⊛

A N T A R C T I C A

POLITICAL WORLD

World Population

How big is a billion? It's hard to imagine. But Earth's population is 7.7 billion and rising, with more than a billion living in both China and India. And more than 80 million people are added to the world each year. Most population growth occurs in the lower-income countries in Africa, Asia, North America, and South America, while some countries in Europe are hardly increasing at all. Population changes can create challenges for countries. Fast-growing countries with young populations need food, housing, and schools. Countries with low growth rates and older populations need workers to sustain their economies.

MOST POPULOUS COUNTRIES

(2019 estimates)	
1. China	1,384,689,000
2. India	1,296,834,000
3. United States	329,256,000
4. Indonesia	262,787,000
5. Brazil	208,847,000

MOST CROWDED COUNTRIES

Population Density (People per sq mi/sq km; 2019 estimates)	
1. Monaco	39,000 / 19,500
2. Singapore	22,280 / 8,602
3. Vatican City	5,886 / 2,272
4. Bahrain	4,917 / 1,898
5. Malta	3,680 / 1,420

◗ **DENSITY.** Demographers, people who study population, use density to measure how concentrated population is, but density is just an average. For example, the population density of Egypt is more than 257 people per square mile (99 people per sq km). This incorrectly assumes that the population is evenly spread throughout the country. Actually, most people live along the Nile River. Likewise, Earth's population is not evenly spread across the land. Some places are almost empty, others are very crowded.

◗ **CITY DWELLERS.**
More than half the world's people have shifted from rural areas to urban centers, with some countries adding more than 100 million to their urban populations between 1950 and 2020 (map, right). In higher-income countries, about 75 percent of the population is urban, compared with just 46 percent in lower-income countries. But the fastest growing urban areas are in less developed countries, where thousands flock to cities, such as Dhaka, Bangladesh (photo, far right), in search of a better life. In 2016, there were 34 cities with a population of 10 million or more.

NORTH AMERICA

Los Angeles

Mexico City

PACIFIC OCEAN

Kilometers
0   1,000   2,000   3,000

Miles
0   1,000   2,000   3,000

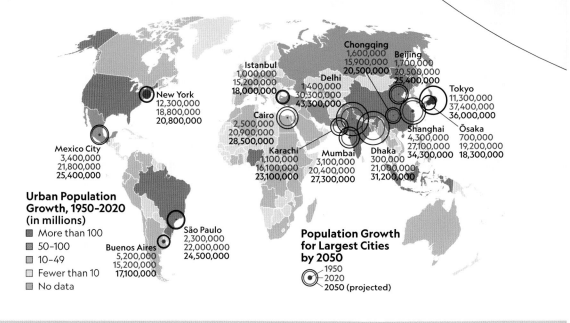

Chongqing
1,600,000
15,900,000
20,500,000

Beijing
1,700,000
20,500,000
25,400,000

Istanbul
1,000,000
15,200,000
18,000,000

Delhi
1,400,000
30,300,000
43,300,000

Tokyo
11,300,000
37,400,000
36,000,000

New York
12,300,000
18,800,000
20,800,000

Cairo
2,500,000
20,900,000
28,500,000

Shanghai
4,300,000
27,100,000
34,300,000

Ōsaka
700,000
19,200,000
18,300,000

Mexico City
3,400,000
21,800,000
25,400,000

Karachi
1,100,000
16,100,000
23,100,000

Mumbai
3,100,000
20,400,000
27,300,000

Dhaka
300,000
21,000,000
31,200,000

Urban Population Growth, 1950–2020 (in millions)
- More than 100
- 50–100
- 10–49
- Fewer than 10
- No data

São Paulo
2,300,000
22,000,000
24,500,000

Buenos Aires
5,200,000
15,200,000
17,100,000

Population Growth for Largest Cities by 2050
- 1950
- 2020
- 2050 (projected)

A.D. 1   50   100   150   200   250   300   350   400   450   500   550   600   650   700   750   800   850
Year

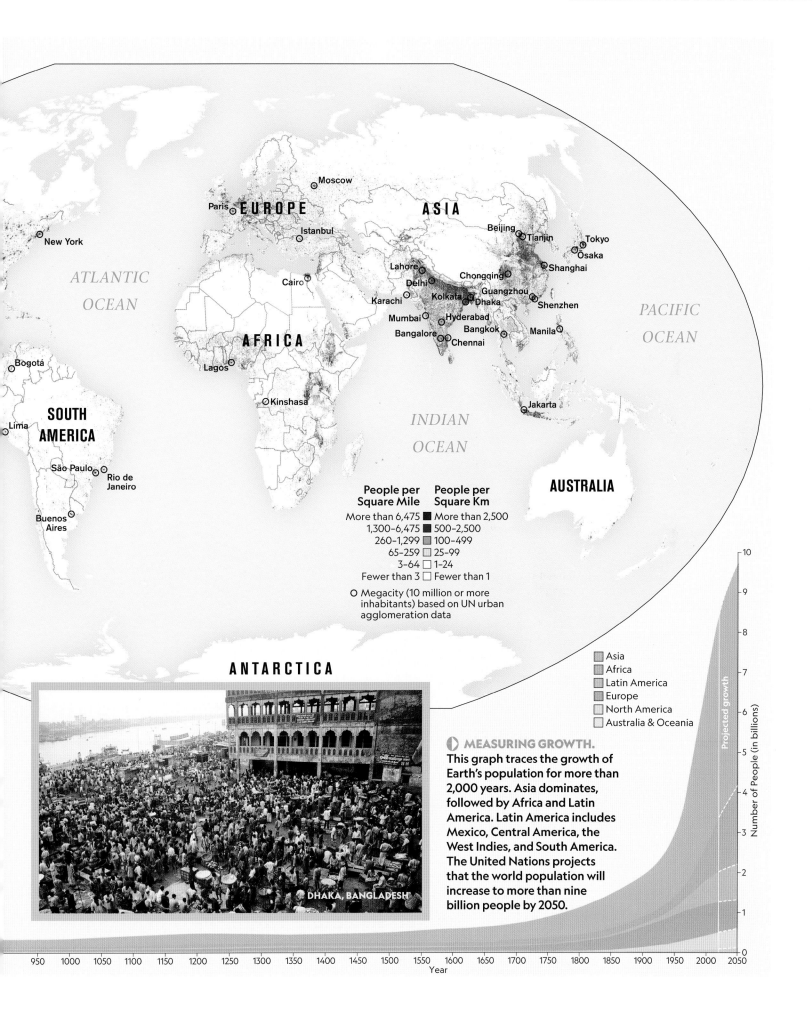

Moscow

Paris EUROPE

ASIA

Beijing
Tianjin
Tokyo
Osaka

New York

Istanbul

ATLANTIC
OCEAN

Lahore
Chongqing
Shanghai

Cairo

Delhi

AFRICA

Karachi
Kolkata Guangzhou
Dhaka
Shenzhen

Mumbai Hyderabad

PACIFIC
OCEAN

Lagos

Bangalore Bangkok Manila
Chennai

Kinshasa

INDIAN

SOUTH
AMERICA

OCEAN

Bogotá

Lima

Jakarta

São Paulo
Rio de
Janeiro

AUSTRALIA

Buenos
Aires

**People per
Square Mile** **People per
Square Km**

More than 6,475 ■ More than 2,500
1,300–6,475 ■ 500–2,500
260–1,299 ■ 100–499
65–259 □ 25–99
3–64 □ 1–24
Fewer than 3 □ Fewer than 1

O Megacity (10 million or more
inhabitants) based on UN urban
agglomeration data

ANTARCTICA

DHAKA, BANGLADESH

Asia
Africa
Latin America
Europe
North America
Australia & Oceania

◗ **MEASURING GROWTH.**
This graph traces the growth of
Earth's population for more than
2,000 years. Asia dominates,
followed by Africa and Latin
America. Latin America includes
Mexico, Central America, the
West Indies, and South America.
The United Nations projects
that the world population will
increase to more than nine
billion people by 2050.

Projected growth

Number of People (in billions)

10
9
8
7
6
5
4
3
2
1
0

950 1000 1050 1100 1150 1200 1250 1300 1350 1400 1450 1500 1550 1600 1650 1700 1750 1800 1850 1900 1950 2000 2050
Year

POLITICAL WORLD

Population Trends

Population growth rates are slowing, total fertility rates are declining, and populations are aging. Nevertheless, world population will continue to increase for many years to come because the base population is so large. More than 80 million people are added, on average, to the world's population each year, 90 percent of whom are born in lower-income countries where poverty is greatest. In more affluent countries, life expectancy is higher and populations are aging. It's estimated that by 2050, one-sixth of the world's population will be 65 years of age or older.

POPULATION GROWTH RATE (%)

Lowest (2019 estimates)	
1. Lebanon	-6.7
2. Lithuania	-1.1
3. Latvia	-1.1
4. Moldova	-1.1
5. Bulgaria	-0.7

POPULATION GROWTH RATE (%)

Highest (2019 estimates)	
1. Syria	4.3
2. Niger	3.7
3. Angola	3.4
4. Benin	3.4
5. Uganda	3.3

◑ **POPULATION GROWTH.**
This map shows projected population change (%) from 2015 to 2050. Russia, China, Japan, and much of Europe face a decline in population due to low birth rates and women waiting longer to have children. Countries in most of Africa can expect to see an opposite trend as fertility rates remain high.

NORTH AMERICA

UNITED STATES

United States
80 years
1.8

Projected Population Change (%), 2015–2050

gain
- More than 100
- 50 to 100
- 0 to 49.9

loss
- -10 to -0.1
- -30 to -10.1
- No data

Other Map Symbols
■ **Life expectancy**
(symbol represents 10 years, both sexes)

🕴 **Fertility rate**
(average number of children born to women in a given population; symbol represents 1 child)

PACIFIC OCEAN

POPULATION PYRAMIDS

A population pyramid compares population by age and sex and can be used to predict future trends. Countries, such as Nigeria, with high birth rates and high percentages of young people have a pyramid-shaped graph, which suggests continued growth. Countries with low birth rates, such as Italy, have narrow bases with bulges in the higher age brackets, indicating an aging population.

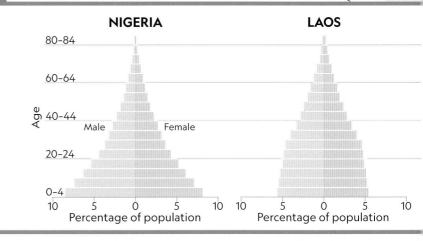

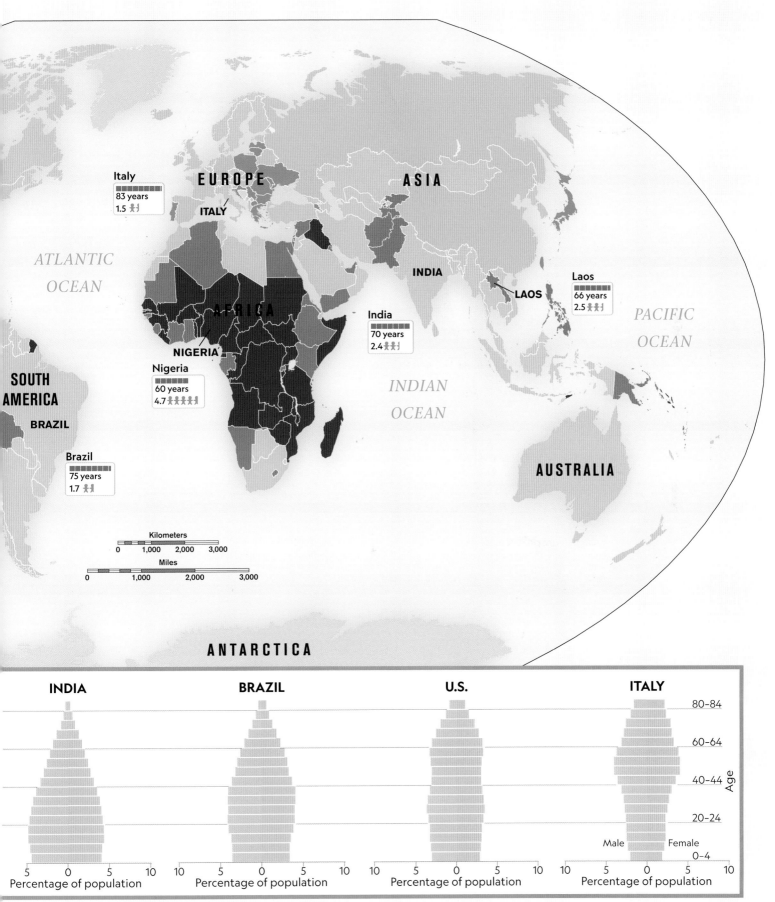

Italy
83 years
1.5

EUROPE

ASIA

ITALY

ATLANTIC
OCEAN

AFRICA

INDIA

Laos
66 years
2.5

LAOS

PACIFIC
OCEAN

NIGERIA

India
70 years
2.4

SOUTH
AMERICA

Nigeria
60 years
4.7

INDIAN
OCEAN

BRAZIL

AUSTRALIA

Brazil
75 years
1.7

Kilometers
0   1,000   2,000   3,000

Miles
0   1,000   2,000   3,000

ANTARCTICA

INDIA

BRAZIL

U.S.

ITALY

80–84

60–64

40–44

Age

20–24

Male   Female
0–4

5   0   5   10   10   5   0   5   10   10   5   0   5   10   10   5   0   5   10
Percentage of population   Percentage of population   Percentage of population   Percentage of population

2019 data

Migration

Why do people move? Many people move for the same reason that animals migrate. They are looking for food, adequate shelter, safety, and better climate conditions.

The forces that draw people to move into a country are called pull factors. Pull factors are positive forces on migration, such as earning more money, being near family, and having freedom and safety. The forces that make people want to leave a country are called push factors. Push factors are negative forces on migration, such as poverty, unemployment, famine, and conflict or war.

By analyzing the map, you will notice that many countries in North America, Europe, Asia, and Australia are shaded in a darker green. Many of these countries offer freedom and job opportunities for immigrants. You will also notice that the countries of Gabon in Africa, French Guiana in South America, and Kazakhstan in Asia are darker green than the countries around them. These countries have attracted migrants due to the job opportunities found there.

NORTH AMERICA

PACIFIC OCEAN

ATLANTIC OCEAN

SOUTH AMERICA

Kilometers
0   1,000   2,000   3,000

Miles
0   1,000   2,000   3,000

Migrant Population
(percentage of total population)

- More than 25
- 15.1–25
- 5.5–15
- 2.5–5.4
- 1.–2.4
- Less than 1
- No data

◗ **BORDER CROSSING.**
Four countries (Zambia, Namibia, Zimbabwe, and Botswana) meet at the Zambezi River. Most travelers and migrants must wait hours to cross the river. Due to heavy migration, the Kazungula Ferry will soon be replaced by a bridge.

EUROPE

ASIA

AFRICA

PACIFIC
OCEAN

INDIAN
OCEAN

AUSTRALIA

ANTARCTICA

REFUGEES. Civil war in a country can create concerns along the borders with neighboring countries. Due to civil unrest and conflict in surrounding countries, refugees arrive in Ruwaished, Jordan, to escape this upheaval and to seek medical attention.

IMMIGRATION INSPECTION. Traveling to a new country can mean a wait in line to have passports checked, as in the photo below from the Miami International Airport in Florida, U.S.A. There are usually separate lines for citizens returning to a country and citizens of other countries.

MIGRANT WORKERS. In 2015, 36 percent of the Chinese workforce was made up of migrant workers who moved from one place to another within China. Every year, many of these workers leave agricultural areas for jobs in urbanized areas. When these workers return home to celebrate the Chinese New Year, their traveling period, called the Chunyun, is considered the world's largest annual human migration.

POLITICAL WORLD

World Languages

Earth's 7.7 billion people live in 195 independent countries, but they speak more than 7,000 languages. Experts believe that humans may once have spoken as many as 10,000 languages. Some countries, such as Germany, have one official language. Other countries, such as Zimbabwe, have many official languages.

Literacy is the ability to read and write in one's native language. High literacy rates are associated with higher-income countries. But literacy is also a gender issue, since women in lower-income countries often lack access to education.

LEADING LANGUAGES

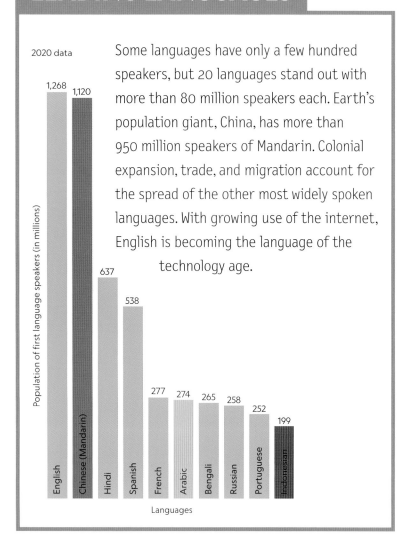

2020 data

Some languages have only a few hundred speakers, but 20 languages stand out with more than 80 million speakers each. Earth's population giant, China, has more than 950 million speakers of Mandarin. Colonial expansion, trade, and migration account for the spread of the other most widely spoken languages. With growing use of the internet, English is becoming the language of the technology age.

Population of first language speakers (in millions)

Language	Speakers
English	1,268
Chinese (Mandarin)	1,120
Hindi	637
Spanish	538
French	277
Arabic	274
Bengali	265
Russian	258
Portuguese	252
Indonesian	199

Languages

NORTH AMERICA

SOUTH AMERICA

PACIFIC OCEAN

⬥ **EDUCATION AND LITERACY.** These Nenet boys in Siberia spend hours learning the national language—Russian—but this may result in the loss of their native language. There are more than 7,000 languages spoken on Earth, but by 2100, experts predict that more than half of those may have disappeared.

& Literacy

POLITICAL WORLD

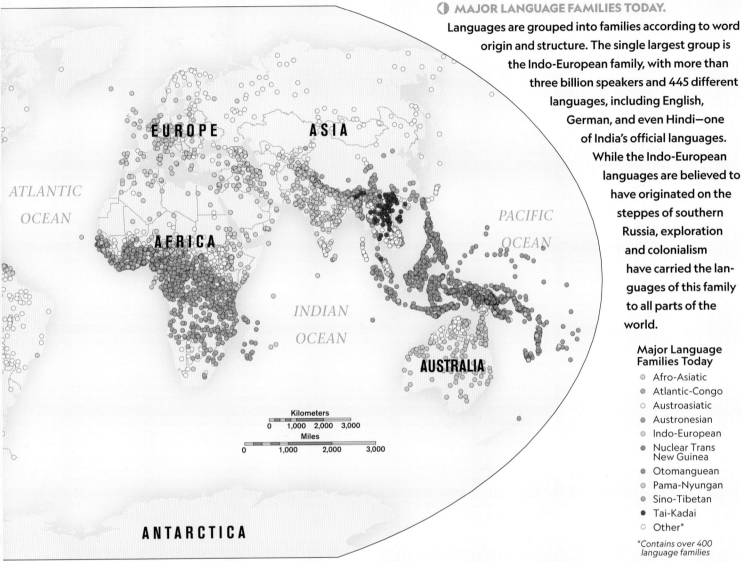

◖ **MAJOR LANGUAGE FAMILIES TODAY.** Languages are grouped into families according to word origin and structure. The single largest group is the Indo-European family, with more than three billion speakers and 445 different languages, including English, German, and even Hindi—one of India's official languages. While the Indo-European languages are believed to have originated on the steppes of southern Russia, exploration and colonialism have carried the languages of this family to all parts of the world.

Major Language Families Today

- ◎ Afro-Asiatic
- ◉ Atlantic-Congo
- ○ Austroasiatic
- ◉ Austronesian
- ◎ Indo-European
- ◉ Nuclear Trans New Guinea
- ◉ Otomanguean
- ◎ Pama-Nyungan
- ◎ Sino-Tibetan
- ● Tai-Kadai
- ○ Other*

Contains over 400 language families

Kilometers
0 1,000 2,000 3,000
Miles
0 1,000 2,000 3,000

⊖ **ONE LANGUAGE, TWO FORMS.** Some languages, including Chinese, use characters instead of letters. The Golden Arches provide a clue to the meaning of the characters on the restaurant sign. Many signs, such as the one in the foreground, also show words in pinyin, a spelling system that uses the Western alphabet.

⊖ **UNIVERSAL LANGUAGE.** The widespread use of technology—for example, the computer that holds the attention of these girls in Indonesia—has crossed the language barrier. Computers, the internet, and electronic communication devices use a universal language that knows no national borders.

POLITICAL WORLD

World Religions

Religion takes many forms. Some belief systems, such as Christianity, Islam, and Judaism, are monotheistic, meaning that followers believe in just one supreme being. Others, like Hinduism, Shintoism, and most indigenous belief systems, are polytheistic, meaning that followers believe in many gods.

All of the major religions have their origins in Asia, but they have spread around the world. Christianity, with the largest number of followers, has three main divisions—Roman Catholic, Eastern Orthodox, and Protestant. Islam, with almost one-fourth of all believers, has two main divisions—Sunni and Shia. Together, Hinduism and Buddhism account for more than another one-fifth of believers. Judaism, dating back some 4,000 years, is the oldest of all the major monotheistic religions.

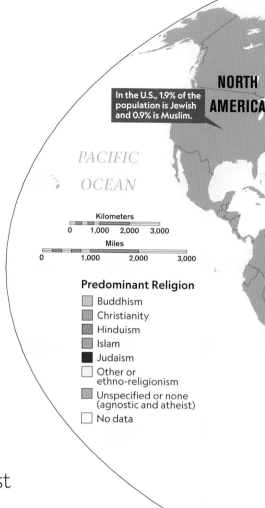

In the U.S., 1.9% of the population is Jewish and 0.9% is Muslim.

NORTH AMERICA

PACIFIC OCEAN

Kilometers
0   1,000   2,000   3,000

Miles
0   1,000   2,000   3,000

Predominant Religion
- Buddhism
- Christianity
- Hinduism
- Islam
- Judaism
- Other or ethno-religionism
- Unspecified or none (agnostic and atheist)
- No data

BUDDHISM

Founded about 2,500 years ago in northern India by a Hindu prince named Gautama Buddha, Buddhism spread throughout eastern and southeastern Asia. Buddhist temples house statues, such as the Mihintale Buddha (above) in Sri Lanka.

CHRISTIANITY

Based on the teachings of Jesus Christ, a Jewish man born some 2,000 years ago in the area of modern-day Israel, Christianity has spread worldwide. Followers in Switzerland (above) participate in a procession with lanterns and crosses.

HINDUISM

Dating back more than 4,000 years, Hinduism is practiced mainly in India. Hindus follow sacred texts known as the Vedas and believe in reincarnation. During the festival of Diwali, Hindus light candles (above) to symbolize the victory of good over evil.

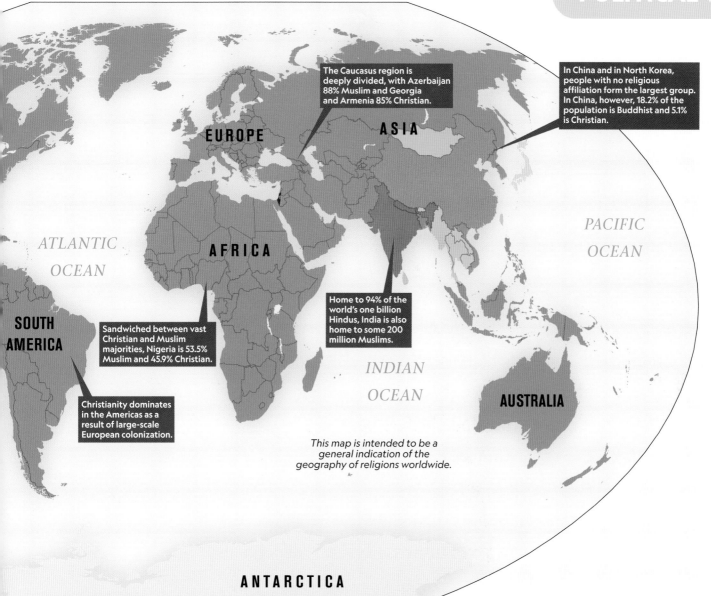

The Caucasus region is deeply divided, with Azerbaijan 88% Muslim and Georgia and Armenia 85% Christian.

In China and in North Korea, people with no religious affiliation form the largest group. In China, however, 18.2% of the population is Buddhist and 5.1% is Christian.

EUROPE

ASIA

ATLANTIC OCEAN

PACIFIC OCEAN

AFRICA

Home to 94% of the world's one billion Hindus, India is also home to some 200 million Muslims.

SOUTH AMERICA

Sandwiched between vast Christian and Muslim majorities, Nigeria is 53.5% Muslim and 45.9% Christian.

INDIAN OCEAN

AUSTRALIA

Christianity dominates in the Americas as a result of large-scale European colonization.

This map is intended to be a general indication of the geography of religions worldwide.

ANTARCTICA

ISLAM

Muslims believe that the Koran, Islam's sacred book, records the words of Allah (God) as revealed to the Prophet Muhammad around 610 C.E. Believers (above) circle the Kabah in the Haram Mosque in Mecca, Saudi Arabia, the spiritual center of the faith.

JUDAISM

The traditions, laws, and beliefs of Judaism date back some 4,000 years to Abraham, its founder, and to the Torah, the first five books of the Old Testament. Followers pray before the Western Wall (above), which stands below Islam's Dome of the Rock in Jerusalem, Israel.

RELIGIOUS FOLLOWERS

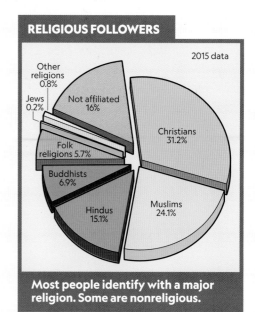

2015 data

Other religions 0.8%

Jews 0.2%

Not affiliated 16%

Folk religions 5.7%

Christians 31.2%

Buddhists 6.9%

Hindus 15.1%

Muslims 24.1%

Most people identify with a major religion. Some are nonreligious.

World Economies

A country's economy can be divided into three parts, or sectors—primary, which includes agriculture, forestry, fishing, and mining; secondary, which includes industry and manufacturing; and tertiary, which includes services ranging from retail sales to mail delivery, to teaching or jobs in medicine. Sometimes a fourth sector, called quaternary, is added. This includes information technology, research, and knowledge creation. The map shows that the economies of the United States, western Europe, and Japan are dominated by service sector jobs. These countries rely heavily on the use of technology and enjoy a high gross domestic product (GDP) per capita—the value of goods and services produced each year, averaged per person in each country. The overall quality of life in these countries is good. In contrast, more than half of the people in Sub-Saharan Africa, South Asia, and Southeast Asia still depend on the primary sector, which generates a low GDP per capita.

UNITED STATES

PACIFIC

OCEAN

**Dominant Economic Sector
(as a percentage of GDP)**

	Agriculture	Industry	Services
70%–100%			
50%–69.9%			
0%–49.9%			
No data			

Services   Agriculture

Industry

INFORMATION. Computers and other technologies have opened employment opportunities dealing with information and knowledge creation. These college students in the United Kingdom learn skills in an information technology lab that will prepare them for 21st-century jobs.

INDUSTRY. A man assembles a hybrid Prius car on an automated assembly line in a Toyota factory in Japan. The manufacture of cars is an important industrial activity and a key part of the global economy.

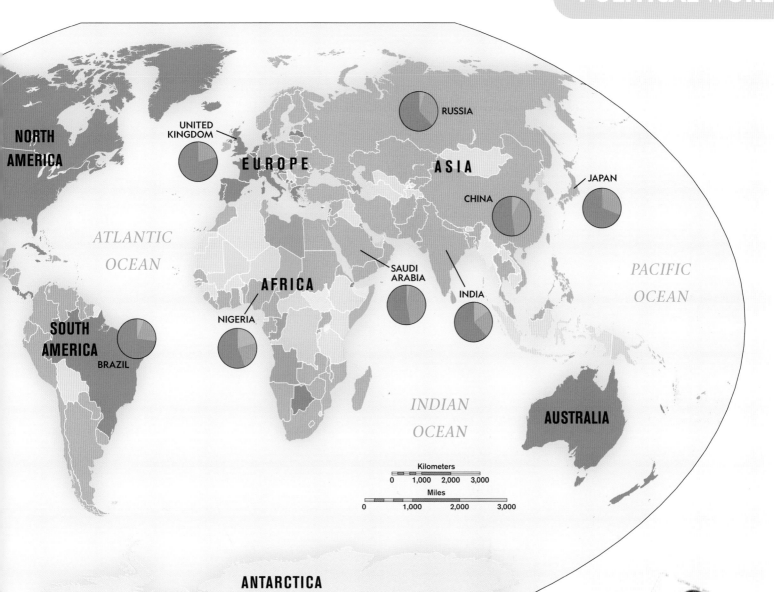

NORTH
AMERICA

UNITED
KINGDOM

EUROPE

RUSSIA

ASIA

JAPAN

CHINA

ATLANTIC
OCEAN

AFRICA

SAUDI
ARABIA

INDIA

PACIFIC
OCEAN

SOUTH
AMERICA

NIGERIA

BRAZIL

INDIAN
OCEAN

AUSTRALIA

Kilometers

0   1,000   2,000   3,000

Miles

0   1,000   2,000   3,000

ANTARCTICA

AGRICULTURE. People in lower-income countries, such as these women in Mozambique, often grow a variety of crops just to support their families. This practice is called subsistence agriculture. In higher-income countries, farmers use machines to produce large quantities of commercial crops.

SERVICES. People employed in the service sector, such as these national forest firefighters in Washington State, U.S.A., use their skills and training to provide services rather than products. Teachers, lawyers, and store clerks, among others, are also part of the service sector.

World Trade

World trade has expanded rapidly since the end of World War II in 1945. In fact, trade has grown faster than world production has. Some countries, such as the United States, China, and Germany, have complex economies that involve trading many different products as well as commercial services, such as financial and information management. But many lower-income countries rely on only a few products—sometimes even just one product—to generate trade income (map, right). Wealthy countries often protect their economies by negotiating agreements and imposing taxes that limit trade in products from other countries. The World Trade Organization works to reduce such trade barriers so that all countries can compete in the global economy.

NORTH AMERICA

PACIFIC OCEAN

Kilometers
0   1,000   2,000   3,000

Miles
0   1,000   2,000   3,000

◗ TRADE. The map (right) shows the richest and poorest economies around the world. The wealth of an economy can be measured in terms of gross national income (GNI) per person—income derived from all economic activity.

TOP MERCHANDISE EXPORTERS

(2019 data, billion U.S. dollars)
1. China	$2,499
2. United States	$1,643
3. Germany	$1,489
4. Netherlands	$709
5. Japan	$705

TOP MERCHANDISE IMPORTERS

(2019 data, billion U.S. dollars)
1. United States	$2,567
2. China	$2,078
3. Germany	$1,234
4. Japan	$720
5. United Kingdom	$695

TOP COMMERCIAL SERVICE EXPORTERS

(2019 data, billion U.S. dollars)
1. United States	$853
2. United Kingdom	$414
3. Germany	$340
4. France	$293
5. Ireland	$247

TOP COMMERCIAL SERVICE IMPORTERS

(2019 data, billion U.S. dollars)
1. United States	$564
2. China	$501
3. Germany	$369
4. Ireland	$331
5. France	$269

◗ GLOBAL EXCHANGE. The world economy depends on container ports where ships deliver goods for sale or redistribution. Some ports, called trans-shipment ports, move containers from one form of transportation (such as a ship) to another (such as a truck) so that goods can be delivered to a final destination.

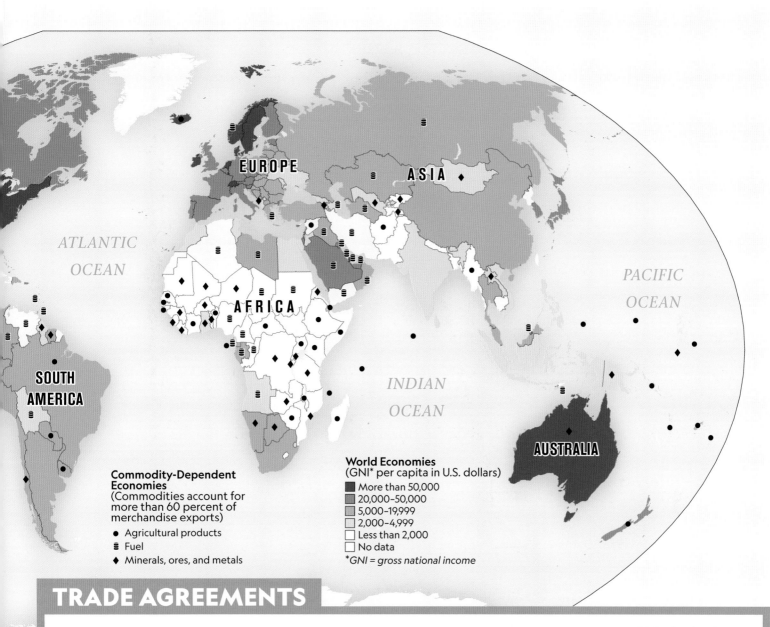

ATLANTIC OCEAN

EUROPE

ASIA

PACIFIC OCEAN

AFRICA

SOUTH AMERICA

INDIAN OCEAN

AUSTRALIA

Commodity-Dependent Economies
(Commodities account for more than 60 percent of merchandise exports)
● Agricultural products
▤ Fuel
◆ Minerals, ores, and metals

World Economies
(GNI* per capita in U.S. dollars)
■ More than 50,000
■ 20,000–50,000
■ 5,000–19,999
□ 2,000–4,999
□ Less than 2,000
□ No data
*GNI = gross national income

TRADE AGREEMENTS

Trade within regions is increasing. Neighboring countries agree to offer each other trade benefits that can improve the economy of the whole region. Such agreements allow products, workers, and money to move more easily among the partners. But these agreements may also prevent trade with other countries that may be able to provide products at a lower cost.

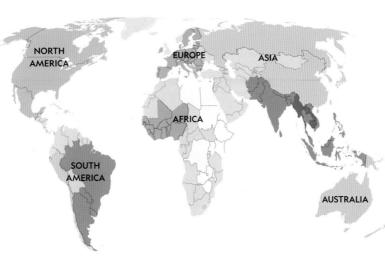

NORTH AMERICA

EUROPE

ASIA

AFRICA

SOUTH AMERICA

AUSTRALIA

Major Regional Trade Agreements
□ **APEC:** Asia-Pacific Economic Cooperation
■ **ASEAN:** Association of Southeast Asian Nations
■ **APEC & ASEAN**
□ **COMESA:** Common Market for Eastern and Southern Africa
■ **ECOWAS:** Economic Community of West African States
■ **EU:** European Union
■ **MERCOSUR:** Southern Common Market
□ **APEC & USMCA:** United States-Mexico-Canada Agreement
■ **SAFTA:** South Asian Free Trade Area

World Water

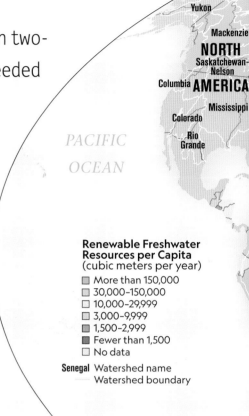

Water is Earth's most precious resource. Although more than two-thirds of the planet is covered by water, freshwater, which is needed by plants and animals—including humans—is only about 2.5 percent of all the water on Earth. Much of this is trapped deep underground or frozen in ice sheets and glaciers. Of the small amount of water that is fresh, less than one percent is available for human use.

The map at right shows each country's access to renewable freshwater supplies. Watersheds are large areas that drain into a particular river or lake. Unfortunately, human activity often puts great stress on watersheds. For example, in Brazil, plans are being made to build large dams on the Amazon. This will alter the natural flow of water in this giant watershed. In the United States, heavy use of chemical fertilizers and pesticides has created toxic runoff that threatens the health of the Mississippi watershed.

Access to clean freshwater is critical for human health. But in many places, safe water is scarce due to population pressure and pollution.

Renewable Freshwater Resources per Capita (cubic meters per year)
- More than 150,000
- 30,000–150,000
- 10,000–29,999
- 3,000–9,999
- 1,500–2,999
- Fewer than 1,500
- No data

Senegal Watershed name
— Watershed boundary

WATER FACTS

Rivers that have been dammed to generate electricity are the source of almost 60 percent of Earth's renewable energy resources.

North America's Great Lakes hold about 20 percent of Earth's available freshwater.

If all the glaciers and ice sheets on Earth's surface melted, they would raise the level of Earth's oceans by about 216 feet (66 m).

If all the world's water could be placed in a gallon jug, the freshwater available for humans to use would equal only about one tablespoon.

⊙ **BIG SPLASH!** Water sports are a favorite recreational activity, especially in hot places such as Albuquerque, New Mexico, U.S.A., where these swimmers cool down in a giant wave pool.

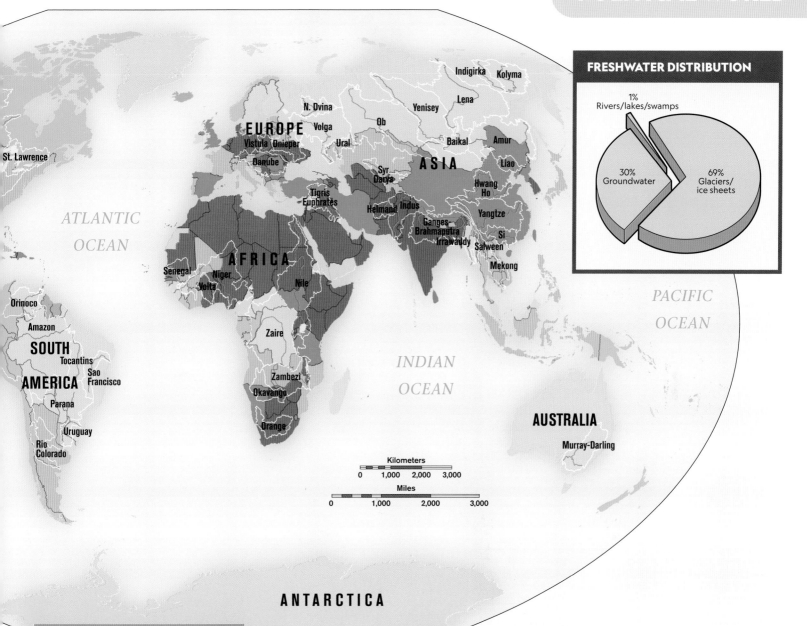

FRESHWATER DISTRIBUTION

1% Rivers/lakes/swamps

30% Groundwater

69% Glaciers/ice sheets

ATLANTIC OCEAN

St. Lawrence

EUROPE

N. Dvina
Volga
Vistula Dnieper
Danube
Ural

Indigirka   Kolyma
Lena
Yenisey
Ob
Baikal
Amur

ASIA

Liao
Hwang Ho
Yangtze
Si
Salween
Mekong

Syr Darya
Tigris Euphrates
Helmand Indus
Ganges-Brahmaputra
Irrawaddy

AFRICA

Senegal
Niger
Volta
Nile

Zaire

Zambezi
Okavango
Orange

Orinoco

Amazon

SOUTH AMERICA

Tocantins
Sao Francisco
Parana
Uruguay
Rio Colorado

INDIAN OCEAN

PACIFIC OCEAN

AUSTRALIA

Murray-Darling

Kilometers
0   1,000   2,000   3,000

Miles
0   1,000   2,000   3,000

ANTARCTICA

WATER CYCLE

The amount of water on Earth has remained more or less constant over the past two billion years—only its form changes. As the sun warms Earth's surface, liquid water is changed to water vapor in a process called evaporation. Plants lose water from their leaves in a process called transpiration. As water vapor rises into the air, it cools and changes again, becoming clouds in a process called condensation. Droplets fall from clouds as precipitation, which travels as groundwater or runoff back to the lakes, rivers, and oceans, where the cycle starts again.

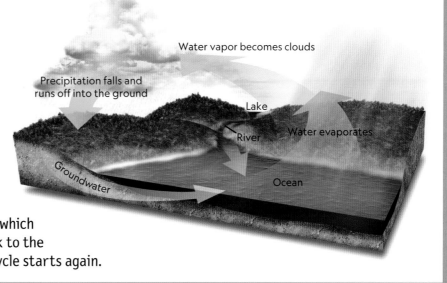

Water vapor becomes clouds

Precipitation falls and runs off into the ground

Lake

River

Water evaporates

Groundwater

Ocean

World Food

Earth produces enough food for all its inhabitants, but not everyone gets enough to eat. Since the 1960s, people in wealthier countries have increased their caloric intake. But many people in poorer countries do not have the same access to food. It's partly a matter of distribution. Agricultural regions (map, right) are unevenly spread around the world, and it is sometimes difficult to move food supplies from areas of surplus to areas of great need. Eastern Africa, in particular, has areas where hunger and malnourishment rob people of healthy, productive lives.

In recent decades, food production has increased, especially production of meats and cereals and the harvesting of fish. As the wealth of a country increases, more people have access to meats, fish, and produce from other regions. Increased production and transportation, along with intensive use of fertilizers and irrigation, create possible threats to the environment.

PACIFIC OCEAN

NORTH AMERICA

Agricultural Land Use

Pasture   Cropland
☐ No data

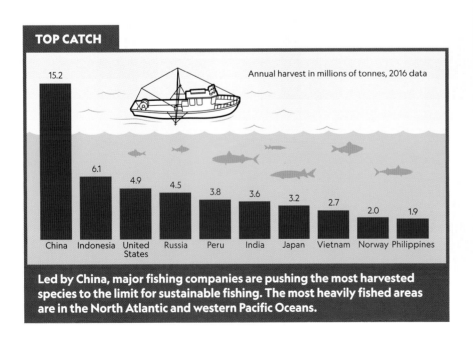

TOP CATCH

Annual harvest in millions of tonnes, 2016 data

Country	Harvest
China	15.2
Indonesia	6.1
United States	4.9
Russia	4.5
Peru	3.8
India	3.6
Japan	3.2
Vietnam	2.7
Norway	2.0
Philippines	1.9

Led by China, major fishing companies are pushing the most harvested species to the limit for sustainable fishing. The most heavily fished areas are in the North Atlantic and western Pacific Oceans.

◯ **HEADED TO MARKET.** A woman inspects a batch of bananas at a banana production facility in Basse-Pointe, Martinique.

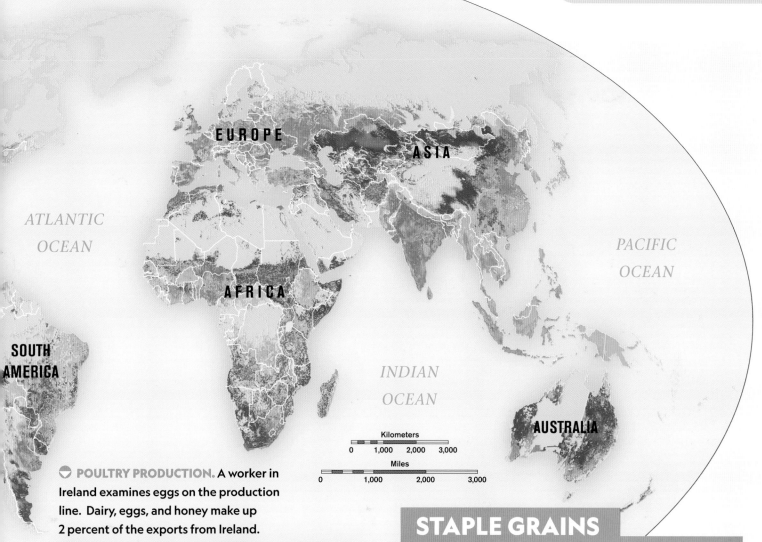

EUROPE

ASIA

ATLANTIC
OCEAN

PACIFIC
OCEAN

AFRICA

SOUTH
AMERICA

INDIAN
OCEAN

AUSTRALIA

Kilometers
0   1,000   2,000   3,000

Miles
0   1,000   2,000   3,000

**POULTRY PRODUCTION. A worker in
Ireland examines eggs on the production
line. Dairy, eggs, and honey make up
2 percent of the exports from Ireland.**

STAPLE GRAINS

CORN. A staple in prehistoric Central
and South America, corn (or maize) is
native to this region. When explorers
first arrived in the New World, corn
was already a hardy crop in much of
North and South America.

WHEAT. One of the two oldest grains
(barley is the other), wheat was
important in ancient Mediterranean
civilizations. Today, it is the most
widely cultivated grain. Wheat grows
best in temperate climates.

RICE. Originating in Asia many
millennia ago, rice is the staple grain
for about half the world's people. It is
a labor-intensive crop that grows
primarily in paddies (flooded fields)
and thrives in the hot, humid tropics.

**CASTING NETS. Fishermen in Orissa, India, cast their nets
on the Birupa River. Fish is an important source of protein in
their diets. Any surplus catch can be sold in the local market.**

World Energy

Almost everything people do requires energy. But energy comes in different forms. Traditional energy sources, such as burning wood and dried animal dung, are still used by many people in lower-income countries. Industrialized countries and urban centers around the world rely on coal, oil, and natural gas—called fossil fuels because they formed long ago from ancient deposits of decayed plant and animal material. As the map shows, these deposits are unevenly distributed on Earth, and many countries frequently cannot afford them.

Carbon dioxide from the burning of fossil fuels along with other emissions contributes to climate change. Concerned scientists are looking at new ways to harness sources of renewable energy, such as water, wind, sun, and biofuels (wood, plant materials, and garbage).

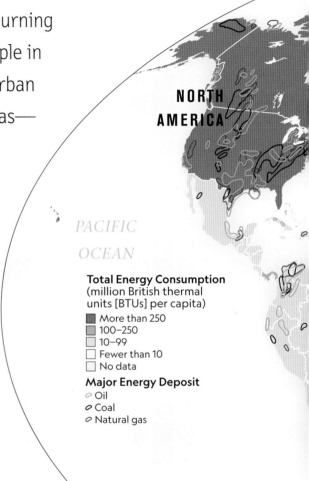

NORTH AMERICA

PACIFIC OCEAN

Total Energy Consumption
(million British thermal units [BTUs] per capita)
- More than 250
- 100–250
- 10–99
- Fewer than 10
- No data

Major Energy Deposit
- Oil
- Coal
- Natural gas

OIL, GAS, AND COAL

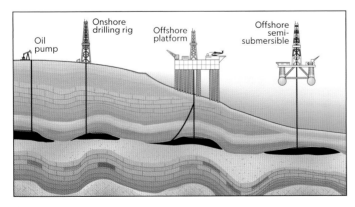

Oil pump · Onshore drilling rig · Offshore platform · Offshore semi-submersible

○ **DRILLING FOR OIL AND GAS.** The type of equipment used depends on whether the oil or natural gas is in the ground or under the ocean. This illustration shows some of the different kinds of onshore and offshore drilling equipment.

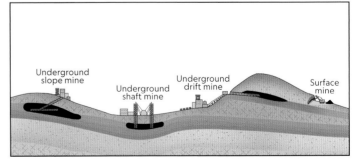

Underground slope mine · Underground shaft mine · Underground drift mine · Surface mine

○ **COAL MINING.** The mining of coal made possible the industrial revolution, which began in the mid-1700s in England, and coal still remains a major energy source. Work that was once done by people using picks and shovels now relies heavily on mechanized equipment. This diagram shows some of the various kinds of mines currently in use.

POLITICAL WORLD

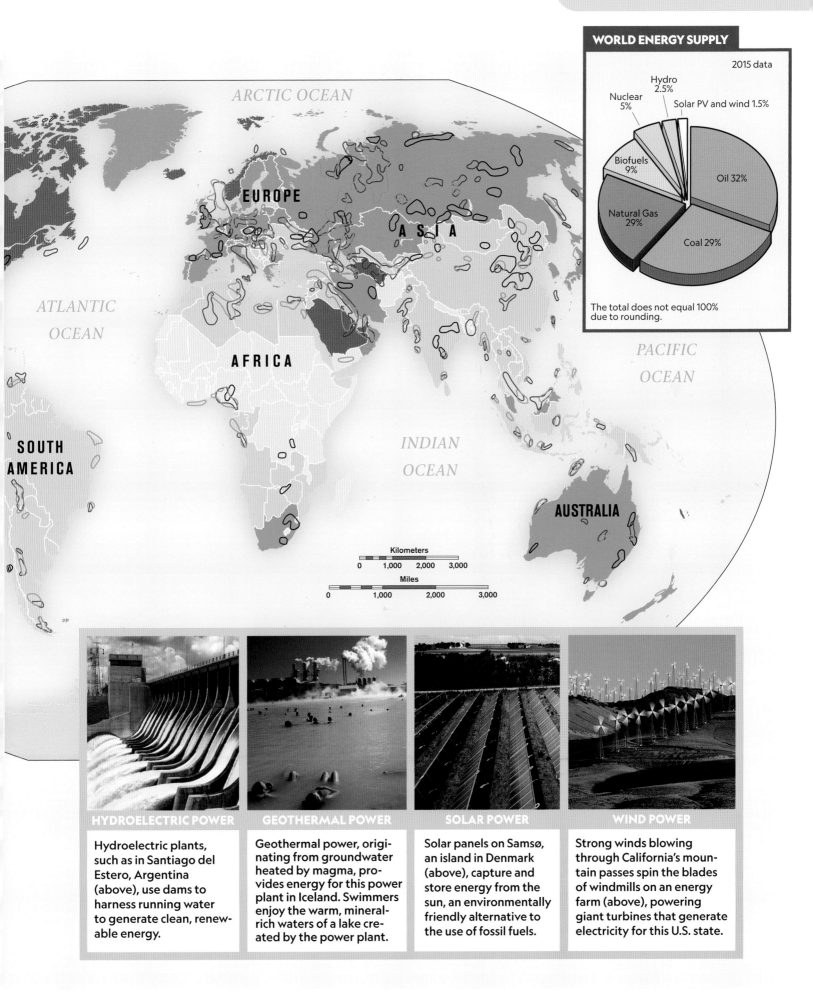

ARCTIC OCEAN

EUROPE

ASIA

ATLANTIC
OCEAN

AFRICA

PACIFIC
OCEAN

INDIAN
OCEAN

SOUTH
AMERICA

AUSTRALIA

Kilometers
0   1,000   2,000   3,000

Miles
0   1,000   2,000   3,000

WORLD ENERGY SUPPLY

2015 data

Hydro
2.5%

Nuclear
5%

Solar PV and wind 1.5%

Biofuels
9%

Oil 32%

Natural Gas
29%

Coal 29%

The total does not equal 100%
due to rounding.

HYDROELECTRIC POWER

Hydroelectric plants, such as in Santiago del Estero, Argentina (above), use dams to harness running water to generate clean, renewable energy.

GEOTHERMAL POWER

Geothermal power, originating from groundwater heated by magma, provides energy for this power plant in Iceland. Swimmers enjoy the warm, mineral-rich waters of a lake created by the power plant.

SOLAR POWER

Solar panels on Samsø, an island in Denmark (above), capture and store energy from the sun, an environmentally friendly alternative to the use of fossil fuels.

WIND POWER

Strong winds blowing through California's mountain passes spin the blades of windmills on an energy farm (above), powering giant turbines that generate electricity for this U.S. state.

THE CONTINENT:
NORTH AMERICA

PHYSICAL			POLITICAL	
TOTAL AREA 9,449,000 sq mi (24,474,000 sq km)	**LOWEST POINT** Death Valley, California, U.S.A. -282 ft (-86 m)	**LARGEST LAKE** Lake Superior, U.S.-Canada 31,700 sq mi (82,100 sq km)	**POPULATION** 592,072,000	**LARGEST COUNTRY** Canada 3,855,101 sq mi (9,984,670 sq km)
HIGHEST POINT Denali (Mount McKinley), Alaska, U.S.A. 20,310 ft (6,190 m)	**LONGEST RIVER** Mississippi-Missouri, United States 3,710 mi (5,971 km)		**LARGEST METROPOLITAN AREA** Mexico City, Mexico Pop. 21,782,000	**MOST DENSELY POPULATED COUNTRY** Barbados 1,765 people per sq mi (681 per sq km)

NORTH AMERICA

North America

2   3   4   5   6   7   8

See inset map on page 66 for the Aleutian Islands and continuation of the Bering Sea.

ARCTIC OCEAN

Wandel Sea
Greenland Sea
Jan Mayen
Oodaaq Island
Peary Land
Lincoln Sea
Faroe Islands

ASIA
Chukchi Sea
St. Lawrence Island
Bering Str.
Point Barrow

QUEEN ELIZABETH IS.
Axel Heiberg I.
Ellesmere I.
Knud Rasmussen Land
ICELAND
ARCTIC CIRCLE

Bering Sea
Seward Peninsula
North Slope
Brooks Range
Beaufort Sea
Borden Island
Mackenzie King I.
Prince Patrick I.
SVERDRUP ISLANDS
PARRY ISLANDS
Hayes Peninsula
GREENLAND
Gunnbjørn
12,119 feet
3,694 meters

Nunivak Island
ALASKA
Yukon
Kuskokwim
Melville Island
Banks Island
Devon I.
Somerset I.
Baffin Bay
Qeqertarsuaq

Highest point in North America
Denali (Mt. McKinley)
20,310 ft
6,190 m
Prince of Wales I.
Boothia Pen.
Baffin Island
Davis Strait

Bristol Bay
Aleutian Range
Alaska Range
Victoria Island
King William I.
Melville Peninsula
Prince Charles I.

Kodiak I.
Kenai Peninsula
Mt. Logan
19,551 ft
5,959 m
Great Bear L.
Southampton Island
Foxe Basin
Hudson Strait
Labrador Sea

Gulf of Alaska
Plateau
CANADA
Ungava Bay
ATLANTIC OCEAN

Glacier Bay
Coast Mountains
Great Slave Lake
Mackenzie Mts.
Slave
Hudson Bay
Ungava Peninsula
LABRADOR

Alexander Archipelago
ROCKY
Peace
Lake Athabasca
CANADIAN
Belcher Islands
James Bay
Island of Newfoundland

Haida Gwaii
Fraser Plateau
Athabasca
Churchill
Saskatchewan
Nelson
SHIELD
Laurentide Scarp
Anticosti Island
Avalon Peninsula

Vancouver Island
Columbia Mts.
MOUNTAINS
GREAT
Lake Winnipeg
Gulf of St. Lawrence
Cape Breton Island
Prince Edward Island

Olympic Peninsula
Columbia
Cascade Range
Missouri
Lake Superior
St. Lawrence
Gaspé Pen.
MOUNTAINS
Nova Scotia

Columbia Plateau
Snake
L. Michigan
Lake Huron
L. Ontario
Bay of Fundy
Gulf of Maine
Cape Cod

Cape Mendocino
Great Basin
Great Salt Lake
L. Erie
APPALACHIAN
Long Island

Sierra Nevada
Mt. Whitney
14,494 feet
4,418 meters
Platte
Missouri
CENTRAL LOWLAND
Chesapeake Bay
Cape Hatteras
Bermuda Islands

Death Valley
-282 ft -86 m
Colorado Plateau
UNITED STATES
Arkansas
Ohio

Lowest point in North America
Grand Canyon
PLAINS
Ozark Plateau
Mississippi
COASTAL

Channel Islands
Colorado
High Plains
Red
Florida
Grand Bahama Island
TROPIC OF CANCER

Guadalupe I.
Sonoran Desert
PLAIN
THE BAHAMAS

Eugenia Point
Baja California
Rio Grande
Florida Keys
Straits of Florida
WEST
Virgin Islands
ST. KITTS & NEVIS

PACIFIC OCEAN
Gulf of California
Sierra Madre Occidental
CUBA
GREATER
HAITI
DOMINICAN REPUBLIC
Puerto Rico
Guadeloupe
ANTIGUA & BARBUDA
DOMINICA

False Cape
MEXICO
Cayman Islands
Hispaniola
INDIES
Martinique

Pico de Orizaba
18,855 ft
5,747 m
Yucatan Peninsula
Cozumel Island
ANTILLES
JAMAICA
ST. LUCIA
BARBADOS

Revillagigedo Islands
Sierra Madre Oriental
Caribbean Sea
Lesser Antilles
ST. VINCENT & THE GRENADINES
GRENADA
TRINIDAD & TOBAGO
Trinidad

Isthmus of Tehuantepec
BELIZE
Gulf of Mexico

Gulf of Tehuantepec
Sierra Madre del Sur
GUATEMALA
HONDURAS
Mosquito Coast

EL SALVADOR
NICARAGUA

Map Key
— Country boundary

Lake Nicaragua
CENTRAL
COSTA RICA

Clipperton

0   600 miles
0   600 kilometers
Azimuthal Equidistant Projection

AMERICA
Isthmus of Panama
PANAMA
Gulf of Panama
Coiba I.
SOUTH AMERICA

Cocos Island

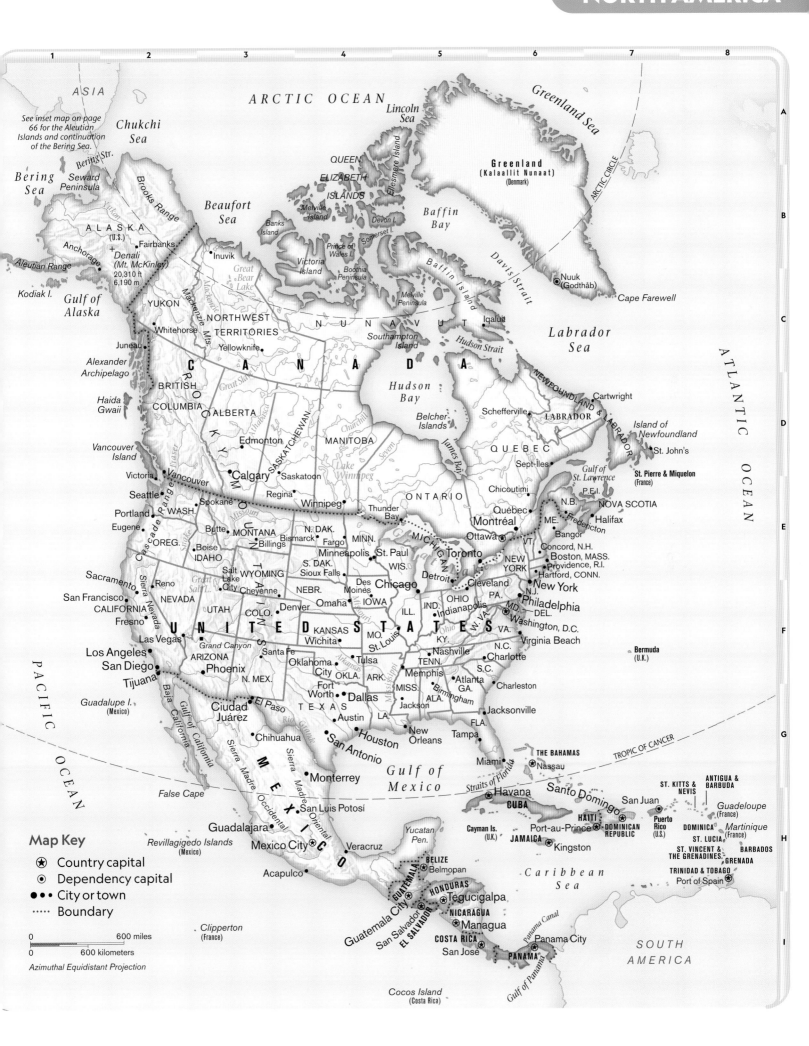

ASIA

See inset map on page 66 for the Aleutian Islands and continuation of the Bering Sea.

ARCTIC OCEAN

Chukchi Sea

Lincoln Sea

Greenland Sea

Bering Str.

Bering Sea

Seward Peninsula

Brooks Range

Beaufort Sea

QUEEN ELIZABETH ISLANDS

Ellesmere Island

Greenland (Kalaallit Nunaat) (Denmark)

ARCTIC CIRCLE

ALASKA (U.S.)

Anchorage

Fairbanks

Denali (Mt. McKinley) 20,310 ft 6,190 m

Inuvik

Great Bear Lake

Banks Island

Melville Island

Victoria Island

Prince of Wales I.

Somerset I.

Devon I.

Baffin Bay

Aleutian Range

Kodiak I.

Gulf of Alaska

YUKON

Mackenzie Mts.

NORTHWEST TERRITORIES

Whitehorse

Yellowknife

Boothia Peninsula

Melville Peninsula

N U N A V U T

Baffin Island

Iqaluit

Davis Strait

Nuuk (Godthåb)

Cape Farewell

Juneau

Alexander Archipelago

C A N A D A

BRITISH COLUMBIA

Great Slave L.

Southampton Island

Hudson Strait

Labrador Sea

Haida Gwaii

ALBERTA

SASKATCHEWAN

MANITOBA

Churchill

Hudson Bay

James Bay

Belcher Islands

Schefferville

NEWFOUNDLAND & LABRADOR

Cartwright

LABRADOR

Vancouver Island

Edmonton

Athabasca

Seven

Lake Winnipeg

QUEBEC

Island of Newfoundland

St. John's

Victoria

Vancouver

Calgary

Saskatoon

Sept-Îles

Gulf of St. Lawrence

St. Pierre & Miquelon (France)

Fraser

Seattle

Spokane

Regina

Winnipeg

Thunder Bay

ONTARIO

Chicoutimi

P.E.I.

N.B.

NOVA SCOTIA

Portland

WASH.

Québec

ME.

Fredericton

Halifax

Eugene

OREG.

Butte

Billings

MONTANA

N. DAK.

Bismarck

Fargo

MINN.

Montréal

Ottawa

MICHIGAN

Toronto

VT

Concord, N.H.

Bangor

Boston, MASS.

Boise

IDAHO

WYOMING

S. DAK.

Minneapolis

St. Paul

WIS.

Detroit

NEW YORK

Providence, R.I.

Hartford, CONN.

Sacramento

Reno

Salt Lake City

Cheyenne

Sioux Falls

NEBR.

Des Moines

IOWA

Chicago

OHIO

Cleveland

PA.

N.J.

New York

San Francisco

NEVADA

UTAH

COLO.

Denver

Omaha

ILL.

IND.

Indianapolis

MD.

Philadelphia

DEL.

Fresno

CALIFORNIA

Grand Canyon

Las Vegas

Santa Fe

KANSAS

MO.

St. Louis

KY.

W. VA.

VA.

Washington, D.C.

Los Angeles

ARIZONA

Phoenix

Oklahoma City

OKLA.

Tulsa

Wichita

Arkansas

Nashville

TENN.

N.C.

Charlotte

Virginia Beach

San Diego

Tijuana

N. MEX.

El Paso

TEXAS

ARK.

Memphis

MISS.

Birmingham

ALA.

Atlanta

GA.

S.C.

Charleston

Guadalupe I. (Mexico)

Baja California

Ciudad Juárez

Fort Worth

Dallas

Jackson

LA.

New Orleans

FLA.

Jacksonville

Chihuahua

Rio Grande

Austin

San Antonio

Houston

Tampa

Gulf of California

Sierra Madre Occidental

Sierra Madre Oriental

Monterrey

Gulf of Mexico

Miami

THE BAHAMAS

Nassau

TROPIC OF CANCER

Bermuda (U.K.)

False Cape

M E X I C O

San Luis Potosí

Straits of Florida

Havana

CUBA

Santo Domingo

San Juan

ST. KITTS & NEVIS

ANTIGUA & BARBUDA

Guadalajara

Cayman Is. (U.K.)

HAITI

Port-au-Prince

DOMINICAN REPUBLIC

Puerto Rico (U.S.)

DOMINICA

Guadeloupe (France)

Martinique (France)

Revillagigedo Islands (Mexico)

Mexico City

Veracruz

Yucatan Pen.

JAMAICA

Kingston

ST. LUCIA

ST. VINCENT & THE GRENADINES

BARBADOS

GRENADA

Acapulco

BELIZE

Belmopan

Caribbean Sea

TRINIDAD & TOBAGO

Port of Spain

GUATEMALA

Guatemala City

HONDURAS

Tegucigalpa

San Salvador

EL SALVADOR

NICARAGUA

Managua

Panama Canal

Panama City

Clipperton (France)

COSTA RICA

San José

PANAMA

Gulf of Panama

SOUTH AMERICA

Cocos Island (Costa Rica)

PACIFIC OCEAN

ATLANTIC OCEAN

Map Key

⊛ Country capital

⊙ Dependency capital

••• City or town

····· Boundary

0 — 600 miles
0 — 600 kilometers

Azimuthal Equidistant Projection

North America

LAND OF CONTRASTS

From the windswept tundra of Alaska, U.S.A., to the rainforest of Panama, the third largest continent stretches 5,500 miles (8,850 km), spanning natural environments that are home to wildlife from polar bears to jaguars. The continent supports 23 countries and 592 million people who live primarily near the coasts and inland water sources. Culturally, the region reflects a mix of people who can trace their ancestry to indigenous people, West African countries, European countries, and elsewhere. Economically, the region's resources have enhanced the growth of North America's countries, as well as provided job opportunities for its people.

QUINCEAÑERA IN CUBA. Upon celebrating her 15th birthday, this young lady enjoys her quinceañera in style along the Malecón (roadway) in Havana, Cuba.

DRESSED TO CELEBRATE. This boy in Mexico's southern state of Chiapas wears traditional clothing, including a charro-style tie with the colors of the Mexican flag and a sombrero used to shade his face from the sun.

⬡ **HOLD TIGHT.** These daring rafters run the roaring rapids of the Kicking Horse River in British Columbia, Canada's westernmost province. Rivers tumbling down the steep slopes of the Rocky Mountains provide many recreational opportunities.

◁ **STREET MUSIC.**
People from around the world visit New Orleans, Louisiana, U.S.A., to hear jazz musicians fill the air with their music.

▷ **COYOTE CALL.**
A coyote sends its mournful howl into the Arizona skies. Members of the dog family, coyotes originated in the southwestern United States but are now found throughout North America—even in urban areas.

more about
North America

◔ **HIGH FLIER.** A young Kutchin boy sails off a snowbank on snowshoes in Canada's Yukon. The Kutchin, an Athabascan tribe, live in the forested lands of eastern Alaska and western Canada. The name Kutchin means "people."

◔ **DWELLINGS FROM THE PAST.** Between 1000 and 1300 c.e., native people known as ancestral Puebloans built cliff dwellings called pueblos, such as this one in Mesa Verde, Colorado, U.S.A.

◔ **MAYA TREASURE.** The Pyramid of the Magician marks the ruins of Uxmal on the Yucatan Peninsula. At least five million people of Maya descent still live in southern Mexico and Central America.

◑ **FROZEN SUMMER.** Because Greenland lies so far north, even summers there are cold. Here, local people navigate their boat among icebergs in waters off the village of Aappilattoq.

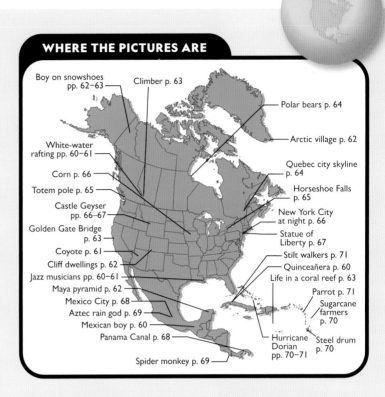

⬆ **SWIMMING FREE.** A variety of fish swim among colorful corals in the clear blue waters of the Caribbean Sea. Tropical waters are the habitat for many species of fish.

WHERE THE PICTURES ARE

Boy on snowshoes pp. 62–63
Climber p. 63
Polar bears p. 64
Arctic village p. 62
White-water rafting pp. 60–61
Corn p. 66
Totem pole p. 65
Castle Geyser pp. 66–67
Golden Gate Bridge p. 63
Coyote p. 61
Cliff dwellings p. 62
Jazz musicians pp. 60–61
Maya pyramid p. 62
Mexico City p. 68
Aztec rain god p. 69
Mexican boy p. 60
Panama Canal p. 68
Spider monkey p. 69
Quebec city skyline p. 64
Horseshoe Falls p. 65
New York City at night p. 66
Statue of Liberty p. 67
Stilt walkers p. 71
Quinceañera p. 60
Life in a coral reef p. 63
Parrot p. 71
Sugarcane farmers p. 70
Steel drum p. 70
Hurricane Dorian pp. 70–71

⬇ **DON'T LOOK DOWN.** Clinging to a rock face, an adventurous climber demonstrates great skill as she scales a steep cliff in Banff National Park in Alberta, Canada. Covering more than 2,500 square miles (6,475 sq km) in the Canadian Rockies, Banff is a major tourist attraction.

⬆ **WESTERN GATEWAY.** The Golden Gate Bridge marks the entrance to San Francisco Bay, U.S.A. Beyond the bridge, captured above, is the California port city that shares a name with the bay.

THE BASICS

STATS

Area
3,855,101 sq mi
(9,984,670 sq km)

Population
35,882,000

Predominant languages
English, French (both official)

Predominant religion
Christianity

GDP per capita
$48,300

Life expectancy
82 years

GEO WHIZ

Nunavut, Canada's newest territory, has issued license plates shaped like a polar bear for cars, motorcycles, and snowmobiles.

Canada's government is a parliamentary democracy that governs under a constitutional monarch, Britain's Queen Elizabeth II.

Canada's Bay of Fundy, located between the eastern provinces of New Brunswick and Nova Scotia, has the highest tides in the world, with a tidal range reaching up to 53 feet (16 m).

Geologists believe the impact of a meteorite may have created Quebec's Réservoir Manicouagan more than 200 million years ago.

Canada

Topped only by Russia in area, Canada has just 36 million people. That's less than the population of the U.S. state of California. Ancient rocks yield abundant minerals. Lakes and rivers in Quebec are tapped for hydropower, and wheat farming and cattle ranching thrive across the western Prairie Provinces. Vast forests attract loggers, and mountain slopes provide a playground for nature lovers. Enormous deposits of oil sands are converted into barrels of oil, exposing the fragile tundra and waterways to possible contamination and habitat disruption. Most Canadians live within a hundred miles (161 km) of the U.S. border in cities, such as Asian-influenced Vancouver, ethnically diverse Toronto, national capital Ottawa, and French-speaking Montreal.

◗ SILENT WATCHERS. Polar bears, North America's largest land carnivores, are adapted to the extreme Arctic environment around Cape Churchill in northern Manitoba. An estimated 16,000 polar bears live in Canada.

LONGEST COASTLINE

Country	Coastline
Canada	151,023 miles (243,042 km)
Indonesia	33,998 miles (54,716 km)
Russia	23,397 miles (37,653 km)
Philippines	22,549 miles (36,289 km)
Japan	18,486 miles (29,751 km)
Australia	16,006 miles (25,760 km)
Norway	15,626 miles (25,148 km)
United States	12,380 miles (19,924 km)
New Zealand	9,404 miles (15,134 km)
China	9,010 miles (14,500 km)

Canada has the longest coastline in the world, and at more than 150,000 miles (243,000 km) it far surpasses the length of coastline of any other country.

◗ FRENCH ENCLAVE.
Château Frontenac sparkles in Quebec City's nighttime skyline. Settled by the French in the early 1600s, the province of Quebec has maintained close ties to its French heritage.

◑ **KNOWING WHO WE ARE.** Native people of the Pacific Northwest preserve family stories and legends in massive carved poles called totems.

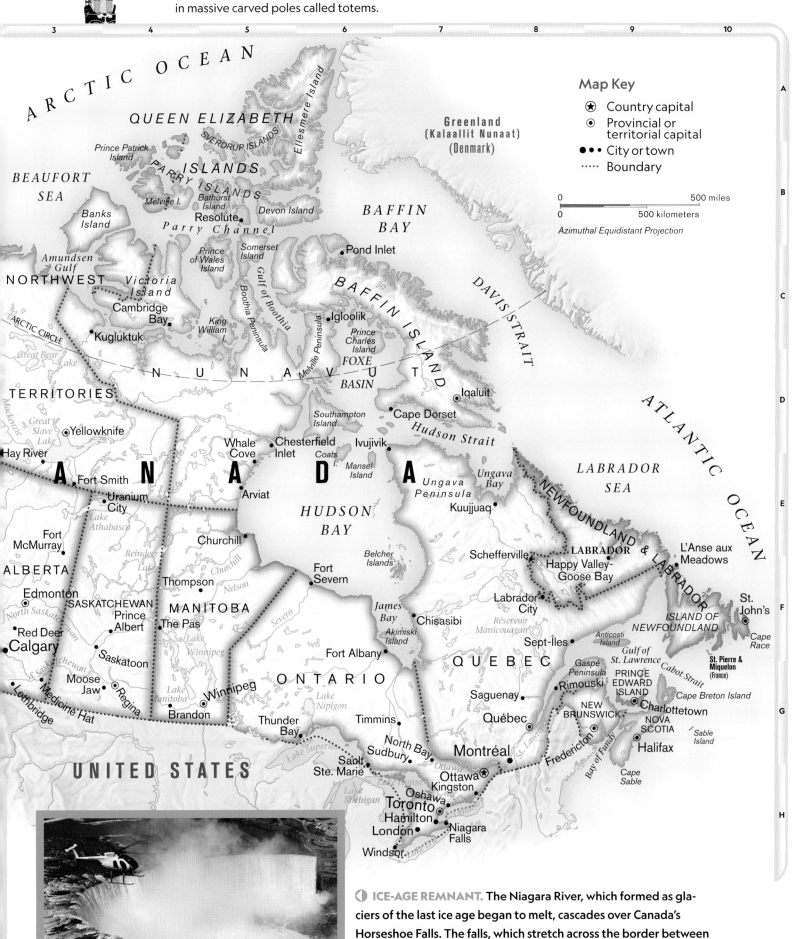

Map Key

★ Country capital
◉ Provincial or territorial capital
●•• City or town
····· Boundary

0 ——————————— 500 miles
0 ——————————— 500 kilometers

Azimuthal Equidistant Projection

ARCTIC OCEAN

QUEEN ELIZABETH
SVERDRUP ISLANDS
Ellesmere Island
Prince Patrick Island
ISLANDS
PARRY ISLANDS
Melville I.
Bathurst Island
Devon Island

BEAUFORT SEA

Greenland
(Kalaallit Nunaat)
(Denmark)

BAFFIN BAY

Banks Island
Resolute
Parry Channel

Amundsen Gulf

NORTHWEST
Victoria Island
Cambridge Bay
Prince of Wales Island
Somerset Island
Gulf of Boothia
Boothia Peninsula

DAVIS STRAIT

ARCTIC CIRCLE
Kugluktuk
King William I.
Melville Peninsula
Igloolik
BAFFIN ISLAND
Prince Charles Island
FOXE BASIN

Great Bear Lake

TERRITORIES
N U N A V U T
Iqaluit

ATLANTIC OCEAN

Great Slave Lake
◉Yellowknife
Southampton Island
Cape Dorset

Hay River
Whale Cove
Chesterfield Inlet
Coats I.
Ivujivik
Hudson Strait

LABRADOR SEA

C A N A D A

Fort Smith
Arviat
Mansel Island
Ungava Peninsula
Ungava Bay

Uranium City
HUDSON BAY
Kuujjuaq
NEWFOUNDLAND & LABRADOR

Lake Athabasca

Fort McMurray
Reindeer Lake
Churchill
Belcher Islands
Scheffersville
LABRADOR
Happy Valley-Goose Bay
L'Anse aux Meadows

ALBERTA
Thompson
Churchill
Fort Severn
Labrador City

Edmonton
Nelson
James Bay
Réservoir Manicouagan
Sept-Îles
ISLAND OF NEWFOUNDLAND
St. John's

SASKATCHEWAN
MANITOBA
Severn
Akimiski Island
Chisasibi
Anticosti Island
Cape Race

Prince Albert
The Pas
Cape Breton Island

Red Deer
Saskatoon
Lake Winnipeg
Fort Albany
Q U E B E C
Gaspé Peninsula
PRINCE EDWARD ISLAND

Calgary
Moose Jaw
Regina
Lake Manitoba
ONTARIO
Saguenay
Rimouski
Charlottetown

Medicine Hat
Winnipeg
Lake Nipigon
Québec
NEW BRUNSWICK
NOVA SCOTIA
Sable Island

Lethbridge
Brandon
Thunder Bay
Timmins
North Bay
Montréal
Fredericton
Halifax

UNITED STATES
Lake Superior
Sault Ste. Marie
Sudbury
Ottawa
Kingston
Bay of Fundy
Cape Sable

Lake Huron
Oshawa
Toronto
Hamilton
London
Niagara Falls
Lake Michigan
Windsor

St. Pierre & Miquelon (France)

Mackenzie
North Saskatchewan
S. Saskatchewan

◑ **ICE-AGE REMNANT.** The Niagara River, which formed as glaciers of the last ice age began to melt, cascades over Canada's Horseshoe Falls. The falls, which stretch across the border between Canada and the United States, are a major tourist attraction.

THE CONTINENT:
NORTH AMERICA

United States

THE BASICS

STATS

Area
3,796,741 sq mi
(9,833,517 sq km)

Population
329,256,000

Predominant languages
English, Spanish

Predominant religion
Christianity

GDP per capita
$59,500

Life expectancy
80 years

GEO WHIZ

Florida is known as the lightning capital of the United States. Breezes from the Gulf of Mexico and Atlantic Ocean collide over the warm Florida peninsula to create thunderstorms and the lightning associated with them.

Hawai'i is politically part of the United States but geographically part of Polynesia, a cultural region of Oceania (pages 156–157).

Lake Michigan is the only one of the Great Lakes located entirely within the United States. Each of the other four lakes spans the U.S.-Canada border.

From "sea to shining sea" the United States is blessed with a rich bounty of natural resources. Mineral treasures abound—oil, coal, iron, and gold—and its croplands are among the most productive in the world. Americans have used this storehouse of raw materials to build an economic base unmatched by that of any other country. An array of high-tech businesses populates the Sunbelt of the South and West. By combining its natural riches and the creative ideas of its ethnically diverse population, this land of opportunity has become a leading global power.

⬢ **STAPLE CROP.**
In 2020, 92 million acres (37 million ha) of corn were planted in the U.S. Most of the crop is used as livestock feed.

◑ **WORLD CITY.** The lights of Manhattan glitter around New York City's Chrysler Building. The city's influence as a financial and cultural center extends across the United States and around the world.

◑ **LETTING OFF STEAM.** Castle Geyser in Wyoming is just one of many active geological features in Yellowstone National Park. The park is part of a region that sits on top of a major tectonic hot spot.

THE CONTINENT:
NORTH AMERICA

LADY LIBERTY. The Statue of Liberty, in New York City's harbor, has become a symbol of hope for millions of immigrants coming to the United States.

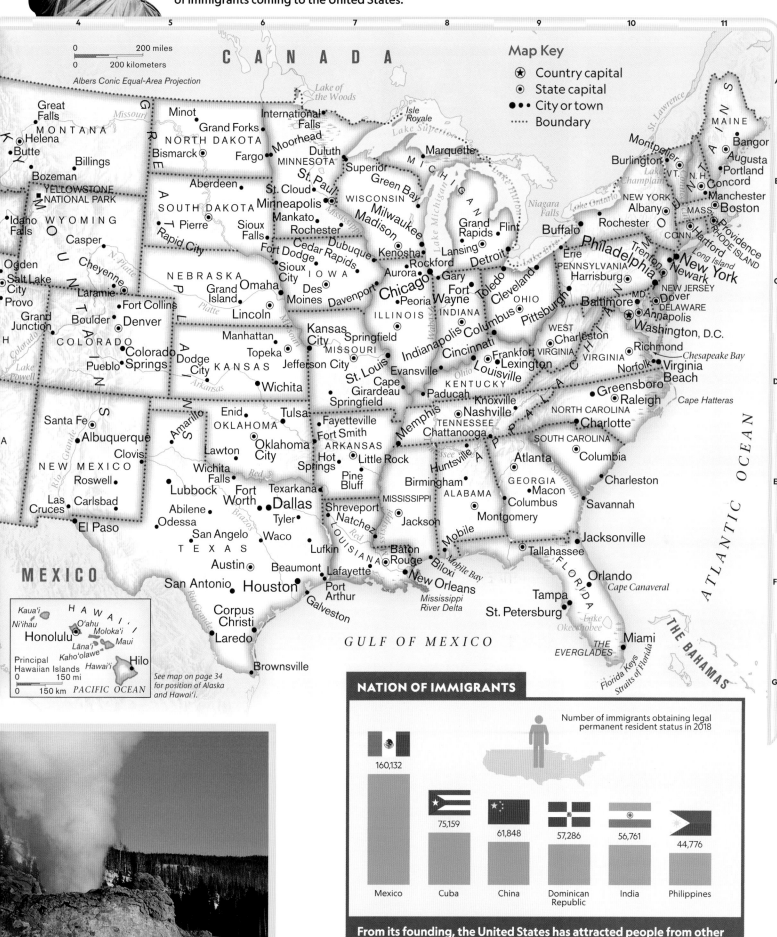

NATION OF IMMIGRANTS

Number of immigrants obtaining legal permanent resident status in 2018

Mexico	Cuba	China	Dominican Republic	India	Philippines
160,132	75,159	61,848	57,286	56,761	44,776

From its founding, the United States has attracted people from other lands. Today, most immigrants come from the Americas and Asia.

THE CONTINENT:
NORTH AMERICA

THE BASICS

STATS

Largest country
Mexico
758,449 sq mi
(1,964,375 sq km)

Smallest country
El Salvador
8,124 sq mi (21,041 sq km)

Most populous country
Mexico
125,959,000

Least populous country
Belize
386,000

Predominant languages
English, Spanish, Mayan,
indigenous languages

Predominant religion
Christianity

Highest GDP per capita
Panama
$25,400

Lowest GDP per capita
Honduras
$5,600

Highest life expectancy
Costa Rica, Panama
79 years

Lowest life expectancy
Belize
69 years

GEO WHIZ

Mexico takes its name from the word Mexica, another name for the Aztec, an indigenous people who ruled the land before it fell to the Spanish in 1521.

Coral colonies growing along much of the coast of Belize form the longest barrier reef in the Western Hemisphere.

Thumb-size vampire bats live throughout Central America.

◗ **URBAN OASIS. Throughout** Mexico City, traditional and modern structures create a vibrant cityscape. After an earthquake in 1985, developers built the Santa Fe neighborhood and La Mexicana Park. To maximize land use, both areas were constructed on a former landfill area.

Mexico & Central America

◗ **VITAL LINK. More than 17,000** oil tankers, cruise ships, and cargo vessels pass through the Panama Canal yearly, avoiding a long trip around South America.

Mexico and most Central American countries share a mountain range, a legacy of powerful First People empires, and an influence from Spanish colonization. Deforestation has destroyed much of the rainforest in the region. Mexico dwarfs its seven Central American neighbors in area, population, and natural resources. Its economy boasts a rich diversity of agricultural crops, highly productive oil fields, and a growing manufacturing base, as well as strong trade with the United States and Canada. Overall, Central American countries rely on agricultural products such as bananas and coffee, though tourism is increasing. Opportunities for jobs and education and concerns over violence increase migration from Central American countries to the northern countries of Mexico and the United States.

Tijuana
Ensenada
Mexicali
BAJA CALIFORNIA
Gulf of California
Nogales
Hermosillo
Guaymas
Yaqui
Ciudad Obregón
Los Mochis
La Paz
False Cape

◑ **MYTHS AND LEGENDS.** The powerful Aztec Empire dominated much of Mexico and Central America from 1427 to 1521.

◑ **TREETOP LIVING.** This spider monkey hangs by its tail in a rainforest on the Osa Peninsula, in Costa Rica. Found in undisturbed forests from southern Mexico to Brazil, spider monkeys spend nearly all their time in trees.

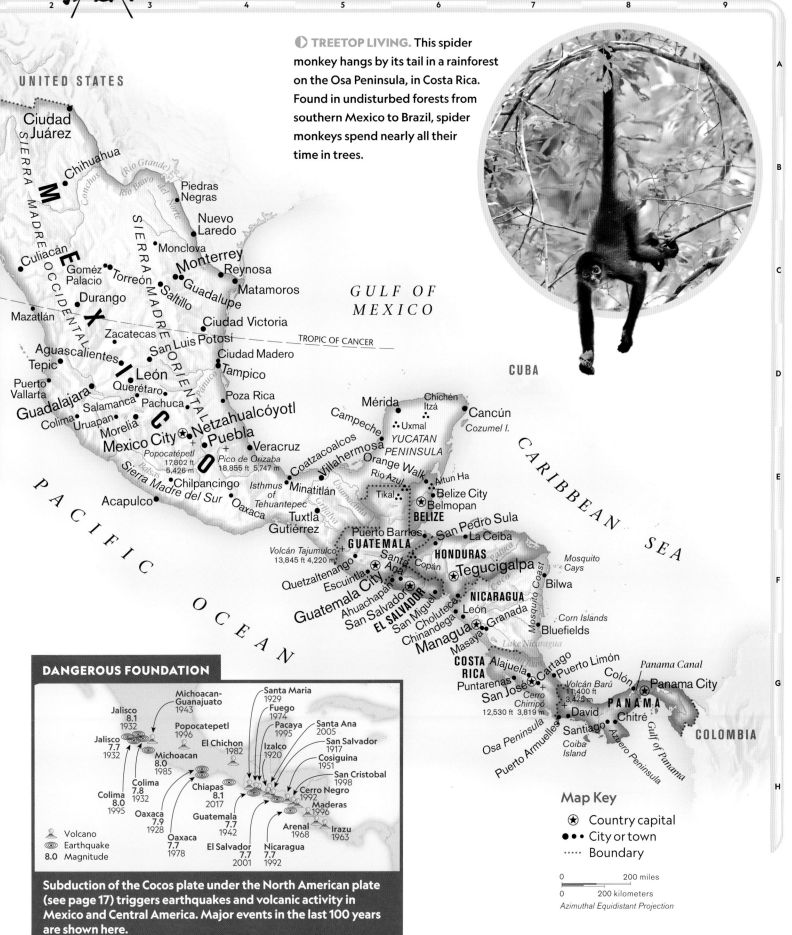

UNITED STATES

Ciudad Juárez
SIERRA MADRE
Chihuahua
Río Grande
Conchos
Río Bravo del Norte
Piedras Negras
Nuevo Laredo
Monclova
M
Culiacán
Goméz Palacio
Torreón
Monterrey
Reynosa
Guadalupe
Saltillo
Matamoros
Durango
Mazatlán
E
Ciudad Victoria
Zacatecas
San Luis Potosí
Aguascalientes
Ciudad Madero
Tampico
Tepic
X
León
Puerto Vallarta
Querétaro
Poza Rica
Guadalajara
Salamanca
Pachuca
Netzahualcóyotl
Colima
Uruapan
Morelia
Mexico City
Puebla
Veracruz
I
Acapulco
Chilpancingo
Sierra Madre del Sur
Oaxaca
Popocatépetl 17,802 ft 5,426 m
Pico de Orizaba 18,855 ft 5,747 m
C
O
Balsas
Isthmus of Tehuantepec
Minatitlán
Tuxtla Gutiérrez
Coatzacoalcos
Villahermosa
Orange Walk
Campeche
YUCATAN PENINSULA
Mérida
Chichén Itzá
Uxmal
Cancún
Cozumel I.
Río Azul
Altun Ha
Tikal
Belize City
Belmopan
BELIZE
San Pedro Sula
La Ceiba
Puerto Barrios
GUATEMALA
Copán
HONDURAS
Tegucigalpa
Mosquito Cays
Bilwa
Volcán Tajumulco 13,845 ft 4,220 m
Santa Ana
Quetzaltenango
Escuintla
Guatemala City
Ahuachapán
San Salvador
EL SALVADOR
San Miguel
Choluteca
Chinandega
León
NICARAGUA
Managua
Masaya
Granada
Lake Nicaragua
Corn Islands
Bluefields
Mosquito Coast
Coco
Patuca
Grijalva
Usumacinta
Pánuco

GULF OF MEXICO
TROPIC OF CANCER
CUBA
CARIBBEAN SEA
PACIFIC OCEAN

COSTA RICA
Alajuela
Puntarenas
San José
Cartago
Puerto Limón
Colón
Panama Canal
Panama City
PANAMA
COLOMBIA
Volcán Barú 11,400 ft 3,475 m
Cerro Chirripó 12,530 ft 3,819 m
David
Chitré
Santiago
Osa Peninsula
Puerto Armuelles
Coiba Island
Azuero Peninsula
Gulf of Panama

DANGEROUS FOUNDATION

Michoacan-Guanajuato 1943
Santa Maria 1929
Jalisco 8.1 1932
Popocatepetl 1996
Fuego 1974
Pacaya 1995
Santa Ana 2005
Jalisco 7.7 1932
El Chichon 1982
Izalco 1920
San Salvador 1917
Michoacan 8.0 1985
Cosiguina 1951
Colima 7.8 1932
Chiapas 8.1 2017
San Cristobal 1998
Colima 8.0 1995
Oaxaca 7.9 1928
Guatemala 7.7
Cerro Negro 1992
Maderas 1996
Oaxaca 7.7 1978
El Salvador 7.7 2001
Nicaragua 7.7 1992
Arenal 1968
Irazu 1963

♨ Volcano
◎ Earthquake
8.0 Magnitude

Subduction of the Cocos plate under the North American plate (see page 17) triggers earthquakes and volcanic activity in Mexico and Central America. Major events in the last 100 years are shown here.

Map Key

⊛ Country capital
●●● City or town
····· Boundary

0 _____ 200 miles
0 _____ 200 kilometers
Azimuthal Equidistant Projection

THE CONTINENT:
NORTH AMERICA

West Indies & The Bahamas

◯ **RHYTHM OF THE TROPICS.**
When traditional drums were banned in Trinidad in 1884, plantation workers looked for new instruments, including 55-gallon (208-L) oil drums, which were the origin of today's steel drums, or "pans."

This region of tropical islands stretches from the Bahamas, off the eastern coast of Florida, to Trinidad and Tobago, off the northern coast of South America. The Greater Antilles—Cuba, Jamaica, Hispaniola, and U.S. territory Puerto Rico—account for nearly 90 percent of the region's land area and most of its 42 million people. An archipelago of smaller islands called the Lesser Antilles, plus the Bahamas, make up the rest of this region. Lush vegetation, warm waters, and scenic beaches attract tourists from across the globe. While these visitors bring much needed income, poverty is still a concern in the region.

◖ **WHITE GOLD.** Sugarcane is an important economic resource throughout the Caribbean. This woman carries freshly cut cane on her head in a field in Barbados.

FUN IN THE SUN

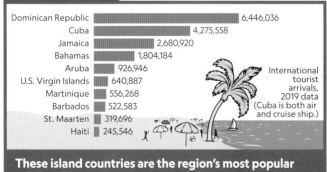

Country	International tourist arrivals
Dominican Republic	6,446,036
Cuba	4,275,558
Jamaica	2,680,920
Bahamas	1,804,184
Aruba	926,946
U.S. Virgin Islands	640,887
Martinique	556,268
Barbados	522,583
St. Maarten	319,696
Haiti	245,546

International tourist arrivals, 2019 data (Cuba is both air and cruise ship.)

These island countries are the region's most popular destinations for tourists seeking sandy beaches, blue waters, and warm breezes.

RARE BIRD. The red-necked Amazon, or Jaco, parrot is found only on the island of Dominica, where it lives on flowers, seeds, and fruits.

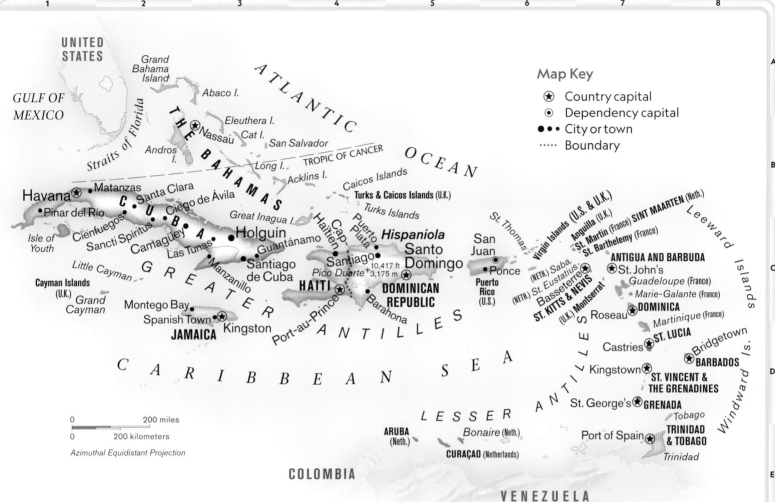

Map Key
- ★ Country capital
- ◉ Dependency capital
- ●●● City or town
- ····· Boundary

UNITED STATES

GULF OF MEXICO

Grand Bahama Island

Abaco I.

ATLANTIC OCEAN

Eleuthera I.
Cat I.
San Salvador

THE BAHAMAS

Nassau

Andros I.

Straits of Florida

Long I. TROPIC OF CANCER

Acklins I.

Caicos Islands

Turks & Caicos Islands (U.K.)

Turks Islands

St. Thomas

Virgin Islands (U.S. & U.K.)

Anguilla (U.K.)

St. Martin (France) SINT MAARTEN (Neth.)

St. Barthelemy (France)

Leeward Islands

Havana ★
Matanzas
Santa Clara
Ciego de Ávila
Pinar del Río
Cienfuegos
Isle of Youth
Sancti Spíritus
Camagüey
Las Tunas
Holguín
Guantánamo
Manzanillo
Santiago de Cuba

CUBA

GREATER

Little Cayman

Cayman Islands (U.K.)
Grand Cayman

Montego Bay
Spanish Town ★
Kingston

JAMAICA

Haitien
Cap-Haitien

Puerto Plata

Hispaniola

Santiago

Santo Domingo

Pico Duarte + 10,417 ft 3,175 m ★

HAITI

Port-au-Prince

DOMINICAN REPUBLIC

Barahona

San Juan

Ponce

Puerto Rico (U.S.)

(NETH.) Saba

St. Eustatius (NETH.)

Basseterre ★

ST. KITTS & NEVIS

Montserrat (U.K.)

ANTIGUA AND BARBUDA

St. John's

Guadeloupe (France)

Marie-Galante (France)

DOMINICA

Roseau

Martinique (France)

ANTILLES

Castries

ST. LUCIA

Bridgetown

BARBADOS

Kingstown ★

ST. VINCENT & THE GRENADINES

St. George's ★ GRENADA

Tobago

Windward Is.

Port of Spain ★

TRINIDAD & TOBAGO

Trinidad

LESSER ANTILLES

CARIBBEAN SEA

ARUBA (Neth.)

Bonaire (Neth.)

CURAÇAO (Netherlands)

COLOMBIA

VENEZUELA

0 ——— 200 miles
0 ——— 200 kilometers
Azimuthal Equidistant Projection

NATURAL DISASTERS. Hurricanes, such as Dorian in 2019, are a reminder of the forces of nature affecting the West Indies and the Bahamas. Islands in the region range in elevation from 0 to 10,000 feet (3,048 m), making them vulnerable to flooding and damage.

CELEBRATION. Stilt walkers in brightly colored costumes tower above this street in Old Havana, Cuba, during the annual celebration of Carnival. Introduced by Catholic colonizers from Spain, this festival occurs prior to the beginning of the religious season of Lent.

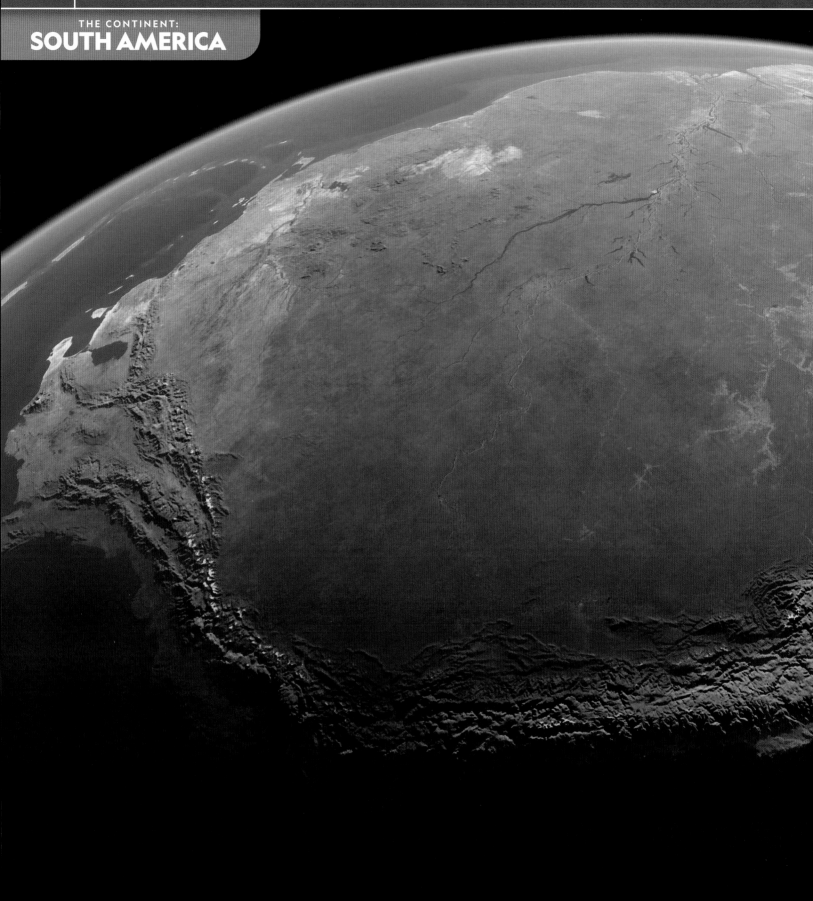

THE CONTINENT:
SOUTH AMERICA

PHYSICAL

TOTAL AREA
6,880,000 sq mi
(17,819,000 sq km)

LOWEST POINT
Laguna del Carbón, Argentina
-344 ft (-105 m)

LARGEST LAKE
Lake Titicaca,
Bolivia-Peru
3,200 sq mi
(8,300 sq km)

HIGHEST POINT
Cerro Aconcagua, Argentina
22,831 ft (6,959 m)

LONGEST RIVER
Amazon
4,150 mi (6,679 km)

POLITICAL

POPULATION
430,760,000

LARGEST METROPOLITAN AREA
São Paulo, Brazil
Pop. 22,043,000

LARGEST COUNTRY
Brazil
3,287,611 sq mi (8,514,877 sq km)

MOST DENSELY POPULATED COUNTRY
Ecuador
150.7 people per sq mi (58.1 per sq km)

SOUTH AMERICA

South America

CARIBBEAN SEA

NORTH
AMERICA

Lake
Maracaibo

Orinoco

Total drop
3,212 ft 979 m

LLANOS

VENEZUELA

Angel Falls

GUYANA

GUIANA

SURINAME

French
Guiana
(France)

HIGHLANDS

COLOMBIA

Malpelo
Island

Galápagos
Islands

EQUATOR

AMAZON

Negro

Amazon

Marajó
Island

ECUADOR

Amazon

Marañón

Madeira

Tapajós

Xingú

São Francisco

Selvas

Ucayali

Purus

BASIN

Teles Pires

Tocantins

BRAZIL

PERU

PACIFIC OCEAN

Lake
Titicaca

BOLIVIA

BRAZILIAN

HIGHLANDS

Altiplano

Salar de Uyuni

Pantanal

Atacama Desert

Paraguay

PARAGUAY

TROPIC OF CAPRICORN

Gran Chaco

Iguazú
Falls

San Félix Island

San Ambrosio Island

Paraná

Paraná

Uruguay

ATLANTIC OCEAN

Cerro
Aconcagua
22,831 ft
6,959 m

Highest point in
South America

Juan Fernández Islands

URUGUAY

River Plate

ANDES

ARGENTINA

PAMPAS

Negro

Valdés Peninsula

Isla Grande
de Chiloé

Gulf of
San Jorge

Taitao
Peninsula

PATAGONIA

Lowest point in
South America

Wellington Island

Laguna del Carbón
-344 ft -105 m

FALKLAND ISLANDS
(ISLAS MALVINAS)

Strait of Magellan

TIERRA DEL FUEGO

Cape Horn

South Georgia

Map Key

— Country boundary

0 ———— 600 miles
0 ———— 600 kilometers

Azimuthal Equidistant Projection

CARIBBEAN SEA

NORTH AMERICA

Santa Marta
Barranquilla
Cartagena
Lake Maracaibo
Maracaibo
Barquisimeto
Caracas
Maracay
Valencia
Ciudad Guayana
Cúcuta
Bucaramanga
San Cristóbal
VENEZUELA
Georgetown
GUYANA
Paramaribo
Medellín
Cayenne
Manizales
GUIANA
HIGHLANDS
SURINAME
French Guiana (France)
Ibagué
Bogotá
Angel Falls
COLOMBIA
Boa Vista
Amapá
Cali

Malpelo Island (Colombia)

Esmeraldas
Pasto
Boundary claimed by Venezuela
Boundary claimed by Suriname
EQUATOR

Quito
Negro
Amazon
Marajó Island
Belém
São Luís
ECUADOR
Manaus
Santarém
Parnaíba
Guayaquil
Amazon (Solimões)
Galápagos Islands (Ecuador)
Cuenca
Iquitos
Madeira
Tapajós
Marabá
Teresina
Fortaleza
Marañón
Selva
Xingu
Natal
Piura
João Pessoa
Chiclayo
s
Campina Grande
Trujillo
BASIN
Purus
Porto Velho
Teles Pires
Recife
Chimbote
Rio Branco
PERU
Tocantins
BRAZIL
Aracaju
Callao
Maceió
Lima
Machu Picchu
BRAZILIAN
Feira de Santana
Ayacucho
Cusco
Trinidad
Salvador (Bahia)
Ucayali
Titicaca
Brasília
São Francisco
Ilhéus
La Paz
HIGHLANDS
Arequipa
BOLIVIA
Goiânia
Altiplano
Cochabamba
Santa Cruz
Arica
Oruro
Uberlândia
Governador Valadares
Salar de Uyuni
Sucre
Campo Grande
Uberaba
Belo Horizonte
Iquique
São José do Rio Preto
Ribeirão Preto
Nova Iguaçu
Tarija
Londrina
Campinas
PARAGUAY
Pantanal
Rio de Janeiro
TROPIC OF CAPRICORN
Antofagasta
Gran Chaco
Paraguay
Asunción (Paraguay)
São Paulo
Santos
Salta
Iguazú Falls
Curitiba
San Félix Island (Chile)
San Ambrosio Island
San Miguel de Tucumán
Resistencia
Corrientes
Passo Fundo
Florianópolis
Paraná
Uruguaiana
La Serena
Cerro Aconcagua 22,831 ft 6,959 m
Córdoba
Uruguay
Santa Maria
Porto Alegre
Santa Fe
ARGENTINA
Valparaíso
Mendoza
PAMPAS
Rosario
URUGUAY
Santiago
ANDES
CHILE
Buenos Aires
Montevideo
Talca
La Plata
River Plate
Juan Fernández Islands (Chile)
Concepción
Mar del Plata
Temuco
Bahía Blanca
Negro
Puerto Montt
Viedma
Isla Grande de Chiloé
Valdés Peninsula
PATAGONIA
Comodoro Rivadavia
Gulf of San Jorge
Taitao Peninsula
Laguna del Carbón -344 ft -105 m
Wellington I.
Falkland Islands (Islas Malvinas) (United Kingdom) Claimed by Argentina
Stanley
Rio Gallegos
Strait of Magellan
Punta Arenas
TIERRA DEL FUEGO
Ushuaia
South Georgia (U.K.)
Cape Horn

PACIFIC OCEAN

ATLANTIC OCEAN

Map Key

⊛ Country capital
⊙ Dependency capital
••• City or town
····· Boundary
····· Claimed boundary

0 ——— 600 miles
0 ——— 600 kilometers
Azimuthal Equidistant Projection

South America

A MIX OF OLD AND NEW

South America stretches from the warm waters of the Caribbean to the frigid ocean near Antarctica. Draining a third of the continent, the mighty Amazon carries more water than the world's next 10 biggest rivers combined. Its basin contains the planet's largest rainforest. The Andes tower along the continent's western edge from Colombia to southern Chile. The Incas, an indigenous civilization, had the largest empire in the Americas, helping influence culture in the Andes region prior to the Spanish and Portuguese colonial period. Centuries of ethnic blending have woven indigenous, European, African, and Asian heritage into South America's rich cultural fabric.

◓ **SILENT STALKER.** The jaguar, an at-risk species, is the largest member of the cat family native to the Americas. These cats are most numerous in remote areas of Central and South America.

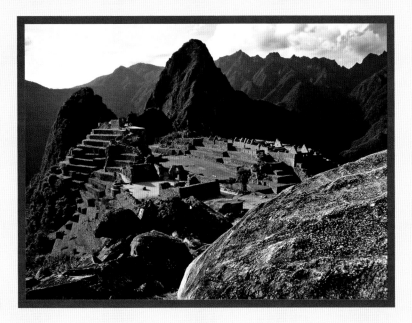

◖ **ROYAL CITY.** Built between 1460 and 1470, Machu Picchu reveals the Inca's skill as stone masons. Massive blocks of granite were carved so carefully that all seams fit tightly without the use of mortar.

◉ SOUTHERN METROPOLIS. A 1,300-foot (396-m)-high block of granite called Sugarloaf dominates the harbor of Brazil's second largest city, Rio de Janeiro. Rio was Brazil's capital until 1960 and remains the country's most popular tourist destination.

◐ NATURAL HERITAGE.
Extending 1.7 miles (2.7 km) along the border between Brazil and Argentina, Iguazú Falls is clouded in mist as the water drops 296 feet (90 m) into the Iguazú River. Iguazú means "great water" in the local Guaraní language.

◑ MOUNTAIN BUDDIES.
An Aymara woman, with her llama, wears the fedora (hat) and shawl distinctive of her culture in the Andes of Peru.

THE CONTINENT:
SOUTH AMERICA

more about
South America

⬬ **STAYING WARM.** The Falkland Islands are home to hundreds of thousands of southern rockhopper penguins. This colony makes up about a third of all rockhoppers found in the world. Seven species of penguins live in South America.

⬬ **ICY COLD.** Rising to an elevation of almost 11,000 feet (3,353 m), Mount Fitz Roy in southern Argentina's Patagonia region presents major challenges to adventurous climbers who must contend with strong winds and bitter cold.

⬬ **QUIET VIGIL.** A Panare Indian sits beside a rushing stream in Venezuela, ready to catch a fish with his spear. The Panare Indians are part of Venezuela's relatively isolated indigenous groups, who make up less than 3 percent of the total population.

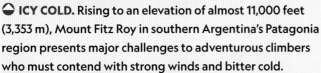

⬡ **JUICY HARVEST.** In Santiago, Chile, grapes hang in heavy clusters ready for harvest. A leading exporter of table grapes, Chile is the major supplier of these grapes for the United States and European Union during their winter months.

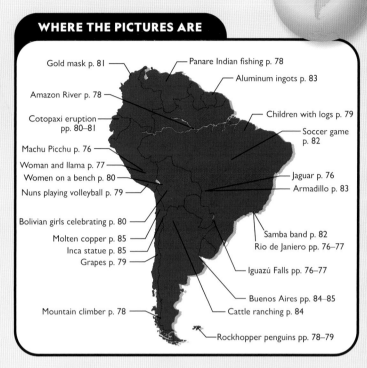

WHERE THE PICTURES ARE

- Gold mask p. 81
- Panare Indian fishing p. 78
- Aluminum ingots p. 83
- Amazon River p. 78
- Children with logs p. 79
- Cotopaxi eruption pp. 80–81
- Soccer game p. 82
- Machu Picchu p. 76
- Woman and llama p. 77
- Women on a bench p. 80
- Jaguar p. 76
- Nuns playing volleyball p. 79
- Armadillo p. 83
- Bolivian girls celebrating p. 80
- Samba band p. 82
- Molten copper p. 85
- Rio de Janiero pp. 76–77
- Inca statue p. 85
- Grapes p. 79
- Iguazú Falls pp. 76–77
- Buenos Aires pp. 84–85
- Mountain climber p. 78
- Cattle ranching p. 84
- Rockhopper penguins pp. 78–79

⬡ **BREAK TIME.** Colonization of South America by Spain and Portugal in the 16th century brought a new religion—Roman Catholicism—to the region. Here, Catholic nuns in Arequipa, Peru, take a break from prayers to engage in a game of volleyball.

⬡ **ENVIRONMENTAL TRAGEDY.** These giants of the rainforest dwarf two children in the Amazon village of Paragominas in Brazil. Harvesting such trees provides income for villagers but poses a serious long-term threat to the environment.

◀ **THE AMAZON RIVER.** Flowing through the Amazon rainforest, the Amazon River in Brazil fills with sediment during the heavy rains. Due to the thick rainforest and lack of roads, the river is the main source of transportation in the region.

THE CONTINENT:
SOUTH AMERICA

Northwestern South America

THE BASICS

STATS

Largest country
Peru 496,224 sq mi
(1,285,216 sq km)

Smallest country
Ecuador
109,483 sq mi (283,561 sq km)

Most populous country
Colombia 48,169,000

Least populous country
Bolivia 11,306,000

Predominant languages
Spanish, indigenous languages, English

Predominant religion
Christianity

Highest GDP per capita
Colombia $14,500

Lowest GDP per capita
Bolivia $7,500

Highest life expectancy
Ecuador 77 years

Lowest life expectancy
Bolivia 69 years

GEO WHIZ

On the llanos of Venezuela, capybaras, the world's largest rodents, are hunted by anacondas. These snakes can weigh as much as 550 pounds (250 kg).

Colombia is the source of some of the world's finest emeralds, a gemstone sacred to the Inca. Mines once operated by the Inca still yield quality stones.

Marine iguanas live only on Ecuador's Galápagos Islands.

◔ **UP HIGH.** La Paz, Bolivia, is located at 11,942 feet (3,639 m) above sea level with summer temperatures ranging from 40 to 60°F (4 to 15°C). Two women enjoy a sunny afternoon while they read the newspaper and eat a snack.

Like a huge letter "C," five countries crest the continent's northwest—Venezuela, Colombia, Ecuador, Peru, and Bolivia. Each has a seacoast, except for landlocked Bolivia. Dominated by the volcano-studded Andes range, the region contains huge rainforests in the upper Amazon and Orinoco River basins. Colombia and Venezuela share an extensive tropical grassland called Los Llanos. Cattle ranching in the region, along with oil and coffee production, are the main economic activities. Due to poverty and politics, the region often experiences civil unrest and demonstrations.

◖ **FOLKLORE CENTER.**
Founded as a mining town, Oruro, Bolivia, is a UNESCO World Heritage site. Each November, people there celebrate traditional Andean culture with ancient dances, music, and rituals.

INDIGENOUS PEOPLE

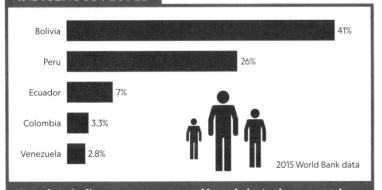

Bolivia	41%
Peru	26%
Ecuador	7%
Colombia	3.3%
Venezuela	2.8%

2015 World Bank data

American Indians are concentrated largely in Andean countries. Almost half of Bolivia's population is made up of these indigenous people.

◖ **VOLCANIC REGIONS.**
Living in the Andes mountain range amid volcanoes means that residents must be aware of potential eruptions. In 2015, residents of Quito, Ecuador, could see the eruption of nearby Cotopaxi.

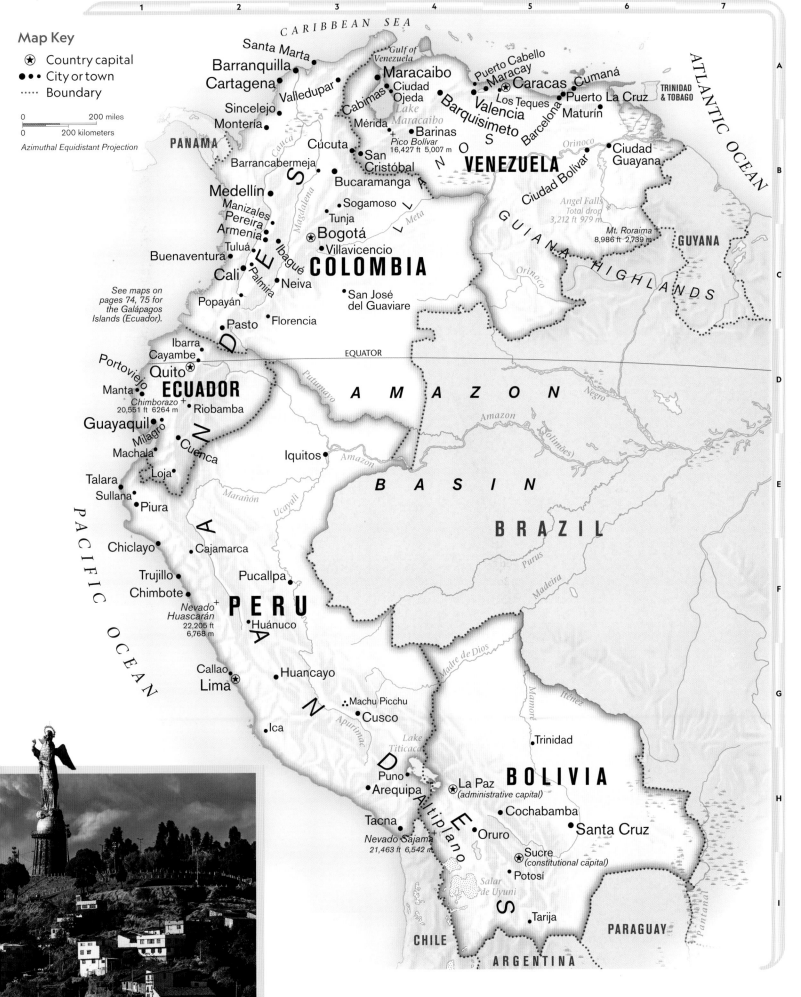

ANCIENT ARTISANS. Early cultures of Colombia left no great stone monuments, but distinguished themselves with fine gold work, such as this mask.

Map Key

⭐ Country capital
●●● City or town
····· Boundary

0 ——— 200 miles
0 ——— 200 kilometers
Azimuthal Equidistant Projection

CARIBBEAN SEA

Gulf of Venezuela

Santa Marta
Barranquilla
Cartagena
Valledupar
Sincelejo
Montería

PANAMA

Maracaibo
Ciudad Ojeda
Cabimas
Lake Maracaibo
Mérida

Puerto Cabello
Maracay
Los Teques
Caracas
Cumaná
Valencia
Barcelona
Puerto La Cruz
Maturín
Barquisimeto

TRINIDAD & TOBAGO

ATLANTIC OCEAN

Barinas
Pico Bolívar
16,427 ft 5,007 m

VENEZUELA

Cúcuta
San Cristóbal
Bucaramanga
Barrancabermeja

Medellín
Manizales
Pereira
Armenia
Tuluá
Buenaventura
Cali
Palmira
Popayán

Sogamoso
Tunja
Bogotá
Villavicencio
Ibagué
Neiva

COLOMBIA

Ciudad Bolívar

Orinoco

GUIANA HIGHLANDS

*Angel Falls
Total drop
3,212 ft 979 m*

Ciudad Guayana

Mt. Roraima
8,986 ft 2,739 m

GUYANA

See maps on pages 74, 75 for the Galápagos Islands (Ecuador).

Pasto
San José del Guaviare
Florencia

Orinoco

Ibarra
Cayambe
Portoviejo
Quito
Manta
Chimborazo
20,551 ft 6264 m
Riobamba

ECUADOR

EQUATOR

Putumayo

Negro

AMAZON

Guayaquil
Milagro
Machala
Cuenca
Loja

Iquitos

Amazon (Solimões)

Amazon

BASIN

BRAZIL

Talara
Sullana
Piura

Marañón
Ucayali

Chiclayo
Cajamarca

Trujillo
Chimbote

Pucallpa

PERU

Purus

Madeira

Nevado Huascarán
22,205 ft 6,768 m
Huánuco

Callao
Lima

Huancayo

Madre de Dios

Mamoré

Iténez

Ica

Machu Picchu
Cusco

Apurímac

PACIFIC OCEAN

Lake Titicaca

Trinidad

Puno
Arequipa

La Paz
(administrative capital)

BOLIVIA

Cochabamba
Santa Cruz

Tacna

Oruro
Nevado Sajama
21,463 ft 6,542 m

Altiplano

Sucre
(constitutional capital)

Potosí

ANDES

Salar de Uyuni

Pantanal

Tarija

CHILE

PARAGUAY

ARGENTINA

Northeastern South America

THE BASICS

STATS

Largest country
Brazil
3,287,611 sq mi (8,514,877 sq km)

Smallest country
Suriname
63,251 sq mi (163,820 sq km)

Most populous country
Brazil 208,847,000

Least populous country
Suriname 598,000

Predominant languages
Portuguese, English,
Dutch, Hindi

Predominant religions
Christianity, Hinduism, Islam

Highest GDP per capita
Brazil $15,600

Lowest GDP per capita
Guyana $8,200

Highest life expectancy
Brazil 74 years

Lowest life expectancy
Guyana 68 years

GEO WHIZ

Guyana's roughly 300 species
of catfish are hunted for the
international aquarium trade.

Brazil's Pantanal is the world's
largest freshwater wetland.

Paramaribo, Suriname's
capital, is a mix of Dutch,
Hindu, Chinese, East Indian,
and Javanese cultures. Dutch
is the only official language.

⬤ **GOAL!** Fans of soccer cheer on the women
from Brazil and Jamaica in the 2019 FIFA
Women's World Cup in Grenoble, France.

Brazil dominates the region as well as the continent in size and population. It is the world's fifth largest country in area, and it is home to about half of South America's 430 million people. São Paulo and Rio de Janeiro are among the world's largest cities, and the country's vast agricultural lands make it a top global exporter of coffee, soybeans, beef, orange juice, and sugar. The Amazon rainforest, once a dense wilderness of unmatched biodiversity, is now threatened by farmers, loggers, and miners. Lands colonized by the British, Dutch, and French make up sparsely settled Guyana and Suriname as well as French Guiana, a French overseas department. Formerly known as the Guianas, these lands are populated by people of African, South Asian, and European heritage.

VAST WATERSHED

The United States and
South America are shown
at the same scale.

Amazon Basin

SOUTH AMERICA

The Amazon River basin includes 2.4 million square
miles (6.1 million sq km). It would cover much of the
contiguous, or lower 48, U.S. states.

◑ **NATIONAL RHYTHM.** Samba, often called Brazil's national
music, combines the music traditions of the country's
populations—Amerindian, Portuguese, and African. Here, a
samba band practices on Rio de Janeiro's Ipanema Beach.

● **THE SIX-BANDED ARMADILLO,** found throughout the dry grassland areas of the region, lives on plants and insects. Unlike others of its species, it remains active during the day.

1 2 3 4 5 6 7 8

VENEZUELA

GUIANA HIGHLANDS

Georgetown
GUYANA
Paramaribo
SURINAME
French Guiana (France)
Cayenne

ATLANTIC OCEAN

COLOMBIA

Boa Vista

Orinoco

Boundary claimed by Venezuela
Boundary claimed by Suriname
Macapá

Pico da Neblina
9,826 ft
2,995 m

EQUATOR

Negro

Itacoatiara

Marajó Island

Belém

São Luís

Parnaíba

Amazon

AMAZON

Manaus

Altamira

Paragominas

Codó
Caxias

Sobral

Fortaleza

Putumayo

Tefé

Coari

Parintins

Santarém

Tucuruí

Marabá

Teresina

Natal

(Solimões)

Tapajós

Imperatriz

Crato

João Pessoa

Selvas

BASIN

Amazon

Madeira

Araguaína

Olinda
Jaboatão
Recife

Cruzeiro do Sul

Purus

Porto Velho

Teles Pires

BRAZIL

Petrolina

Arapiraca
Maceió

Rio Branco

Ariquemes

Alta Floresta

Palmas

Gurupi

Aracaju

PERU

Ji-Paraná

Xingu

Barreiras

Feira de Santana
Alagoinhas

Madre de Dios

Juruena

Alvorado

BRAZILIAN

Jequié

Salvador (Bahia)

Guaporé

Araguaia

Tocantins

Itabuna
Ilhéus

Lake Titicaca

Várzea Grande
Cuiabá

Vitória da Conquista

São Francisco

BOLIVIA

Mamoré

Rondonópolis

HIGHLANDS

Teófilo Otoni
Governador Valadares

Goiânia
Anápolis

Uberlândia

Linhares

Pantanal

Belo Horizonte

Vitória
Vila Velha

CHILE

Campo Grande

São José do Rio Preto

Ribeirão Preto

Juiz de Fora

TROPIC OF CAPRICORN

Paraná

Paraguay

São José dos Campos

Nova Iguaçu

Duque de Caxias

Niterói

São Paulo

Guaratinguetá

Rio de Janeiro

PARAGUAY

Londrina

Santo André
Santos

Iguazú Falls

ARGENTINA

Curitiba
Paranaguá

Joinville

Uruguay

Florianópolis

Caxias do Sul
Criciúma

Santa Maria
Novo Hamburgo
Canoas
Porto Alegre

Patos Lagoon

Pelotas

URUGUAY

Map Key
⊛ Country capital
●●● City or town
····· Boundary
····· Claimed boundary

0 ————— 400 miles
0 ————— 400 kilometers

Azimuthal Equidistant Projection

● **BAUXITE TO ALUMINUM.** By exploiting rich deposits of bauxite, the ore from which aluminum is made, and inexpensive hydropower, Suriname produces aluminum ingots, such as these headed for global markets.

THE BASICS

STATS

Largest country
Argentina
1,073,518 sq mi (2,780,400 sq km)

Smallest country
Uruguay
68,037 sq mi (176,215 sq km)

Most populous country
Argentina 44,694,000

Least populous country
Uruguay 3,369,000

Predominant languages
Spanish, Guaraní, English,
Italian, German, French

Predominant religion
Christianity

Highest GDP per capita
Chile $24,500

Lowest GDP per capita
Paraguay $9,800

Highest life expectancy
Chile 79 years

Lowest life expectancy
Argentina, Paraguay, Uruguay
77 years

GEO WHIZ

The Itaipú Dam, which spans the Paraná River between Paraguay and Brazil, is currently the world's second largest operating hydroelectric power plant.

Guanacos, llama-like animals that live mainly in the Patagonia region of Argentina and Chile, keep enemies at bay by spitting at them.

Southern South America

Four countries make up this region, which is sometimes called the Southern Cone because of its shape. Long north-south distances in Chile and Argentina result in varied environments. Chile's Atacama Desert in the north contrasts with much cooler, moister lands in the country's south, where there are fjords and glaciers. Almost half of Chileans live in and around the country's booming capital, Santiago. Similarly, most neighboring Argentinians live in the central Pampas region, where wheat and cattle flourish on the fertile plains. Farther south lie the arid, windswept plateaus of Patagonia. Landlocked Paraguay is small in comparison, less urbanized, and one of South America's poorest countries. Uruguay is smaller still, but it possesses a strong agricultural economy, including cattle- and sheep-raising.

◖ **COWBOYS OF THE PAMPAS.** Cattle are herded by gauchos, the Argentine term for cowboys. The country's pampas, extensive grass-covered plains, support grain and cattle production on ranches called estancias.

◖ **GATEWAY CITY.** Skyscrapers in the modern skyline rise above Buenos Aires, capital of Argentina and second largest metropolitan area in South America. Situated on the Rio de la Plata, the city was established in 1536 by Spanish explorers. Its port is one of the busiest in South America.

WORLD BEEF EXPORTS

Country	Percentage
Brazil	19.3%
India	18.1%
Australia	15.4%
United States	13.1%
New Zealand	5.4%
Canada	4.6%
Uruguay	4%
Paraguay	3.8%
European Union	3.5%
Argentina	3.3%

Data from FAS/USDA, 2018

Almost 30 percent of world beef exports originate in South America. Uruguay is the leading consumer of beef, at more than 124 pounds (56 kg) per capita annually.

◀ **INCA TREASURE.** Near the frozen summit of Argentina's Cerro Llullaillaco, archaeologists uncovered well-preserved Inca mummies and 20 clothed statues, such as this one.

🌑 **DESERT RICHES.** Molten copper is poured into molds at a refinery near Chuquicamata, a mine that has operated since 1910 in Chile's Atacama Desert. Chile produces 28 percent of the world's copper.

PERU

BOLIVIA

BRAZIL

Arica
Iquique
Chuquicamata
Calama
Antofagasta
Copiapó
La Serena
Coquimbo
San Juan
Viña del Mar
Valparaíso
Santiago
Rancagua
Curicó
Talca
Chillán
Concepción
Los Ángeles
Temuco
Valdivia
Osorno
Puerto Montt

Atacama Desert

Cerro Llullaillaco
22,057 ft
6,723 m

ANDES

Cerro Aconcagua
22,831 ft 6,959 m

Puerto Bahía Negra
La Esmeralda
Concepción

PARAGUAY

TROPIC OF CAPRICORN

San Salvador de Jujuy
Salta
San Miguel de Tucumán
Catamarca
La Rioja
Córdoba
Río Cuarto
Mendoza
Godoy Cruz
San Luis

Gran Chaco

Asunción (Paraguay)
Ciudad del Este
Itaipú Dam
Formosa
Villarrica
Resistencia
Corrientes
Posadas

Paraná
Iguazú Falls

Uruguay

Santiago del Estero
Santa Fe
Concordia
Paraná
Rosario
San Nicolás
San Justo
Buenos Aires
La Plata

Salto
Rivera

URUGUAY

Patos Lagoon

River Plate
Montevideo

ARGENTINA

PAMPA

Bahía Blanca
Mar del Plata

Neuquén

Colorado
Río Negro

PACIFIC OCEAN

ATLANTIC OCEAN

San Matías Gulf
Valdés Peninsula

Isla Grande de Chiloé

PATAGONIA

Comodoro Rivadavia
Gulf of San Jorge

Wellington Island

Laguna del Carbón
-344 ft -105 m

Río Gallegos

Punta Arenas

Strait of Magellan

TIERRA DEL FUEGO

Ushuaia
Cape Horn

Map Key
⊛ Country capital
⊙ Dependency capital
●●● City or town
····· Boundary

0 ___ 200 miles
0 ___ 200 kilometers
Azimuthal Equidistant Projection

Falkland Islands
(Islas Malvinas)
(United Kingdom)
Claimed by Argentina

⊙ Stanley

THE CONTINENT:
EUROPE

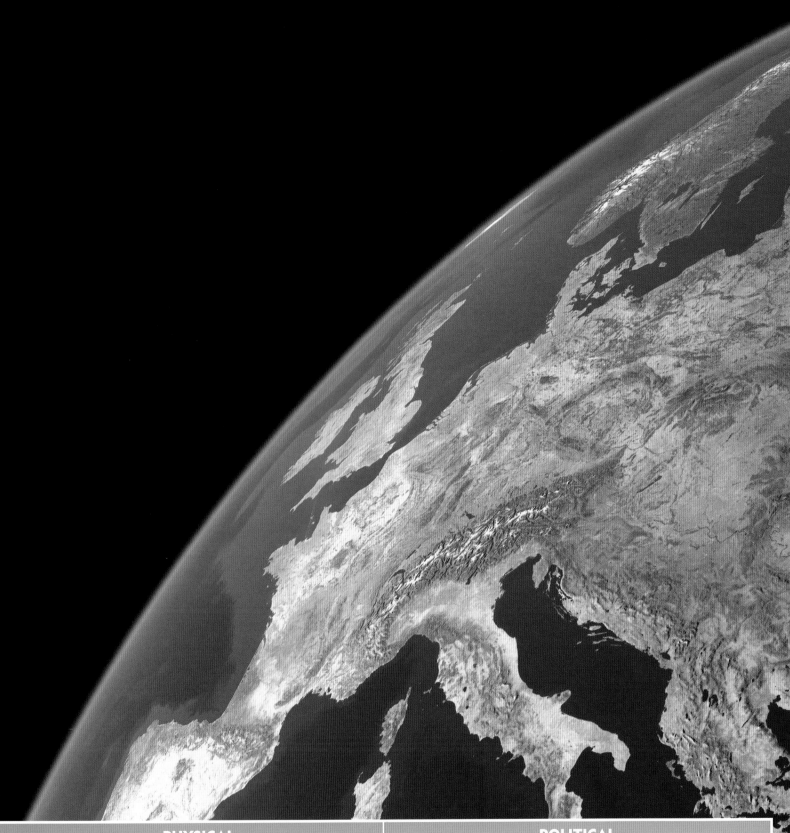

PHYSICAL			POLITICAL	
TOTAL AREA 3,841,000 sq mi (9,947,000 sq km)	**LOWEST POINT** Caspian Sea -92 ft (-28 m)	**LARGEST LAKE ENTIRELY IN EUROPE** Ladoga, Russia 6,800 sq mi (17,700 sq km)	**POPULATION** 747,636,000	**LARGEST COUNTRY ENTIRELY IN EUROPE** France 248,573 sq mi (643,801 sq km)
HIGHEST POINT El'brus, Russia 18,510 ft (5,642 m)	**LONGEST RIVER** Volga, Russia 2,290 mi (3,685 km)		**LARGEST METROPOLITAN AREA** Moscow, Russia Pop. 12,410,000	**MOST DENSELY POPULATED COUNTRY** Monaco 39,000 people per sq mi (19,500 per sq km)

EUROPE

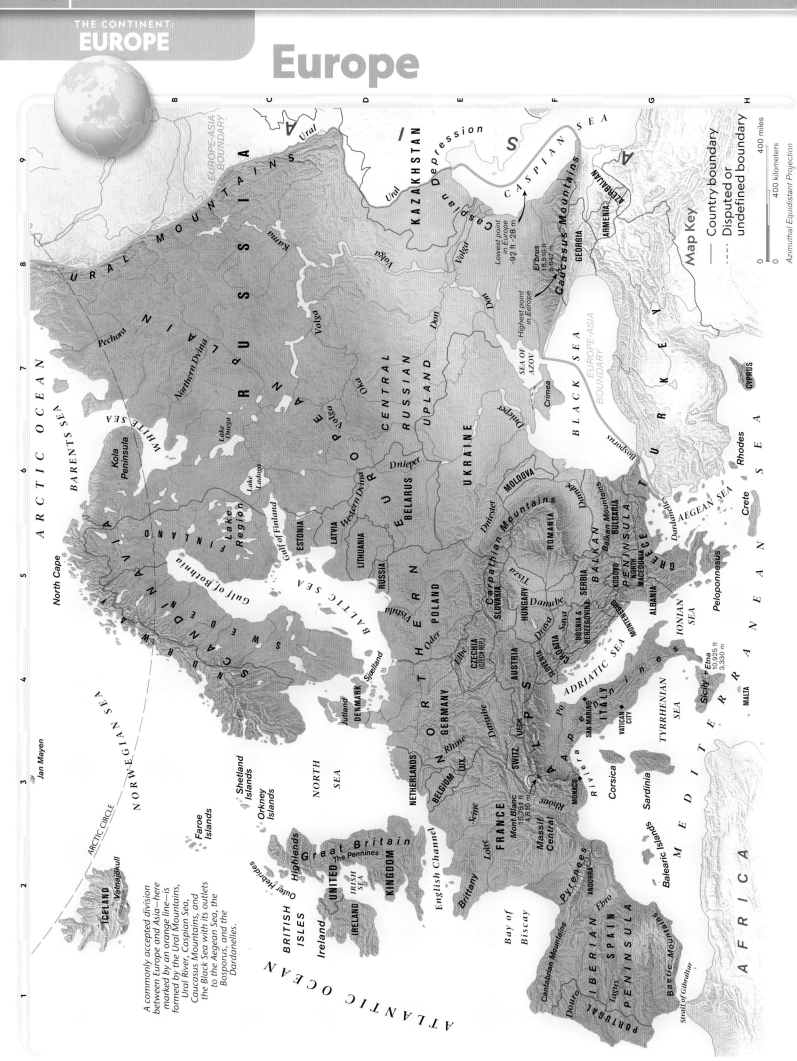

Europe

Map Key

—— Country boundary

- - - - Disputed or undefined boundary

400 miles
400 kilometers

Azimuthal Equidistant Projection

A commonly accepted division between Europe and Asia—here marked by an orange line—is formed by the Ural Mountains, Ural River, Caspian Sea, Caucasus Mountains, and the Black Sea with its outlets to the Aegean Sea, the Bosporus, and the Dardanelles.

EUROPE-ASIA BOUNDARY

KAZAKHSTAN

Caspian Depression

CASPIAN SEA

Lowest point in Europe −92 ft −28 m

El'brus 18,510 ft 5,642 m

Highest point in Europe

Caucasus Mountains

AZERBAIJAN

ARMENIA

GEORGIA

TURKEY

Ural

Ural

Volga

Volga

Don

Don

Kama

Pechora

Northern Dvina

URAL MOUNTAINS

RUSSIA

R U S S I A N P L A I N

Lake Onega

Lake Ladoga

Oka

Volga

Dnieper

CENTRAL RUSSIAN UPLAND

SEA OF AZOV

Crimea

BLACK SEA

EUROPE-ASIA BOUNDARY

Bosporus

Dardanelles

AEGEAN SEA

Rhodes

Crete

CYPRUS

ARCTIC OCEAN

BARENTS SEA

Kola Peninsula

WHITE SEA

North Cape

LAPLAND

FINLAND

Lake Region

Gulf of Finland

ESTONIA

LATVIA

LITHUANIA

Western Dvina

BELARUS

UKRAINE

MOLDOVA

Dniester

Dnieper

ROMANIA

Carpathian Mountains

Danube

Balkan Mountains

BULGARIA

SERBIA

KOSOVO

NORTH MACEDONIA

BALKAN PENINSULA

GREECE

ALBANIA

IONIAN SEA

Peloponnesus

MEDITERRANEAN SEA

Jan Mayen

NORWEGIAN SEA

ARCTIC CIRCLE

ICELAND

Vatnajökull

Shetland Islands

Orkney Islands

Faroe Islands

Outer Hebrides

Highlands

Great Britain

The Pennines

UNITED KINGDOM

IRISH SEA

Ireland

IRELAND

BRITISH ISLES

NORTH SEA

BALTIC SEA

Gulf of Bothnia

SCANDINAVIA

NORWAY

SWEDEN

Sjælland

Jutland

DENMARK

POLAND

Vistula

Oder

Elbe

CZECHIA (CZECH REP.)

SLOVAKIA

HUNGARY

Tisza

Danube

Drava

Sava

CROATIA

BOSNIA & HERZEGOVINA

SLOVENIA

MONTENEGRO

ADRIATIC SEA

Po

Apennines

ITALY

SAN MARINO

VATICAN CITY

TYRRHENIAN SEA

Sicily

Etna 10,925 ft 3,330 m

MALTA

Sardinia

Corsica

Balearic Islands

NETHERLANDS

BELGIUM

LUX.

GERMANY

NORTHERN

Rhine

LIECH.

SWITZ.

AUSTRIA

ALPS

Mont Blanc 15,781 ft 4,810 m

FRANCE

Seine

Loire

Brittany

Massif Central

Rhône

Riviera

MONACO

Bay of Biscay

English Channel

ATLANTIC OCEAN

Pyrenees

ANDORRA

SPAIN

Ebro

IBERIAN PENINSULA

PORTUGAL

Douro

Tagus

Cantabrian Mountains

Baetic Mountains

Strait of Gibraltar

AFRICA

Danube

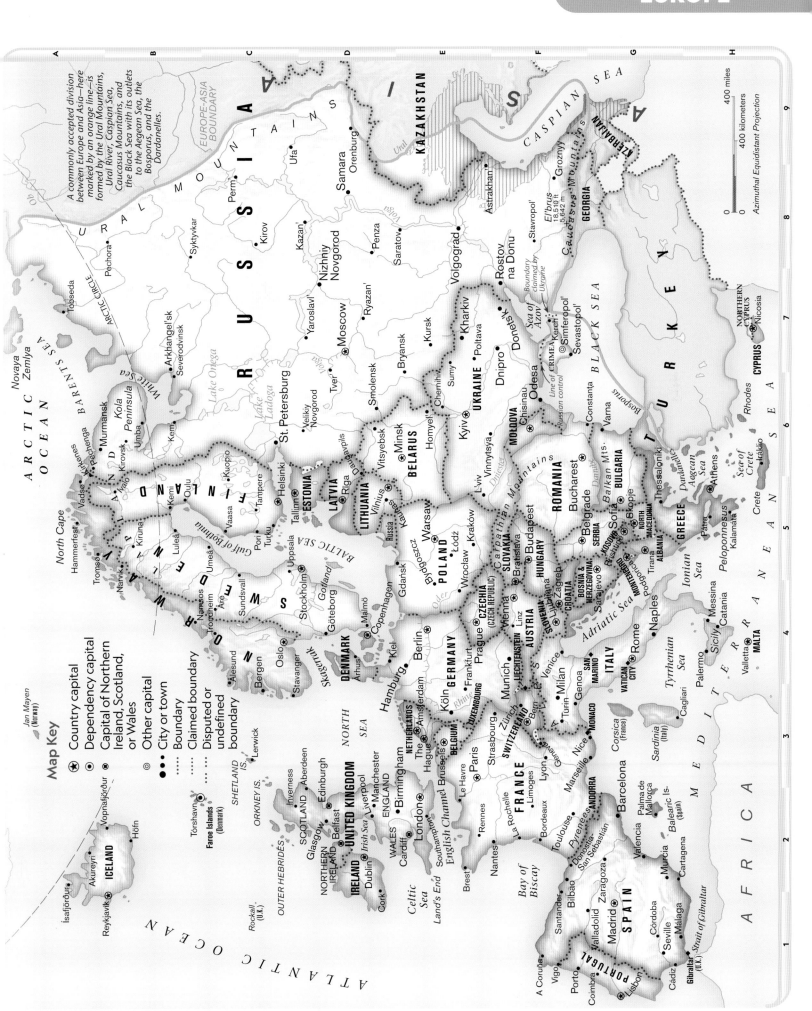

THE CONTINENT:
EUROPE

Europe

SMALL SPACES, DIVERSE PLACES

◑ WIND POWER.
A traditional windmill stands silent in Spain, as most electricity comes from nonrenewable sources. Modern windmills, along with hydroelectricity and solar, provide 49 percent of Spain's renewable energy.

A cluster of islands and peninsulas jutting west from Asia, Europe is bordered by two oceans and more than a dozen seas, which are linked to inland areas by canals and navigable rivers such as the Rhine and Danube. The fertile Northern European Plain sweeps west from the Urals. Rugged uplands form part of Europe's western coast, while the Alps shield Mediterranean lands from frigid northern winds. Here, first Greek and then Roman civilizations laid Europe's cultural foundation. Its colonial powers built wealth from vast empires, while its inventors and thinkers influenced world industry, economy, and politics. Today, the European Union seeks to achieve political and economic cooperation among member countries.

◐ CHEERY GREETINGS. Laughing children clown for the camera in Klaipėda, Lithuania. The city is the northernmost ice-free port on the eastern coast of the Baltic Sea.

NOTRE DAME. In 2019, stunned citizens of Paris, France, and the world watched as the centuries-old cathedral burned during renovations. It is currently undergoing restoration supported by donations.

ROCKY SENTINEL. Towering 14,692 feet (4,478 m) in elevation, the Matterhorn, on the border between Switzerland and Italy, is one of Europe's most famous mountains. Frequent avalanches on its steep slopes pose challenges for mountain climbers.

WINDOW ON THE PAST. The brightly painted houses of Nyhavn (New Harbor), once the homes and warehouses of wealthy Copenhagen merchants, are now shops and restaurants and one of the most popular tourist attractions in Denmark's capital city.

THE CONTINENT:
EUROPE

more about
Europe

AGELESS TIME. This famous astronomical clock, built in 1410 in Prague, Czechia, has an astronomical dial on top of a calendar dial. Together, the dials keep track of time as well as the movement of the sun, moon, and stars.

CLIFF DWELLERS. The town of Positano clings to the rocky hillside along Italy's Amalfi coast. In the mid-19th century, more than half the town's population emigrated, mainly to the United States. The economy today is based on tourism.

SEABIRDS OF THE NORTH. Colorful Atlantic puffins perch on a grass-covered cliff in Iceland, Europe's westernmost country. These birds are skilled fishers but have difficulty becoming airborne and often crash as they attempt to land.

FAMILY BUSINESS. A father and son monitor and gather cherry tomatoes on their farm in Portugal. In the most recent agricultural census (2009), 90 percent of Portugal's farms were family-owned, with most of the work being completed by family members.

🔵 **GLIMPSE OF THE PAST.** Rome's Colosseum is a silent reminder of a once powerful empire that stretched from the British Isles to Persia (now Iran). The concrete, stone, and brick structure could seat as many as 50,000 people.

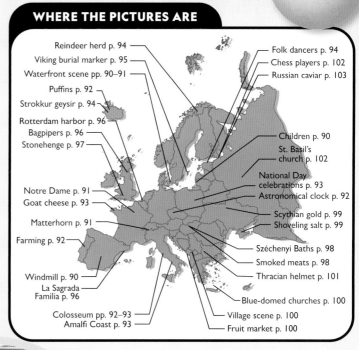

WHERE THE PICTURES ARE

Reindeer herd p. 94
Viking burial marker p. 95
Waterfront scene pp. 90–91
Puffins p. 92
Strokkur geysir p. 94
Rotterdam harbor p. 96
Bagpipers p. 96
Stonehenge p. 97
Notre Dame p. 91
Goat cheese p. 93
Matterhorn p. 91
Farming p. 92
Windmill p. 90
La Sagrada Familia p. 96
Colosseum pp. 92–93
Amalfi Coast p. 93

Folk dancers p. 94
Chess players p. 102
Russian caviar p. 103
Children p. 90
St. Basil's church p. 102
National Day celebrations p. 93
Astronomical clock p. 92
Scythian gold p. 99
Shoveling salt p. 99
Széchenyi Baths p. 98
Smoked meats p. 98
Thracian helmet p. 101
Blue-domed churches p. 100
Village scene p. 100
Fruit market p. 100

◀️ **LUNCHTIME!** Varieties of creamy, fresh goat cheese are displayed in a market in the Brittany region of northern France.

🔵 **NATIONAL PRIDE.** Women carry banners in a parade marking Poland's National Day. Celebrated each year on May 3, it is the anniversary of the 1997 proclamation of the Polish Constitution.

THE CONTINENT: EUROPE

Northern Europe

This region lies in latitudes similar to Canada's Hudson Bay, but the warm North Atlantic Drift current moderates temperatures from volcanically active Iceland to Denmark and Norway. Sparsely populated but mostly urban, northern Europe is home to slightly more than 33 million people. The region's better farmlands lie in southern Sweden and Denmark's lowlands. Forested Finland shares a border with Russia. Estonia, Latvia, and Lithuania—the so-called Baltic States—are former republics of the Soviet Union.

THE BASICS

STATS

Largest country
Sweden
173,860 sq mi (450,295 sq km)

Smallest country
Denmark
16,639 sq mi (43,094 sq km)

Most populous country
Sweden 10,041,000

Least populous country
Iceland 344,000

Predominant languages
Swedish, Danish, Finnish, Norwegian, Lithuanian, Latvian, Estonian, Russian, Icelandic

Predominant religion
Christianity

Highest GDP per capita
Norway $71,800

Lowest GDP per capita
Latvia $27,600

Highest life expectancy
Iceland 83 years

Lowest life expectancy
Latvia, Lithuania 75 years

GEO WHIZ

Vatnajökull, in Iceland, is the largest glacier in Europe.

The inventors of LEGO blocks opened their first business in 1932 in Billund, Denmark, manufacturing stools and wooden toys.

In Tromsø, Norway, which is north of the Arctic Circle, the sun does not rise from November to January.

NORDIC HERDERS. The Sami, indigenous people of northern Europe, herd their reindeer across the borders of Norway, Sweden, Finland, and Russia. Some use snowmobiles instead of horses.

STROKKUR GEYSIR. The word "geysir" comes from the Icelandic verb, *geysa,* which means "to gush." Every 5 to 10 minutes, to the delight of tourists, Strokkur in Iceland erupts. From 2011 to 2018, Iceland experienced a huge increase in tourism, leading to concerns for natural areas.

COLORFUL TRADITION.
Costumed folk dancers perform traditional dances at an open-air museum in Tallinn, Estonia's capital city.

NORTHERN FISHERIES

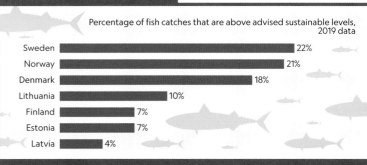

Percentage of fish catches that are above advised sustainable levels, 2019 data

Country	Percentage
Sweden	22%
Norway	21%
Denmark	18%
Lithuania	10%
Finland	7%
Estonia	7%
Latvia	4%

Profits from the fishing industry conflict with conservation interests to protect the North Sea from overfishing.

◐ **MARKER FROM THE PAST.** This stone memorial in Sweden marks the burial site of Viking warriors. Although known for their fierce raids, Vikings were mainly farmers and traders.

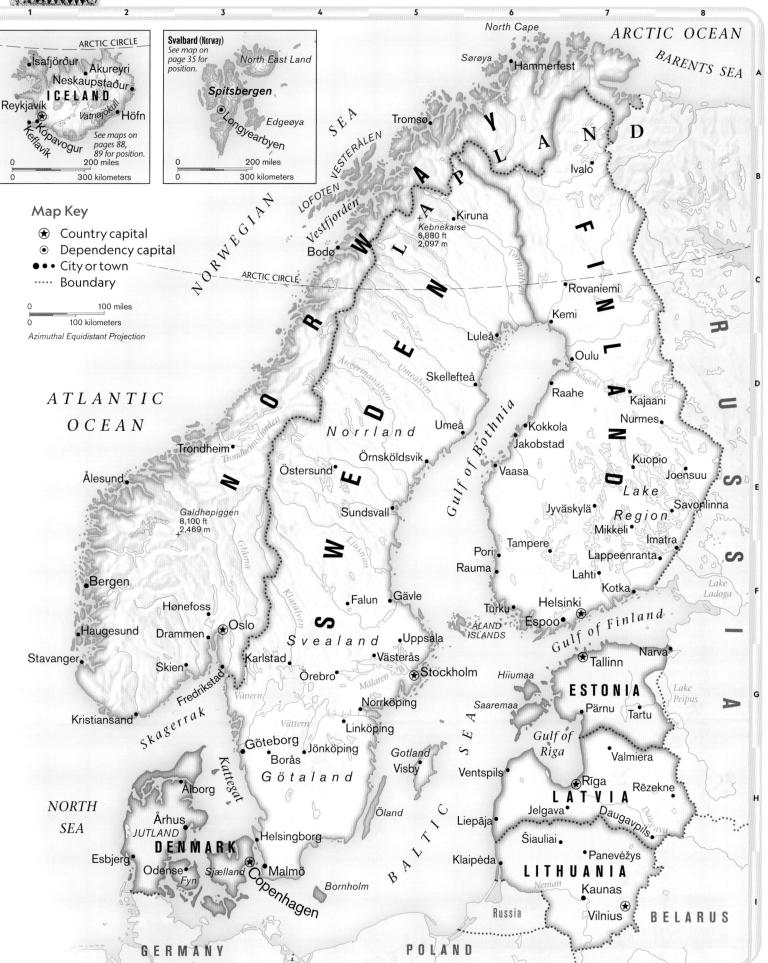

ARCTIC CIRCLE

• Ísafjörður
Akureyri •
Neskaupstaður •
ICELAND
Reykjavik •
⊛ *Vatnajökull* • Höfn
Kópavogur •
Keflavik •

See maps on pages 88, 89 for position.

0 ——— 200 miles
0 ——— 300 kilometers

Svalbard (Norway)
See map on page 35 for position.

North East Land

Spitsbergen

⊙ Longyearbyen   *Edgeøya*

0 ——— 200 miles
0 ——— 300 kilometers

Map Key

⊛ Country capital
⊙ Dependency capital
••• City or town
···· Boundary

0 ——— 100 miles
0 ——— 100 kilometers
Azimuthal Equidistant Projection

North Cape

ARCTIC OCEAN
BARENTS SEA

Søroya
Hammerfest •

Tromsø •

SEA

VESTERÅLEN

LOFOTEN

Vestfjorden

Bodø •

NORWEGIAN

ARCTIC CIRCLE

L A P L A N D

Ivalo •

+ Kebnekaise
6,880 ft
2,097 m
Kiruna •

Tornealven

F I N L A N D

R U S S I A

Rovaniemi •

Kemi •

Luleå •

Oulu •

Oulujoki

Skellefteå •

Raahe •

Kajaani •

Nurmes •

ATLANTIC OCEAN

N O R R L A N D

Ångermanälven

Umeälven

Örnsköldsvik •

Umeå •

Norrland

Östersund •

Trondheim •
Trondheimsfjorden

Ålesund •

+ Galdhøpiggen
8,100 ft
2,469 m

Glåma

Bergen •

Hønefoss •

Drammen •
Haugesund •

Skien •

Stavanger •

Kristiansand •

Skagerrak

NORTH SEA

Esbjerg •

JUTLAND

Ålborg •

Århus •

Odense •
Fyn

DENMARK

Helsingborg •

Sjælland
⊛ Copenhagen
Malmö •

Bornholm

Kattegat

Göteborg •
Borås •
Götaland

Jönköping •

Linköping •

Karlstad •

Vänern

Örebro •

Vättern

Falun •

Gävle •

Ljusnan

S V E D E N

Sundsvall •

Klarälven

⊛ Oslo

N O R W A Y

S V E A L A N D

Svealand

Uppsala •

Västerås •

Mälaren

⊛ Stockholm

Norrköping •

Gotland
Visby •

Öland

Gulf of Bothnia

Kokkola •
Jakobstad •

Vaasa •

Kuopio •

Joensuu •

Savonlinna •

Lake Region

Jyväskylä •

Mikkeli •

Imatra •

Tampere •

Lappeenranta •

Pori •
Rauma •

Lahti •

Kotka •

Turku •

Helsinki •

Espoo •

ÅLAND ISLANDS

Hiiumaa

⊛ Tallinn

Narva •

Saaremaa

ESTONIA

Pärnu •

Tartu •

Lake Peipus

Gulf of Finland

B A L T I C   S E A

Gulf of Riga

Ventspils •

Valmiera •

⊛ Rīga

Rēzekne •

LATVIA

Jelgava •

Daugava

Daugavpils •

Liepāja •

Šiauliai •

Panevėžys •

Klaipėda •

LITHUANIA

Neman

Kaunas •

⊛ Vilnius

Russia

BELARUS

GERMANY

POLAND

Lake Ladoga

THE CONTINENT:
EUROPE

Western Europe

Eighteen countries crowd this diverse region, which has enjoyed a central role in world affairs for centuries. Over time, bitter rivals have become allies, with today's European Union growing out of the need to rebuild economic and political stability after World War II. Fertile soil in the many river valleys across the Northern European Plain and on Mediterranean hillsides gives rise to abundant harvests of a wide variety of crops. France leads in agricultural production and area, while Germany is the most populous country.

MONUMENT TO FAITH. The towering spires of La Sagrada Familia (The Holy Family) rise above Barcelona, Spain. This massive Roman Catholic church has been under construction for more than a century.

HIGHLAND TUNE. Bagpipers in formal dress parade through the streets of Edinburgh, Scotland, in the United Kingdom. Bagpipes may have arrived centuries ago with Roman invaders, but today they are most associated with the Scottish Highlands.

HOW BIG IS A COUNTRY?

MONACO
VATICAN CITY
SAN MARINO
Rhode Island
ANDORRA
LIECHTENSTEIN
MALTA

Area of Rhode Island
1,034 sq mi (2,678 sq km)

Europe's six smallest countries (for areas, see pages 176–185) would fit inside Rhode Island, the smallest U.S. state, with room to spare.

MODERN SPAN.
Tall red arches support the Willem Bridge across the Maas River in Rotterdam, Netherlands. The Maas, which flows into the North Sea, is a major trade and transport artery, linking the Netherlands to the rest of Europe.

◑ **CELTIC POWER.** These rock pillars, part of Stonehenge in southern England, United Kingdom, were placed more than 5,000 years ago and may be associated with sun worship.

0 ——— 200 miles
0 ——— 200 kilometers
Azimuthal Equidistant Projection

Map Key

⊛ Country capital
⊗ Capital of Northern Ireland, Scotland, or Wales
•·· City or town
···· Boundary

ATLANTIC OCEAN

Rockall
(United Kingdom)

Shetland Islands

Orkney Islands

Outer Hebrides
Inner Hebrides

Inverness

SCOTLAND Aberdeen
Perth Dundee
Edinburgh ⊗
Glasgow

Londonderry
NORTHERN IRELAND
Belfast ⊗

IRELAND (ÉIRE) ⊛
Limerick Dublin ⊛
Waterford
Cork

IRISH SEA
Isle of Man

CELTIC SEA

Liverpool
Manchester
Birmingham
WALES
Cardiff
Bristol
Plymouth
Southampton

GREAT BRITAIN

UNITED KINGDOM
Newcastle
Sunderland
Leeds
Kingston upon Hull
Sheffield
Nottingham
ENGLAND
London ⊛

NORTH SEA

ENGLISH CHANNEL
Strait of Dover
Channel Islands (U.K.)
Brest
Le Havre
Caen
Rennes
Le Mans
Angers
Nantes

FINLAND

NORWAY

SWEDEN

ESTONIA

BALTIC SEA

DENMARK
Kiel
Rostock
Lübeck
Oldenburg
Hamburg
Berlin
POLAND

Frisian Islands
Groningen
NETHERLANDS
Amsterdam (official capital)
The Hague (administrative capital)
Utrecht
Rotterdam
Brugge
Antwerp
Brussels ⊛
BELGIUM
Lille
Amiens
Charleroi
Luxembourg ⊛
LUXEMBOURG
Rouen
Reims
Metz
Nancy
Strasbourg

Bremen
Hannover
Bielefeld
Magdeburg
Dortmund
Essen
Köln
GERMANY
Bonn
Frankfurt
Mainz
Mannheim
Karlsruhe
Stuttgart
Nürnberg
Augsburg
Munich

Leipzig
Erfurt
Dresden
Chemnitz
CZECHIA (CZECH REPUBLIC)
Linz
Vienna ⊛
Salzburg
AUSTRIA
Graz

SLOVAKIA

HUNGARY

Seine
Marne
Seine
Orléans
Paris ⊛
Tours
Loire
Vichy
Limoges
FRANCE
Clermont-Ferrand
MASSIF CENTRAL
Bordeaux
Garonne
Toulouse
PYRENEES
Donostia-San Sebastián

Dijon
Besançon
Mulhouse
Basel
Lausanne
Geneva
Bern ⊛
SWITZERLAND
Zürich
LIECHTENSTEIN
Freiburg
Innsbruck
Bolzano
Trento
ALPS
Mont Blanc 15,781 ft 4,810 m
Matterhorn 14,692 ft 4,478 m
Lyon
St.-Étienne
Rhône
Nîmes
Avignon
Aix-en-Provence
Montpellier
Marseille
Toulon
Nice
MONACO

SLOVENIA
Trieste
Verona
Padova
Venice
Milan
Turin
Po
Modena
Ferrara
Bologna
Florence
Genoa
Pisa
Perugia
LIGURIAN SEA
CORSICA
Bastia
Ajaccio

CROATIA
BOSNIA & HERZEGOVINA
SERBIA
MONTENEGRO
ALBANIA

ADRIATIC SEA
SAN MARINO
Ancona
Pescara
VATICAN CITY
Rome ⊛
ITALY
Terni
Vesuvius 4,203 ft 1,281 m
Naples
Salerno
Foggia
Bari
Taranto
Lecce
Gulf of Taranto

APENNINES

BAY OF BISCAY

A Coruña
Gijón
Santander
Bilbao
Vigo
Santiago de Compostela
Oviedo
León
Vitoria-Gasteiz
Pamplona
ANDORRA ⊛
Andorra la Vella
Perpignan
Braga
Porto
Bragança
Viseu
Coimbra
PORTUGAL
Lisbon ⊛
Setúbal
Burgos
Valladolid
Zaragoza
Lleida
Sabadell
Martaró
Tarragona
Barcelona
Castelló de la Plana
Salamanca
Madrid ⊛
Toledo
SPAIN
Valencia
Albacete
Alicante
Murcia
Cartagena
Almería
Badajoz
SIERRA MORENA
Córdoba
Jaén
Granada
Málaga
Huelva
Seville
Jerez
Cádiz
Algeciras
Gibraltar (U.K.)
Ceuta (Spain)
Strait of Gibraltar
ALBORAN SEA
Melilla (Spain)
MOROCCO

Duero
Douro
Tágus
Guadiana
Ebro

BALEARIC SEA
Minorca
Majorca
Palma de Mallorca
BALEARIC ISLANDS

SARDINIA
Sassari
Cagliari

TYRRHENIAN SEA

IONIAN SEA
Cosenza
Reggio di Calabria
Messina
Palermo
Marsala
SICILY
Mt. Etna 10,925 ft 3,330 m
Taormina
Catania
Syracuse

MEDITERRANEAN SEA

ALGERIA
TUNISIA

MALTA ⊛
Valletta

THE CONTINENT:
EUROPE

Eastern Europe

TIME TO EAT.

Smoked sausages and
bacon, ready for pur-
chase in the market, are
an important part of the
diet in the countries of
eastern Europe.

Eastern Europe stretches from
the Baltic Sea southeast to
the Black Sea. Before
1991, the former
republics of Ukraine,
Belarus, and
Moldova were
controlled by the
Soviet Union,
with the region's
other countries
heavily influenced by it. Kaliningrad,
a small region of Russia separated
from the main country, lies just north
of Poland. Much of the region has a
continental climate similar to that of the
U.S. Midwest. Nearly the size of Texas,
Ukraine is the region's largest country in
both population and area. Like Poland, it holds
rich agricultural and industrial resources. Warsaw is
the region's largest city, while historic Prague and Budapest
are popular tourist stops. With the exceptions of Hungarians and
Moldovans, most people in these lands are linked by branches of
Slavic language and ethnicity.

HEALING WATERS.

Budapest's Széchenyi Baths, built
between 1909 and 1913, are famous for
their thermal waters, discovered in 1879.
A total of 15 baths, as well as saunas and
steam rooms, are housed in buildings
decorated with sculptures and mosaics
by Hungary's leading artists.

◐ **ANCIENT GOLD.** Scythians, who occupied the area from what is now Ukraine into Russia from the third century B.C.E. to the second century C.E., crafted this gold collar.

⬡ **MOUNTAIN OF SALT.** Workers shovel salt in Ukraine, where the mineral is a symbol of friendship.

SEA

LATVIA

LITHUANIA

Russia

Gdynia
Gdańsk
Olsztyn
Bydgoszcz
Toruń
Białystok

Vistula

Hrodna

Western Dvina

Vitsyebsk
Orsha
Barysaw
Mahilyow
⊛ Minsk

B E L A R U S

Baranavichy
Babruysk
Homyel'

Dnieper

LAND
⊛ Warsaw
Łódź
Radom
Częstochowa
Kielce
Bytom
Katowice
Tychy
Kraków

Brest
Pinsk
Pinsk Marshes
Mazyr

Lublin
Vistula
Rzeszów
Tarnów

Chernihiv
Chernobyl'

Sumy

R U S S I A

C A R P A T H I A N

Luts'k
Rivne
Zhytomyr ⊛ Kyiv
Bila Tserkva

Kharkiv
Poltava

OVAKIA

Košice
Uzhhorod
Miskolc
Budapest
Nyiregyháza
Debrecen

Tisza

NGARY

L'viv
Dniester
Ternopil'
Khmel'nyts'kyy
Ivano-Frankivs'k
Kam'yanets'-Podil's'kyy
Chernivtsi

U K R A I N E

Vinnytsya
Cherkasy
Oleksandriya
Kirovohrad
Dniprodzerzhyns'k
Kryvyy Rih

Kremenchuk
Dnipro
Zaporizhzhya

Slov"yans'k
Kramators'k
Kostyantynivka
Horlivka
Donets'k

Lysychans'k
Kadivka
Luhans'k
Alchevs'k
Krasnyy Luch
Yenakiyeve
Makiyivka

M O U N T A I N S

Dniester
Bălți
TRANSNISTRIA
MOLDOVA
Chisinau ⊛
Tiraspol

Nikopol'
Melitopol'

Mariupol'
Berdyans'k

R O M A N I A

Szeged

SERBIA

Since 1990, Transnistria, a self-proclaimed breakaway state in Moldova's predominantly Russian-speaking area east of the Dniester River, has remained unrecognized by any UN member state.

Mykolayiv
Dnieper
Kherson
Odesa

Prut

Line of Russian control

SEA OF AZOV

Boundary claimed by Ukraine

CRIMEA

Danube

B L A C K   S E A

Map Key

- ⊛ Country capital
- ◎ Other capital
- ●●● City or town
- ⋯⋯ Boundary
- ⋯⋯ Claimed boundary
- ⋯ ⋯ Disputed or undefined boundary

| 0 | 200 miles |
| 0 | 200 kilometers |

Azimuthal Equidistant Projection

UNDISTURBED FOREST

DENMARK
BALTIC SEA
LATVIA
LITHUANIA
Russia

GERMANY
POLAND
BELARUS

■ Old-growth forest

| 0 | 300 miles |
| 0 | 300 kilometers |

SWITZ.
CZECHIA
SLOVAKIA
AUSTRIA
SLOVENIA
HUNGARY
ITALY
CROATIA
SERBIA
BOSNIA & HERZEGOVINA

UKRAINE
MOLDOVA
ROMANIA

RUSSIA

CRIMEA
BLACK SEA

Old-growth forests have minimal signs of human interaction and are usually found in remote areas.

THE CONTINENT:
EUROPE

The Balkans & Cyprus

THE BASICS

STATS

Largest country
Romania
92,043 sq mi (238,391 sq km)

Smallest country
Cyprus
3,572 sq mi (9,251 sq km)

Most populous country
Romania 21,457,000

Least populous country
Montenegro 614,000

Predominant languages
Romanian, Greek, Serbian,
Croatian, Bulgarian, Albanian,
Turkish, English

Predominant religions
Christianity, Islam

Highest GDP per capita
Cyprus $37,000

Lowest GDP per capita
Kosovo $10,500

Highest life expectancy
Greece 81 years

Lowest life expectancy
Bulgaria, Romania
75 years

GEO WHIZ

The Dalmatian, a popular
breed of dog, is named for
the region where it
originated: Dalmatia, along
the Adriatic coast of the
Balkan Peninsula.

Dracula tours are popular in
Romania, home of Vlad
Dracula (Vlad the Impaler),
who ruled the region
between the Danube and the
Transylvanian Alps in the
15th century.

The Balkans—named for a Bulgarian mountain range—make up a rugged land with a rough history. Ethnic and religious conflicts have long troubled the area. After 1991, seven new countries stretching from Slovenia to North Macedonia emerged as a result of the breakup of Yugoslavia. Kosovo is the most recent. The Danube River winds east across the Balkans, separating Bulgaria from Romania, the region's largest country. Rimmed by four seas—the Black, Aegean, Ionian, and Adriatic—the Balkans, particularly Greece, have a long maritime history. In 2004, Cyprus, which has been uneasily divided for three decades into Turkish and Greek sections, joined the European Union along with Greece.

RURAL LIFE. Villagers walk down a cobbled street in Gusinje, a rural town in northeastern Montenegro. A place of rugged mountains, Montenegro is one of the countries that emerged from the former Yugoslavia.

SEISMIC HISTORY. Blue-domed Greek Orthodox churches on the island of Thira (Santorini) cling to cliffs above the remains of a volcano that erupted more than 3,000 years ago.

COLORFUL BOUNTY. An open-air fruit market in Kotor, Montenegro, overflows with grapes, plums, apples, and other produce that grow in the moderate climate of the Mediterranean region. Warm, dry summers and cool, rainy winters provide ideal growing conditions for a variety of fruits, many of which had their origins in the region.

ANCIENT WARRIORS. Soldiers and horsemen from Thrace, an ancient territory in present-day Bulgaria and Greece, wore battle masks, such as this one.

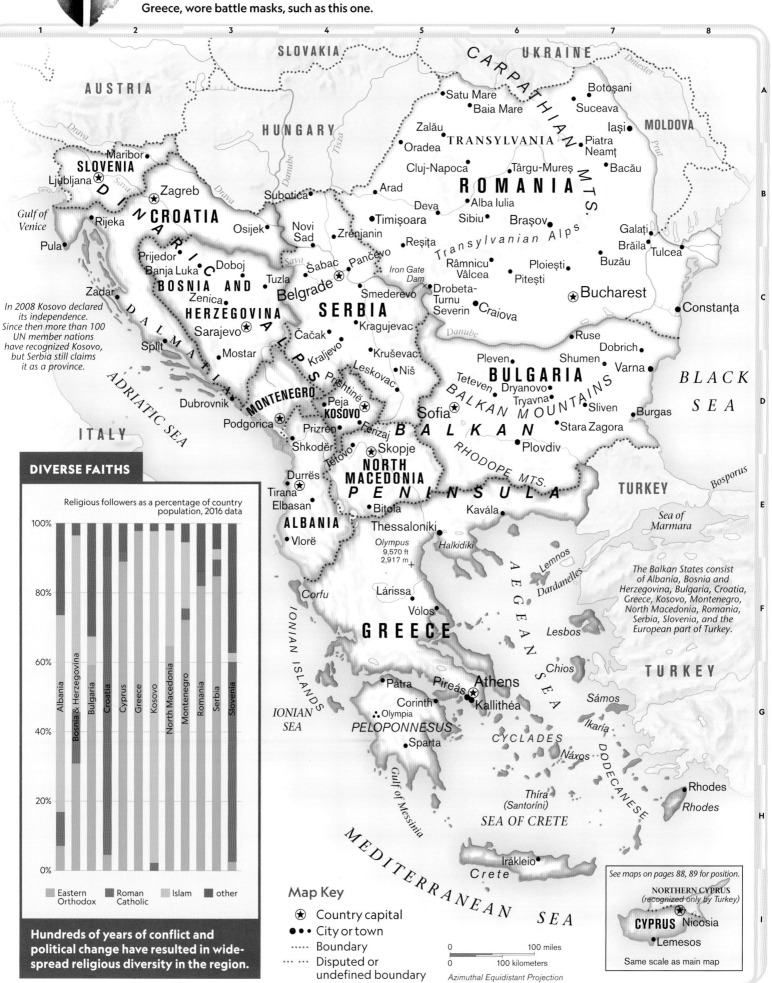

SLOVAKIA

UKRAINE

AUSTRIA

HUNGARY

Drava

Tisza

Danube

CARPATHIAN MTS.

MOLDOVA

Satu Mare • • Botoşani
Baia Mare • • Suceava
Zalău • Iaşi
Oradea • TRANSYLVANIA Piatra Neamţ •
Cluj-Napoca • Târgu-Mureş • • Bacău
Arad • ROMANIA
Deva • Alba Iulia •
Timişoara • Sibiu • Braşov • Galaţi •
Reşiţa • *Transylvanian Alps* Brăila • • Tulcea
Râmnicu Vâlcea • Ploieşti • Buzău •
Drobeta-Turnu Severin • Piteşti •
⊛ Bucharest
Craiova • • Constanţa

SLOVENIA
Maribor •
Ljubljana ⊛
Sava
Zagreb ⊛
CROATIA
Gulf of Venice
Rijeka •
Pula •
Drava
Subotica •
Novi Sad •
Osijek •
Zrenjanin •
Danube
Prijedor • Doboj •
Banja Luka • Tuzla •
Zadar • BOSNIA AND Zenica •
HERZEGOVINA
Sarajevo ⊛
Split •
Mostar •

Sava
Šabac • Pančevo •
Belgrade ⊛
Smederevo •
SERBIA
Kragujevac •
Čačak •
Kraljevo • Kruševac •
Leskovac • Niš •

In 2008 Kosovo declared its independence. Since then more than 100 UN member nations have recognized Kosovo, but Serbia still claims it as a province.

Iron Gate Dam
Danube
Ruse •
Dobrich •
Pleven • Shumen •
Teteven • Varna •
Dryanovo • BULGARIA
Sofia ⊛ Tryavna • Sliven •
BALKAN MOUNTAINS
Stara Zagora •
Plovdiv •
RHODOPE MTS.

ITALY

ADRIATIC SEA

DALMATIA

DINARIC ALPS

Dubrovnik •
MONTENEGRO
Podgorica ⊛
Prishtinë ⊛
Peja • KOSOVO •
Prizren •
Ferizaj •
Shkodër •
Tetovo •
Skopje ⊛
NORTH MACEDONIA
Durrës •
Tirana ⊛
Elbasan •
Bitola •
ALBANIA
Vlorë •

BALKAN PENINSULA

BLACK SEA

Bosporus

TURKEY

Sea of Marmara

Kavála •
Thessaloníki •
Olympus 9,570 ft 2,917 m +
Halkidikí
Lemnos
Dardanelles

The Balkan States consist of Albania, Bosnia and Herzegovina, Bulgaria, Croatia, Greece, Kosovo, Montenegro, North Macedonia, Romania, Serbia, Slovenia, and the European part of Turkey.

Corfu
IONIAN ISLANDS
IONIAN SEA
Lárissa •
Vólos •
GREECE
PELOPONNESUS
Pátra •
Corinth •
Olympia ⋄
Sparta •
Pireás • ⊛ Athens
Kallithéa •

AEGEAN SEA
Lesbos
Chios
Sámos
Ikaría
Náxos
CYCLADES
DODECANESE

TURKEY

Rhodes •
Rhodes

Gulf of Messinia

Thíra (Santoríni)
SEA OF CRETE
Irákleio •
Crete

MEDITERRANEAN SEA

DIVERSE FAITHS

Religious followers as a percentage of country population, 2016 data

100%

80%

60%

40%

20%

0%

Albania | Bosnia & Herzegovina | Bulgaria | Croatia | Cyprus | Greece | Kosovo | North Macedonia | Montenegro | Romania | Serbia | Slovenia

■ Eastern Orthodox ■ Roman Catholic ■ Islam ■ other

Hundreds of years of conflict and political change have resulted in widespread religious diversity in the region.

Map Key

⊛ Country capital
• • • City or town
····· Boundary
··· Disputed or undefined boundary

0 — 100 miles
0 — 100 kilometers
Azimuthal Equidistant Projection

See maps on pages 88, 89 for position.

NORTHERN CYPRUS
(recognized only by Turkey)
CYPRUS ⊛ Nicosia
Lemesos •

Same scale as main map

THE CONTINENT:
EUROPE

European Russia

GEO WHIZ

St. Petersburg's many canals
and hundreds of bridges have
earned the city the nickname
Venice of the North.

The fertile Northern
European Plain, west of
the Urals, is home to most
of Russia's population and
industry, whereas most of
its mineral resources lie east
of the Urals in the Asian
portion of the country.

Arkhangel'sk, founded in 1584,
is Russia's oldest Arctic port.
The timber resources that are
its chief export have been
nicknamed "green gold."

The Kremlin is a walled
fortress in Moscow, Russia's
capital city, that houses the
official residence of the
country's president.

⬤ CHECKMATE! Bystanders watch intently as one
player prepares to make his move in this chess game in
a park in St. Petersburg. In Russia, chess is a national
pastime, popular with people from all walks of life.

Home to four-fifths of
Russia's 144 million people,
European Russia contains
most of the country's
agriculture and industry.
Prior to 1991, Russia was
the largest of the former
republics of the Soviet
Union. Here also is Moscow,
its capital and Europe's
largest city. Far to the north, Murmansk provides a year-round
seaport—a gift of the warming currents of the North Atlantic
Drift. This European region of Russia, spanning 994
miles (1,600 km), is home to the Volga, Europe's
longest river, and Mount El'brus, its highest peak.
The Caucasus and Urals form a natural boundary
between Europe and Asia. Although parts of
Azerbaijan, Georgia, and Kazakhstan span the
continental boundary, only Russia is
counted as part of Europe.

EUROPE'S GREAT RIVERS

Volga	2,290 mi (3,685 km)
Danube	1,795 mi (2,888 km)
Dnieper	1,423 mi (2,290 km)
Rhine	820 mi (1,320 km)
Elbe	678 mi (1,091 km)
Vistula	651 mi (1,047 km)
Tagus	645 mi (1,038 km)
Loire	629 mi (1,012 km)
Rhône	497 mi (800 km)
Po	405 mi (652 km)

**Europe's rivers, many linked by canals, form a
transportation network that connects the continent's people and places to each other and the
world beyond.**

◖ CATHEDRAL ON
THE SQUARE. The
onion-shaped domes
atop the towers of
St. Basil's are a key
landmark on Red
Square in Moscow. Built
between 1555 and 1561
to commemorate mili-
tary campaigns led by
Ivan the Terrible, the
building is rich in
Christian symbolism.

RUSSIAN DELICACY. Caviar is the eggs (called roe) of sturgeon fish caught in the Caspian Sea. The eggs are aged in a salty brine, then packaged in cans (left) for export.

Map Key

★ Country capital
◎ Other capital
●•• City or town
····· Boundary
····· Claimed boundary
··· Disputed or undefined boundary

0   200 miles
0   200 kilometers

Azimuthal Equidistant Projection

See map on pages 112–113 for the Asian part of Russia.

Russia invaded Crimea in 2014 and, after secession from Ukraine was approved in a disputed and boycotted referendum held in Crimea, the Russian parliament voted to annex Crimea into the Russian Federation.
The United Nations General Assembly subsequently adopted a nonbinding resolution declaring the annexation invalid and affirming Ukraine's territorial jurisdiction. As of 2019, Russia administers and controls all aspects of the peninsula, while Ukraine continues to maintain that Crimea is its sovereign territory.

ARCTIC OCEAN
NOVAYA ZEMLYA
KARA SEA
Yamal Peninsula
Gulf of Ob
BARENTS SEA
Kolguyev I.
Kanin Peninsula
NORWAY
Murmansk
Vorkuta
Kola Peninsula
ARCTIC CIRCLE
Usinsk
LAPLAND
SWEDEN
WHITE SEA
Pechora
Ob
URAL
SIBERIA
FINLAND
Severodvinsk
Arkhangel'sk
Sosnogorsk
Gulf of Bothnia
Ukhta
Pechora
Petrozavodsk
Zheleznodorozhnyy
Syktyvkar
Lake Ladoga
Lake Onega
Northern Dvina
Kotlas
Gulf of Finland
St. Petersburg
Berezniki
ESTONIA
Lake Peipus
Cherepovets
Vologda
Sukhona
EUROPE-ASIA BOUNDARY
BALTIC SEA
Pskov
Velikiy Novgorod
Rybinsk Reservoir
Kirov
Perm'
NORTHERN
Velikiye Luki
Rybinsk
Kostroma
Izhevsk
Kama
Tver'
Yaroslavl'
Ivanovo
Nizhniy Novgorod
Kazan'
Naberezhnyye Chelny
Russia
LATVIA
Moscow
Vladimir
Ufa
LITHUANIA
Smolensk
Volga
Cheboksary
Ul'yanovsk
Magnitogorsk
POLAND
Kaluga
Oka
Ryazan'
Saransk
Syzran'
Tol'yatti
Sterlitamak
EUROPEAN
Tula
Penza
Samara
Dnieper
BELARUS
CENTRAL
Bryansk
Orel
Oka
Lipetsk
Tambov
Saratov
Orenburg
Novotroitsk
RUSSIA
RUSSIAN
Kursk
Voronezh
Balakovo
Orsk
Belgorod
Engels
Belaya
Ural
UPLAND
Kamyshin
KAZAKHSTAN
UKRAINE
Don
Donets
Volgograd
Volzhskiy
MOLDOVA
Shakhty
Don
Volga
Ural
Dnieper
Rostov na Donu
CASPIAN DEPRESSION
Taganrog
Line of Russian control
SEA OF AZOV
Boundary claimed by Ukraine
CRIMEA
Yevpatoriya
Kerch
Astrakhan'
Simferopol'
Novorossiysk
Krasnodar
Stavropol'
Sevastopol'
Maykop
Pyatigorsk
CASPIAN SEA
El'brus 18,510 ft 5,642 m
CHECHNYA
BLACK SEA
Sochi
Groznyy
Makhachkala
CAUCASUS MOUNTAINS
Vladikavkaz
GEORGIA
TURKEY
ARMENIA
AZERBAIJAN

THE CONTINENT:
ASIA

PHYSICAL

TOTAL AREA 17,208,000 sq mi (44,570,000 sq km)	**LOWEST POINT** Dead Sea, Israel-Jordan -1,424 ft (-434 m)	**LARGEST LAKE** **ENTIRELY IN ASIA** Lake Baikal 12,200 sq mi (31,500 sq km)
HIGHEST POINT Mount Everest, China-Nepal 29,035 ft (8,850 m)	**LONGEST RIVER** Yangtze (Chang), China 3,880 mi (6,244 km)	

POLITICAL

POPULATION 4,641,055,000	**LARGEST COUNTRY ENTIRELY IN ASIA** China 3,705,405 sq mi (9,596,960 sq km)
LARGEST METROPOLITAN AREA Tokyo, Japan Pop. 37,468,000	**MOST DENSELY POPULATED COUNTRY** Singapore 22,281 people per sq mi (8,603 per sq km)

ASIA

Asia

A commonly accepted division
between Asia and Europe—here marked
by an orange line—is formed by the
Ural Mountains, Ural River, Caspian Sea,
Caucasus Mountains, and the Black Sea
with its outlets to the Aegean Sea,
the Bosporus, and the Dardanelles.

ATLANTIC
OCEAN

NORTH AMERICA

Aleutian Islands

PACIFIC OCEAN

Mariana Islands

Nanpo Islands

TROPIC OF CANCER

CAROLINE ISLANDS

EQUATOR

NEW GUINEA

AUSTRALIA

ARAFURA SEA

TIMOR SEA

BANDA SEA

EAST TIMOR
TIMOR-LESTE
Timor

LESSER SUNDA ISLANDS

Commander Islands

Kamchatka Peninsula

Chukchi Peninsula

Bering Strait

Chukchi Peninsula

BERING SEA

Kuril Islands

Hokkaido

SEA OF OKHOTSK

Sakhalin

J A P A N

Honshu

Shikoku

Kyushu

SEA OF JAPAN
(EAST SEA)

Ryukyu Islands

EAST CHINA SEA

TAIWAN

PHILIPPINE SEA

PHILIPPINE ISLANDS

Luzon

PHILIPPINES

Mindanao

CELEBES SEA

SULU SEA

MOLUCCAS

Celebes

GREATER SUNDA ISLANDS

Flores Sea

JAVA SEA

Java

Borneo

MALAYSIA

BRUNEI

SINGAPORE

Sumatra

ARCTIC OCEAN

North Pole

North Magnetic Pole

ARCTIC CIRCLE

Franz Josef Land

Greenland

North Land

New Siberian Islands

Wrangel Island

EAST SIBERIAN SEA

Kolyma Range

Kolyma

Chersky Range

Aldan

Verkhoyansk Range

Lena

LAPTEV SEA

Taymyr Peninsula

Gulf of Ob

KARA SEA

BARENTS SEA

Yenisey

CENTRAL SIBERIAN PLATEAU

S I B E R I A

Tunguska

Angara

Ob

WEST SIBERIAN PLAIN

Irtysh

Ob

R U S S I A

Ural Mountains

Ural

THE STEPPES

Volga

EUROPE

RUSSIA

Baltic Sea

EUROPE-ASIA BOUNDARY

KAZAKHSTAN

Lake Balkhash

Aral Sea

Syr Darya

Amu Darya

UZBEKISTAN

TURKMENISTAN

Caspian Depression

Caspian Sea

Caucasus Mts.

BLACK SEA

ANATOLIA

TURKEY

GEORGIA

ARMENIA

AZERBAIJAN

Elburz Mountains

IRAN

Zagros Mountains

Persian Gulf

QATAR

BAHRAIN

UNITED ARAB EMIRATES

Gulf of Oman

OMAN

Rub' al Khali

ARABIAN PENINSULA

SAUDI ARABIA

YEMEN

Gulf of Aden

RED SEA

AFRICA

Mediterranean Sea

Aegean Sea

Sinai

LEBANON

ISRAEL

Jordan R.

SYRIA

Syrian Desert

Euphrates

Mesopotamia

Tigris

KUWAIT

IRAQ

Suez Canal

Dead Sea
-1,424 ft
-434 m
World's
lowest point

ALTAI MOUNTAINS

MONGOLIA

GOBI

TIEN SHAN

TARIM BASIN

Taklimakan Desert

KUNLUN MOUNTAINS

Qaidam Basin

PLATEAU OF TIBET

Mt. Everest
29,035 ft
8,850 m
World's highest point

HIMALAYA

Ganges

Brahmaputra

DECCAN PLATEAU

Eastern Ghats

Western Ghats

INDIA

PAKISTAN

AFGHANISTAN

Indus

Thar Desert

Great Indian Desert

BANGLADESH

MYANMAR (BURMA)

NEPAL

BHUTAN

BAY OF BENGAL

Andaman Islands

Nicobar Islands

ANDAMAN SEA

SRI LANKA

LACCADIVE SEA

MALDIVES

ARABIAN SEA

INDIAN OCEAN

EQUATOR

C H I N A

Greater Khingan Range

Northeast China Plain

North China Plain

Yellow

Yellow (Huang)

YELLOW SEA

NORTH KOREA

SOUTH KOREA

Amur

Sikhote Alin Range

Yangtze

Sichuan Basin

Three Gorges

Hengduan Shan

Yangtze

Hainan

SOUTH CHINA SEA

Gulf of Thailand

THAILAND

CAMBODIA

VIETNAM

LAOS

Mekong

MALAY PENINSULA

Map Key

— Country boundary

- - - Disputed or
undefined boundary

1,000 miles

0

0   1,000 kilometers

Two-Point Equidistant Projection

A   B   C   D   E   F   G   H

9   8   7   6   5   4   3   2   1

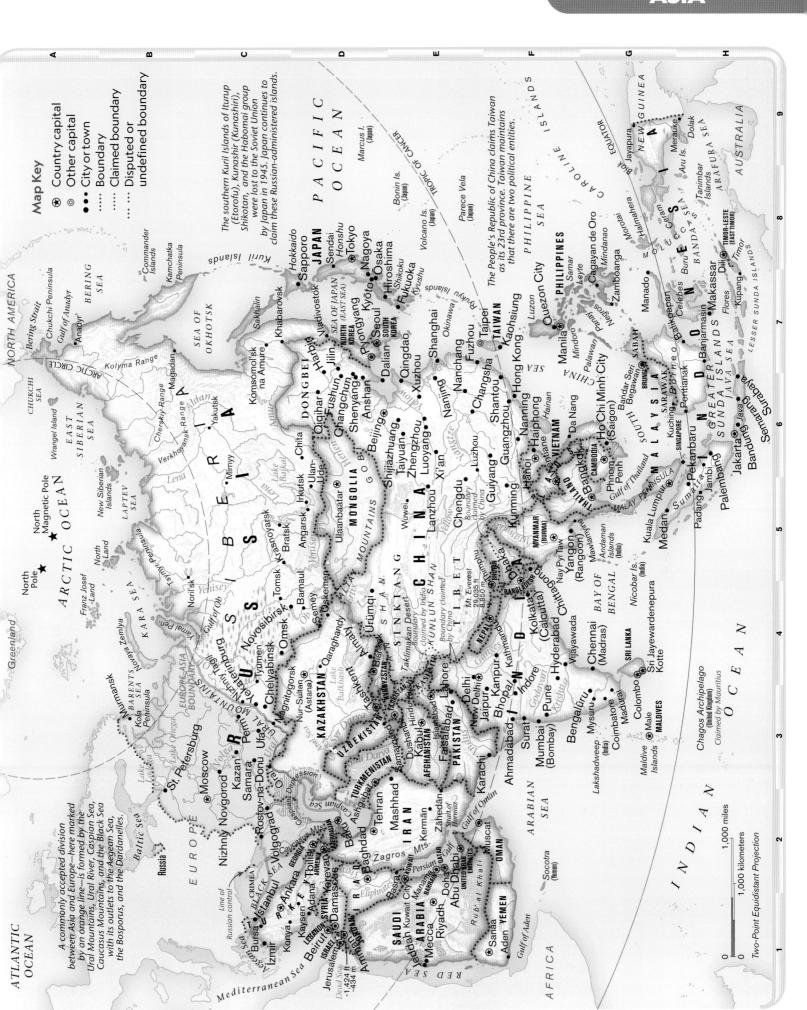

Map Key
- ⊛ Country capital
- ◎ Other capital
- • City or town
- •••• Boundary
- •••• Claimed boundary
- •••• Disputed or undefined boundary

A commonly accepted division between Asia and Europe—here marked by an orange line—is formed by the Ural Mountains, Ural River, Caspian Sea, Caucasus Mountains, and the Black Sea, with its outlets to the Aegean Sea, the Bosporus, and the Dardanelles.

The southern Kuril Islands of Iturup (Etorofu), Kunashir (Kunashiri), Shikotan, and the Habomai group were lost to Japan in 1945. Japan continues to claim these Russian-administered islands.

The People's Republic of China claims Taiwan as its 23rd province. Taiwan maintains that there are two political entities.

ATLANTIC OCEAN

NORTH AMERICA

ARCTIC OCEAN

North Pole ★
North Magnetic Pole ★

Greenland

PACIFIC OCEAN

R U S S I A

S I B E R I A

C H I N A

I N D I A

INDIAN OCEAN

AUSTRALIA

AFRICA

1,000 miles
1,000 kilometers
Two-Point Equidistant Projection

Asia
WORLD CHAMPION

🔵 **TASTY SNACK.** This giant panda, native to China, munches on a stalk of bamboo, the mainstay of its diet.

From Turkey to the eastern tip of Russia, Asia sprawls across nearly 180 degrees of longitude—almost half the globe! It boasts the highest (the Himalaya) and lowest (the Dead Sea) places on Earth's surface. Then there are Asia's people—more than four billion of them. More people live here than on all the other continents put together. Asia has both the most farmers and the most million-plus cities. The world's first civilization arose in Sumer, in what is now southern Iraq. Rich cultures also emerged along rivers in present-day India and China, strongly influencing the world ever since.

🔵 **CULTURE.** An Afghan woman wearing a traditional burka, a loose garment worn by women in some branches of Islam, sits with young girls in Kabul. In Afghanistan the burka is known as a chadri.

◑ **LUNAR NEW YEAR.** Men carry a writhing paper dragon on poles in this Chinese New Year's parade in Singapore.

◐ **WINGED HUNTER.** A Kazakh falconer sits astride his pony as he releases his golden eagle to pursue prey on the dry Asian steppe.

◑ **TOURISM.** One of the world's most popular hot air ballooning destinations is in Cappadocia, Turkey. Riders soar through valleys and above volcanic formations in Göreme National Park.

THE CONTINENT:
ASIA

more about
Asia

⬤ **EASTERN BELIEF.** From its origins in the foothills of the Himalaya, Buddhism has spread across much of eastern Asia. Statues of the Buddha, such as this one in Bangkok, Thailand, are an important part of the region's cultural landscape.

⬤ **RECREATION.** Rich in oil and natural gas, Qatar has developed areas with grassy fields and trails for recreation. With the skyline of Doha behind her, this woman runs along the Corniche, a popular trail that follows the Persian Gulf coast.

⬤ **FINAL TOUCH.** A silk kimono and makeup identify a maiko, or apprentice geisha, in Kyoto, Japan. Geishas are entertainers who perform traditional Japanese songs and dances.

STONE BARRIER. Built as a defense against invaders in the northeastern part of China, the Great Wall's construction started in 220 B.C.E.

WHERE THE PICTURES ARE

Kyrgyz goat herder p. 114
Samarqand market p. 115
Baikonur Cosmodrome p. 114
Saiga antelope p. 115
Girls talking p. 120
Stone head p. 119
Galata Bridge p. 118
Hot air balloons pp. 108–109
3D ruins p. 119
Petra p. 118
Ring p. 121
Horse and car p. 120
Runner p. 110
Musicians p. 120
Afghan girls p. 108
Taj Mahal p. 122
Hindu god Shiva p. 123
Tigers p. 111
Mountain climbers p. 123

Natural gas well p. 113
Ger and yak p. 117
Falconer p. 109

Nenet woman and child p. 112
Lenin's head p. 113
Brown bears p. 112
Great Wall of China pp. 110–111
Woman in lab p. 116
Tokyo city street pp. 116–117
Geisha p. 110
Terra-cotta soldiers p. 117
Panda p. 108
Jeepney p. 125
Philippine tarsier p. 124
Buddhist monk p. 124
Container terminal p. 124
Rainforest p. 127
Boy with flag p. 126
Orangutan p. 127
Terraced rice fields p. 111
Ceremonial mask p. 127

Golden Buddha p. 110
Petronas Twin Towers p. 125
Chinese New Year p. 109
Man and his cow p. 122 Jakarta at night p. 126

MOUNTAIN STAIRWAY. Terraces cut into a steep mountainside create fields for rice on the island of Bali, in Indonesia. Rice is a staple grain crop in much of eastern Asia. In the foreground, a man climbs a palm tree to harvest coconuts.

MOTHER KNOWS BEST.
A Bengal tiger gently moves her cub to a safe hiding place before stalking her prey in India's Bandhavgarh National Park. Tigers are an endangered species.

THE CONTINENT:
ASIA

THE BASICS

STATS

Area
6,601,665 sq mi
(17,098,234 sq km)

Population
144,478,000

Predominant language
Russian (official)

Predominant religions
Christianity, Islam

GDP per capita
$27,800

Life expectancy
71 years

*Note: These figures are for all of Russia. For European Russia, see pages 102–103.

GEO WHIZ

The name Siberia comes from the Turkic language and means "sleeping land."

It takes at least six days to travel 6,000 miles (9,656 km) on the Trans-Siberian Railway from Moscow to the Pacific port of Vladivostok. The trip crosses eight time zones.

Lake Baikal, nicknamed Siberia's "blue eye," is home to 1,500 unique species of plants and animals, including the nerpa, the world's only freshwater seal.

The Chukchi, the largest group of indigenous people in Siberia, take their name from a word meaning "rich in reindeer." They share their name with their homeland, a peninsula bordered by the Arctic and Pacific Oceans.

A region of northern coniferous forest called taiga stretches across northern Russia as far as Norway.

Asian Russia

🌐 **NOMADIC HERDERS.** A Nenet woman and her grandson prepare to follow the family reindeer herd to northern Siberia for spring and summer grazing.

Forming more than half of Russia, this region stretches from the Ural Mountains east to the Pacific, and from the Arctic Ocean south to mountains and deserts along borders with Central Asia, Mongolia, China, and North Korea. Siberia, as this region is commonly known, has limited croplands but bountiful forests (the taiga) and rich mineral resources such as oil, natural gas, and gold. The Trans-Siberian Railway, built between 1891 and 1905, opened up the region for settlement, but not too much. Fewer than 33 million people—23 percent of Russia's population—live in sprawling Siberia.

See map on page 103 for European part of Russia.

◐ **FISHING FOR A MEAL.**
A brown bear and her cubs hunt for fish in a river below the slopes of a volcano on Russia's Kamchatka Peninsula. Part of the Pacific Ring of Fire, this peninsula has 29 active volcanoes.

◐ **REVOLUTIONARY LEADER.** Vladimir Ilyich Lenin, a founder of the Soviet Union, was honored with many statues. This one in Siberia is the largest still standing in Russia.

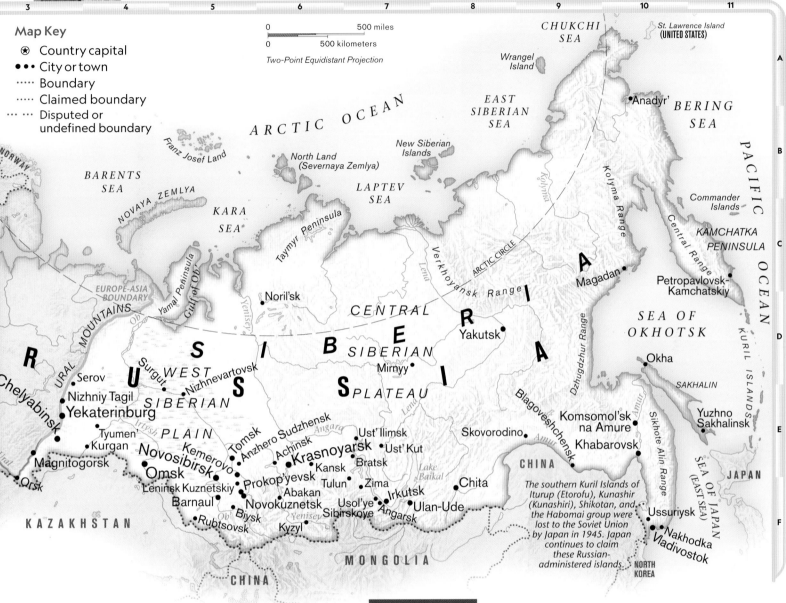

Map Key

- ✪ Country capital
- ••• City or town
- ‥‥ Boundary
- ‥‥ Claimed boundary
- ‥‥ Disputed or undefined boundary

0   500 miles
0   500 kilometers
Two-Point Equidistant Projection

The southern Kuril Islands of Iturup (Etorofu), Kunashir (Kunashiri), Shikotan, and the Habomai group were lost to the Soviet Union by Japan in 1945. Japan continues to claim these Russian-administered islands.

DEEPEST LAKE

Lake Baikal	Lake Tanganyika	Caspian Sea	Lake Malawi	Ysyk-Köl	Great Slave Lake	Crater Lake
5,369 ft (1,637 m)	4,708 ft (1,435 m)	3,104 ft (946 m)	2,316 ft (706 m)	2,297 ft (700 m)	2,015 ft (614 m)	1,943 ft (592 m)

Most of Earth's freshwater surface water is stored in lakes. The deepest of all is Lake Baikal, which contains about 20 percent of Earth's total surface freshwater.

◐ **COLD POWER.** A liquefied natural gas well on the Yamal Peninsula in northwestern Siberia taps into Russia's largest gas reserves. Bitterly cold Arctic winters are a major challenge to this project.

Central Asia

Located along the historic Silk Road, Central Asia is made up of five former republics of the Soviet Union, often referred to as the stans, or "homelands." This region's population includes Kazakhs, Turkmen, Uzbeks, Tajiks, Kyrgyz, and Russians. The population is largely Muslim. Kazakhstan's short-grass steppes give way to deserts, arid plateaus, and rugged mountains to the south. The Amu Darya and the Syr Darya provide water for irrigating wheat, rice, cotton, and fruit crops. Although this landlocked region lies far from any ocean, it includes several large bodies of water, including the Caspian Sea, which is actually a saltwater lake.

⬥ **BEST FRIENDS.** A boy carries his goat in mountainous Kyrgyzstan, where almost half the land is used for pasture and hay to support herds of goats and sheep.

THE BASICS

STATS

Largest country
Kazakhstan 1,052,089 sq mi
(2,724,900 sq km)

Smallest country
Tajikistan 55,637 sq mi
(144,100 sq km)

Most populous country
Uzbekistan 30,024,000

Least populous country
Turkmenistan 5,411,000

Predominant languages
Russian, Kazakh, Uzbek,
Kyrgyz, Tajik, Turkmen

Predominant religions
Islam, Christianity

Highest GDP per capita
Kazakhstan $26,300

Lowest GDP per capita
Tajikistan $3,200

Highest life expectancy
Uzbekistan 74 years

Lowest life expectancy
Tajikistan 68 years

GEO WHIZ

The main musical instrument of the steppes in Kazakhstan is the dombra, a long-necked lute with two strings.

Uzbekistan, one of the world's top gold-producing countries, has the world's deepest open-pit gold mine. Muruntau Mine is said to hold more gold reserves than any other mine in the world.

Mountains, including the ranges Pamir and Tian Shan, cover more than 90 percent of Tajikistan.

◗ **INTO SPACE.** Baikonur Cosmodrome, located east of the Aral Sea in Kazakhstan, has been the launch site for Russian space missions since Sputnik 1 in 1957. U.S. astronauts have taken off from here to the International Space Station.

◖ **CRITICALLY ENDANGERED.** Loss of habitat, illegal hunting, and disease have put the saiga antelope, found mainly in Kazakhstan, at risk.

◖ **WHERE BARGAINING IS AN ART.**
Two men bargain over the price of cherries in a bazaar in Samarqand, Uzbekistan. Located on the fabled Silk Road, the country relies on agriculture, especially cotton production, to support its economy.

VANISHING SEA

The Aral Sea has lost more than 90 percent of its area because water from feeder rivers is being used to irrigate millions of acres of cotton and rice.

THE CONTINENT:
ASIA

Eastern Asia

THE BASICS

STATS

Largest country
China 3,705,405 sq mi
(9,596,960 sq km)

Smallest country
South Korea
38,502 sq mi (99,720 sq km)

Most populous country
China 1,384,689,000

Least populous country
Mongolia 3,103,000

Predominant languages
Standard Chinese (Mandarin),
Japanese, Korean, Mongol

Predominant religions
Daoism, Buddhism, Shintoism,
Christianity, Confucianism

Highest GDP per capita
Japan $42,800

Lowest GDP per capita
North Korea $1,700

Highest life expectancy
Japan 85 years

Lowest life expectancy
Mongolia
70 years

GEO WHIZ

The only surviving breed of
wild horse, the Przewalski, is
named for the count who
"discovered" it in Mongolia in
the 1880s. Careful breeding
has saved it from extinction.
About 2,000 remain.

Each year on October 9, people
in South Korea celebrate their
alphabet, which was created
in 1446 to increase literacy.

China, Mongolia, the Koreas, and Japan make up eastern Asia. Rich river valleys have supported Chinese civilization for more than four millennia. The Tibetan Plateau, dry basins, and the towering Himalaya border China to the west. Mongolia, the land of Genghis Khan, lies to China's north. Japan and South Korea have used technology and manufacturing to become economic powerhouses. While China has opened to global markets, North Korea has remained a communist government that leans toward isolation. North Korea's isolation creates a lack of economic opportunity, and its people remain poor.

HIGH TECH. This South Korean woman works in a laboratory that makes microcircuits in a semi-conductor plant in Seoul.

NIGHTLIGHTS. Tokyo's Shinjuku is both a shopping center and a theater district, as well as the city's busiest train station. It averages more than 3.6 million passengers daily.

AUTO GIANTS

2018 Production Statistics in millions

Country	Production (millions)
China	23.5
Japan	8.4
Germany	5.1
India	4.1
South Korea	3.7
USA	2.7
Brazil	2.4
Spain	2.3
France	1.8
Mexico	1.6

Once the leader in car production, the United States now ranks sixth. Holding first place, China's production is almost triple that of second-ranked Japan.

◑ **HOME ON THE STEPPE.** A *ger* is the traditional Mongolian dwelling. The cowlike yak works as a pack animal and is a source of milk.

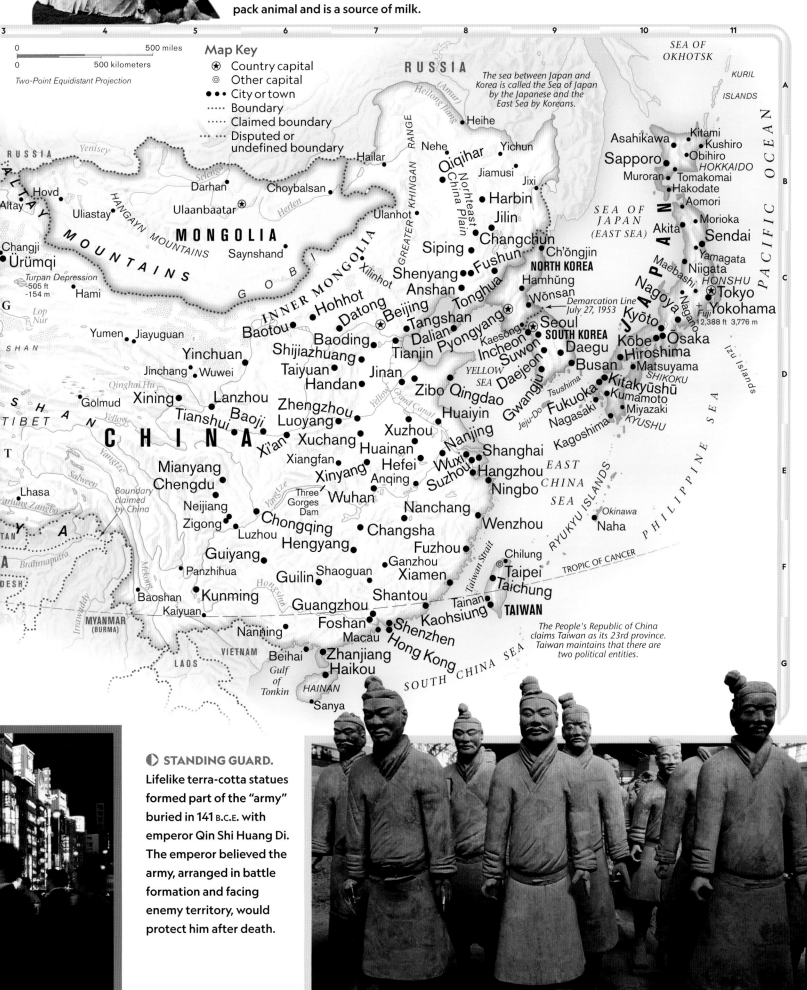

Map Key
★ Country capital
◎ Other capital
•••• City or town
····· Boundary
····· Claimed boundary
····· Disputed or undefined boundary

0 ——— 500 miles
0 ——— 500 kilometers
Two-Point Equidistant Projection

The sea between Japan and Korea is called the Sea of Japan by the Japanese and the East Sea by Koreans.

The People's Republic of China claims Taiwan as its 23rd province. Taiwan maintains that there are two political entities.

RUSSIA
SEA OF OKHOTSK
KURIL ISLANDS
PACIFIC OCEAN
MONGOLIA
Ulaanbaatar ★
INNER MONGOLIA
GOBI
RUSSIA
ALTAY MOUNTAINS
HANGAYN MOUNTAINS
GREATER KHINGAN RANGE
Heilong Jiang (Amur)
Heihe
Nehe
Yichun
Jiamusi
Jixi
Qiqihar
Northeast China Plain
Harbin
Jilin
Changchun
Hailar
Ulanhot
Siping
Shenyang
Fushun
Ch'ŏngjin
NORTH KOREA
Hamhŭng
Wŏnsan
Demarcation Line July 27, 1953
Pyongyang ◎
Kaesŏng
Seoul ★
SOUTH KOREA
Incheon
Suwon
Daejeon
Daegu
Busan
Gwangju
YELLOW SEA
Jeju-Do
Tsushima
SEA OF JAPAN (EAST SEA)
JAPAN
HOKKAIDO
Sapporo
Asahikawa
Kitami
Kushiro
Obihiro
Muroran
Tomakomai
Hakodate
Aomori
Morioka
Akita
Yamagata
Sendai
Niigata
Maebashi
Nagano
HONSHU
Nagoya
Tokyo ★
Yokohama
Kyōto
Ōsaka
Kōbe
Hiroshima
Matsuyama
SHIKOKU
Fukuoka
Kitakyūshū
Kumamoto
Nagasaki
Miyazaki
KYUSHU
Kagoshima
Fuji 12,388 ft 3,776 m
Izu Islands
PHILIPPINE SEA
EAST CHINA SEA
RYUKYU ISLANDS
Okinawa
Naha
Hovd
Altay
Changji
Ürümqi
Turpan Depression -505 ft -154 m
Hami
Yumen
Jiayuguan
Darhan
Choybalsan
Uliastay
Saynshand
Xilinhot
Hohhot
Baotou
Datong
Beijing ★
Tangshan
Dalian
Tianjin
Baoding
Shijiazhuang
Taiyuan
Handan
Jinan
Zibo
Qingdao
Huaiyin
Anshan
Tonghua
CHINA
SHAN
Yinchuan
Jinchang
Wuwei
Lanzhou
Xining
Golmud
Qinghai Hu
TIBET
SHAN
Lhasa
Yarlung Zangbo
Boundary claimed by China
Brahmaputra
Yellow
Tianshui
Baoji
Zhengzhou
Luoyang
Xi'an
Xuchang
Xuzhou
Nanjing
Shanghai
Wuxi
Suzhou
Hangzhou
Ningbo
Huainan
Hefei
Anqing
Wenzhou
Xinyang
Xiangfan
Mianyang
Chengdu
Neijiang
Zigong
Luzhou
Chongqing
Three Gorges Dam
Wuhan
Nanchang
Changsha
Fuzhou
Ganzhou
Xiamen
Shantou
Chilung
Taipei ◎
Taichung
Tainan
Kaohsiung
TAIWAN
Taiwan Strait
Guiyang
Guilin
Shaoguan
Shaoshan
Panzhihua
Baoshan
Kunming
Kaiyuan
Nanning
Beihai
Guangzhou
Foshan
Shenzhen
Macau
Hong Kong
Zhanjiang
Haikou
HAINAN
Sanya
Gulf of Tonkin
SOUTH CHINA SEA
VIETNAM
LAOS
MYANMAR (BURMA)
Irrawaddy
Mekong
Hongshui
Yangtze
Salween
Hengyang
Xiangfan
Yenisey
Selenga
Herlen
Grand Canal
TROPIC OF CANCER

◑ **STANDING GUARD.** Lifelike terra-cotta statues formed part of the "army" buried in 141 B.C.E. with emperor Qin Shi Huang Di. The emperor believed the army, arranged in battle formation and facing enemy territory, would protect him after death.

THE CONTINENT:
ASIA

Eastern Mediterranean

THE BASICS

STATS

Largest country
Turkey
302,535 sq mi (783,562 sq km)

Smallest country
Lebanon
4,015 sq mi (10,400 sq km)

Most populous country
Turkey 81,257,000

Least populous country
Armenia 3,038,000

Predominant languages
Turkish, Arabic, Azerbaijani, Hebrew, Georgian, Armenian, English, French, Kurdish

Predominant religions
Islam, Judaism, Christianity

Highest GDP per capita
Israel $36,300

Lowest GDP per capita
Syria $2,900

Highest life expectancy
Israel 82 years

Lowest life expectancy
Azerbaijan 73 years

GEO WHIZ

Some English and Spanish words have origins in Arabic, such as algebra, coffee, and hasta (until).

Israelis capture runoff from seasonal rains to support crops in the Negev, a desert region that extends across more than half their country.

⬖ **ANCIENT MYSTERY.**
A camel walks past Al-Khazneh in Petra, a World Heritage site in Jordan. Carved out of a mountainside more than 2,500 years ago, Petra was the capital of the Nabateans.

This region forms a bridge between Europe and Asia, from the Caucasus Mountains to the desert lands of Jordan. Turkey, framed by the Black, Aegean, and Mediterranean Seas, leads the region in population and area. The historic and life-giving Tigris and Euphrates Rivers begin in Turkey and flow southeast through arid Syria and Iraq. Israel, Lebanon, Syria, and Turkey share the Mediterranean shore. While Islam claims the majority of followers across these lands, Judaism, Christianity, and other faiths are present. Many of the holiest sites for Christians, Jews, and Muslims are found in this region.

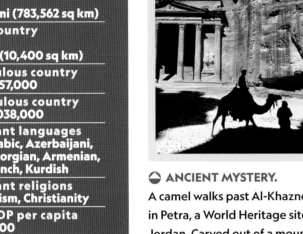

BULGARIA
Edirne
GREECE
Tekirdağ
AEGEAN SEA
Dardanelles
İzmir
Aydın
DODECANESE

BELOW SEA LEVEL

sea level

Empire State Building (U.S.A.)

-1,401 ft
(-427 m)

1,250 ft
(381 m)

Dead Sea

Not every place with an elevation below sea level is under the ocean. The Dead Sea, in western Asia, plunges to -1,401 feet (-427 m) below sea level. That's deeper than the Empire State Building is tall.

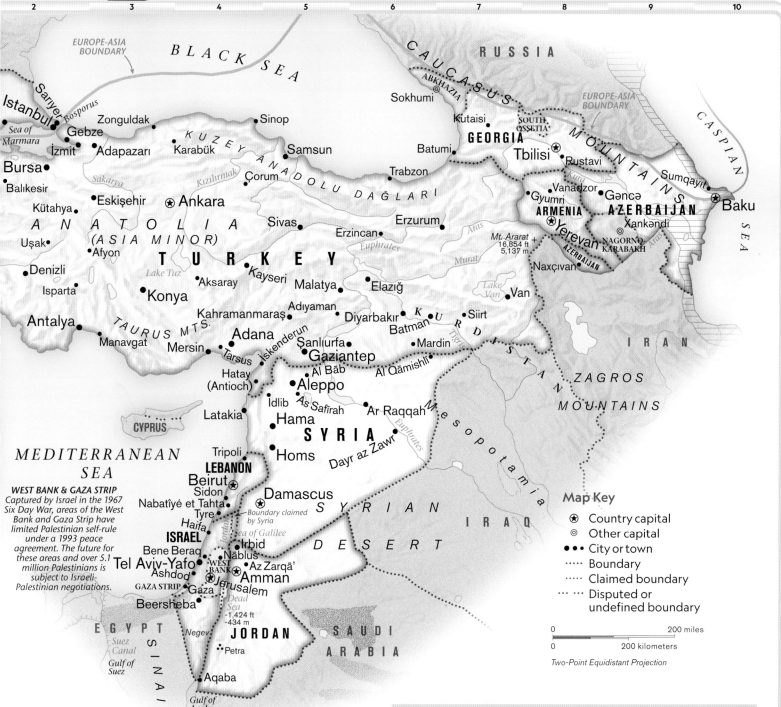

◑ **WATCHERS FROM THE PAST.** Giant stone heads, representing Greek gods, guard the first-century B.C.E. burial site of King Antiochus I in southeastern Turkey.

Map Key

⊛ Country capital
◎ Other capital
••• City or town
····· Boundary
····· Claimed boundary
···· Disputed or undefined boundary

0		200 miles
0		200 kilometers

Two-Point Equidistant Projection

WEST BANK & GAZA STRIP
Captured by Israel in the 1967 Six Day War, areas of the West Bank and Gaza Strip have limited Palestinian self-rule under a 1993 peace agreement. The future for these areas and over 5.1 million Palestinians is subject to Israeli-Palestinian negotiations.

◑ **BETWEEN TWO WORLDS.** The Galata Bridge crosses the Golden Horn, connecting the Asian part of Istanbul, Turkey (foreground), to the Galata area in the city's European part.

◑ **AN INSIDE LOOK.** Visitors to the Bonn Bundeskunsthalle in Bonn, Germany, can experience 3D views of the ruins of Mosul, Iraq, and the Syrian cities Aleppo and Palmyra. The three cities sustained significant destruction during the Syrian civil war that began in March 2011.

THE CONTINENT:
ASIA

Southwestern Asia

⊙ **GIRL TALK. Young
Iranian girls get together
at a film festival in Tehran.
They are wearing hijabs,
a head covering worn by
many Muslim women.**

This region, made up largely of deserts and mountains, includes the countries of the Arabian Peninsula and those that border the Persian Gulf. Islam is the dominant religion, and the two holiest places for Muslims—Mecca and Medina—are here. Arabic is the main language everywhere but Iran, where most people speak Persian (Farsi). While water has been the most important natural resource here for millennia, global attention has focused in recent decades on the region's extensive oil reserves. Ongoing conflict and political tensions also have kept this region in headlines around the world.

⊙ **THEY'VE GOT THE BEAT.**
Omani musicians play for a tribal
dance in Muscat, Oman, preserv-
ing their heritage through music.

WORLD OIL RESERVES

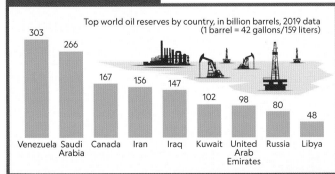

Top world oil reserves by country, in billion barrels, 2019 data
(1 barrel = 42 gallons/159 liters)

Venezuela	Saudi Arabia	Canada	Iran	Iraq	Kuwait	United Arab Emirates	Russia	Libya
303	266	167	156	147	102	98	80	48

Saudi Arabia, second in oil reserves, and four other
southwestern Asia countries account for almost
46 percent of all oil production.

⊙ **MERGING WORLDS. This roadside meeting in Qatar highlights
the transportation options and heritage of southwestern Asia. The oil
industry and horse breeding support economic growth in the region.**

🔵 **LOST AND FOUND.** Ancient treasures were destroyed, lost, or stolen during the 2003 invasion of Iraq. This ring is among the few items recovered.

THE CONTINENT:
ASIA

1   2   3   4   5   6   7   8

BLACK SEA

GEORGIA

TURKEY

ARMENIA   AZERBAIJAN

CASPIAN SEA

TURKMENISTAN

K U R D I S T A N

Orūmīyeh   Marand

Zakho   Tabrīz   Ardabīl

Tigris

Urmia

Miāndoāb   Rasht   Gorgān   Bojnūrd

Gondad-e Kāvūs

Tall 'Afar   Dihok   Zanjān   Sārī

Nineveh   As   Qazvīn   Sabzevār   Mashhad

MEDITERRANEAN SEA

SYRIA

Mosul   Erbil

Kirkuk   Sulaymānīyah   Tehran   Semnān

Sanandaj   +Kūh-e Damāvand 18,602 ft 5,670 m

K H O R Ā S Ā N

LEBANON

Tikrīt   Kermānshāh   Hamadān   Qom   Gonābad

Euphrates

Sāmarrā'

Dasht-e Kavīr (Kavir Desert)

ISRAEL

I R A Q

S Y R I A N

Baghdad   Arāk   I R A N

Birjand

JORDAN

Turaybīl   Ar Ramādī

Al Fallūjah   Z A G R O S   Isfahan

Karbalā'   Dezful

Al Hillah   Nippur   Qomsheh

Dasht-e Lūt

Al Qurayyāt   D E S E R T   An Najaf   Al 'Amārah   Yazd   Zābol

EGYPT

'Ar'ar   Sakākā   Ur   M O U N T A I N S   Ahvāz   Kermān   Noşratābād

Al Jawf   An Nāşirīyah   Al Başrah   Persepolis

Gulf of Aqaba

Tabūk   Ābādān   F Ā R S   Zāhedān

Az Zubayr   Shīrāz   Sa'īdābād

An Nafūd

KUWAIT   Marv Dasht   Bam   Īrānshahr

Būshehr   Jahrom   Fasā   Tārom

Kuwait City

Ha'il   *Historically and most commonly known as the Persian Gulf, this body of water is referred to by some as the Arabian Gulf.*

Bandar 'Abbās   *Strait of Hormuz*   Angohrān

BALUCHISTAN

AFGHANISTAN

PAKISTAN

N

P E R S I A N   Qeshm   Chāh Bāhar

A L   H I J A Z

Al Jubayl   Ra's al-Khaimah   OMAN

Buraydah   Ad Dammām

S A U D I   Manama   BAHRAIN   Sharjah   *GULF OF OMAN*

Medina   Al Mubarraz   Dubai   Suḩār

A R A B I A   Doha   *GULF*   Al Ain   TROPIC OF CANCER

Riyadh   Al Hufūf   QATAR   Muscat

R E D   Abu Dhabi   Quraggāt

Yanbu' al Bahr   Al Hillah   UNITED ARAB EMIRATES   'Ibrī   Sūr

A R A B I A N   Nizwá

Jeddah   Ad Dahnā'   Khalūf

Mecca   At Ta'if   P E N I N S U L A   *Al Hadīdah (meteorite craters)*   O M A N

SUDAN

S E A   Qal'at Bīshah   Masira

Al Qunfudhah   *Jabal Tuwayq*   *Rub' al Khali (Empty Quarter)*   Duqm

ARABIAN SEA

Abā as Sa'ūd   Z U F Ā R

Jīzān   Mirbāţ

ERITREA   Hawf   Şalālah

Hadramawt

Sanaa   Nishtūn

Al Hudaydah   Dhamār   Y E M E N

Ridā'   Ash Shiḩr

Ibb   Al Mukallā   *Socotra (Yemen)*

Ta'izz

Lahij   *GULF OF ADEN*

ETHIOPIA   Aden

DJIBOUTI

SOMALIA

Map Key

✪ Country capital
●●● City or town
····· Boundary

0   300 miles
0   300 kilometers

Two-Point Equidistant Projection

THE CONTINENT:
ASIA

Southern Asia

THE BASICS

STATS

Largest country
India 1,269,219 sq mi
(3,287,263 sq km)

Smallest country
Maldives 115 sq mi (298 sq km)

Most populous country
India 1,296,834,000

Least populous country
Maldives 392,000

Predominant languages
Hindi, English, Punjabi,
Bangla, Dari, Burmese,
Pashto, Urdu, Sinhala,
Nepali, Dzongkha

Predominant religions
Hinduism, Islam, Buddhism

Highest GDP per capita
Maldives $19,100

Lowest GDP per capita
Afghanistan $2,000

Highest life expectancy
Sri Lanka 77 years

Lowest life expectancy
Afghanistan 52 years

GEO WHIZ

India's rail system transports
8.4 billion passengers each
year across nearly 41,890
miles (67,415 km) of track.

Bhutan, a Himalayan country
known as Land of the Thunder Dragon, is the world's
only Buddhist kingdom.

⊙ **TAJ MAHAL.** In 1631 in Agra, India,
the Mughal emperor Shah Jahan began
construction of this magnificent marble
memorial to his deceased wife.

This region is home to the world's highest peaks. Three of the world's famous rivers—the Indus, Ganges, and Brahmaputra—support the hundreds of millions of people who live here. India is at the center, greater in area than the other countries combined and more than double their population. Hinduism and Buddhism originated in India where Hinduism continues to be the main religion. There are large numbers of Buddhists in Bhutan, Nepal, Sri Lanka, and Myanmar, and Muslims form the majority in Afghanistan, Pakistan, and Bangladesh. Poverty and prosperity live side by side across the region, with streams of migrants flowing from rural areas to mushrooming cities.

◖ **GOLDEN GRAIN.**
A man leads his cow
past a rice field
south of Rangpur,
Bangladesh. Rice
is the staple food
for 159 million
Bangladeshis
and provides
employment
for a lot of the
rural population.

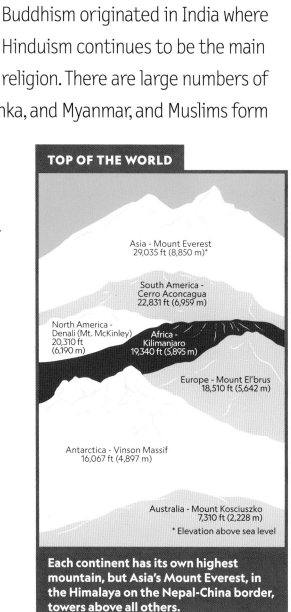

TOP OF THE WORLD

Asia - Mount Everest
29,035 ft (8,850 m)*

South America -
Cerro Aconcagua
22,831 ft (6,959 m)

North America -
Denali (Mt. McKinley)
20,310 ft
(6,190 m)

Africa -
Kilimanjaro
19,340 ft (5,895 m)

Europe - Mount El'brus
18,510 ft (5,642 m)

Antarctica - Vinson Massif
16,067 ft (4,897 m)

Australia - Mount Kosciuszko
7,310 ft (2,228 m)
* Elevation above sea level

Each continent has its own highest
mountain, but Asia's Mount Everest, in
the Himalaya on the Nepal-China border,
towers above all others.

◖ **EASTERN BELIEF.** The god Shiva (left) is part of the Hindu trinity, which also includes the gods Brahma and Vishnu. Hinduism is the world's third largest religion (after Christianity and Islam), with more than a billion followers.

1 2 3 4 5 6 7 8 9

TURKMENISTAN

IRAN

Balkh Faizabad
Mazar-e Sharif
Herat Kunduz Charikar
Baghlan HINDU KUSH TAJIKISTAN
Bamyan Jalalabad Peshawar
Kabul ✪ Mardan
AFGHANISTAN
Ghazni Khost Kohat Islamabad
Gardez Rawalpindi
Kandahar Jammu
Dera Ismail Khan LINE OF CONTROL
Quetta Gujranwala Amritsar Simla
Faisalabad Lahore
PAKISTAN Multan Ludhiana
Jacobabad Bahawalpur Chandigarh
BALUCHISTAN Larkana Sadiqabad
Turbat Dadu Sukkur Nawabshah GREAT INDIAN DESERT
Jodhpur Ajmer
Karachi Hyderabad Pali Udaipur

Boundary claimed by India
K2 (Godwin Austen) 28,250 ft 8,611 m
KUNLUN SHAN
KASHMIR
Srinagar

India and Pakistan both claim Kashmir—a disputed region of some 18 million people. India administers only the area south of the line of control; Pakistan controls northwestern Kashmir. China controls parts of eastern Kashmir that it took from India in a 1962 war.

C H I N A

Boundary claimed by China

TIBET
Brahmaputra
HIMALAYA
Mt. Everest 29,035 ft 8,850 m
Thimphu Dibrugarh
Kathmandu Gangtok BHUTAN Jorhat
Dehra Dun NEPAL Shiliguri Guwahati Kohima
Meerut Bareilly Lalitpur Purnia Rangpur Imphal Myitkyina
Delhi Budaun Lucknow Biratnagar Silchar
New Delhi Agra Kanpur Patna BANGLADESH Aizawl
Jaipur Etawah Varanasi Asansol Dhaka
Gwalior Fatehpur Mirzapur Haora Khulna Chittagong
Kota Jhansi Allahabad Ranchi Kolkata (Calcutta) Monywa Mandalay
Gandhinagar Sagar Raurkela Jamshedpur Mouths of the Ganges Bagan Taunggyi
Ahmadabad INDIA Bilaspur Sambalpur Sittwe MYANMAR
Bhuj Narmada Bhopal Jabalpur Raipur Puri Bhubaneshwar Nay Pyi Taw ✪ Pyinmana
Rajkot SATPURA RANGE Nagpur Brahmapur (BURMA)
Porbandar Bharuch Vijayawada Vizianagaram Insein Bago
Bhavnagar Nasik Aurangabad Chandrapur Rajahmundry Vishakhapatnam Pathein Yangon (Rangoon)
Surat DECCAN Eluru Kakinada BAY OF BENGAL Mawlamyine
Kalyan Pune Hyderabad Machilipatnam
Mumbai (Bombay) PLATEAU Krishna Guntur Dawei
Kolhapur Belgavi Chitradurga Ongole Myeik
Hubballi Nellore
Bengaluru Cuddapah
Mangaluru Mysuru Chittoor Chennai (Madras)
Lakshadweep Salem Puducherry
Kozhikode Tiruchchirappalli
Coimbatore Dindigul Madurai
Kochi Jaffna Rajapalaiyam
Thiruvananthapuram Tuticorin SRI LANKA (CEYLON)
Nagercoil Kandy
Colombo ✪ (commercial capital) Sri Jayewardenepura Kotte (official capital)

Godavari
Eastern Ghats
Western Ghats

Narmada

Harirud
Helmand
Indus
Ganges
Brahmaputra
Salween
Salween
Mekong
Irrawaddy
Malay Peninsula

ARABIAN SEA
TROPIC OF CANCER
Mouths of the Indus

INDIAN OCEAN

Maldive Islands
Minicoy
Male ✪
MALDIVES

EQUATOR
Fua Mulaku
Gan

Cape Comorin

ANDAMAN ISLANDS (India)
ANDAMAN SEA
Isthmus of Kra
NICOBAR ISLANDS (India)

LAOS
THAILAND

Map Key
✪ Country capital
●●● City or town
⋯⋯ Boundary
⋯⋯ Claimed boundary
⋯⋯ Disputed or undefined boundary

0 _____ 300 miles
0 _____ 300 kilometers
Two-Point Projection

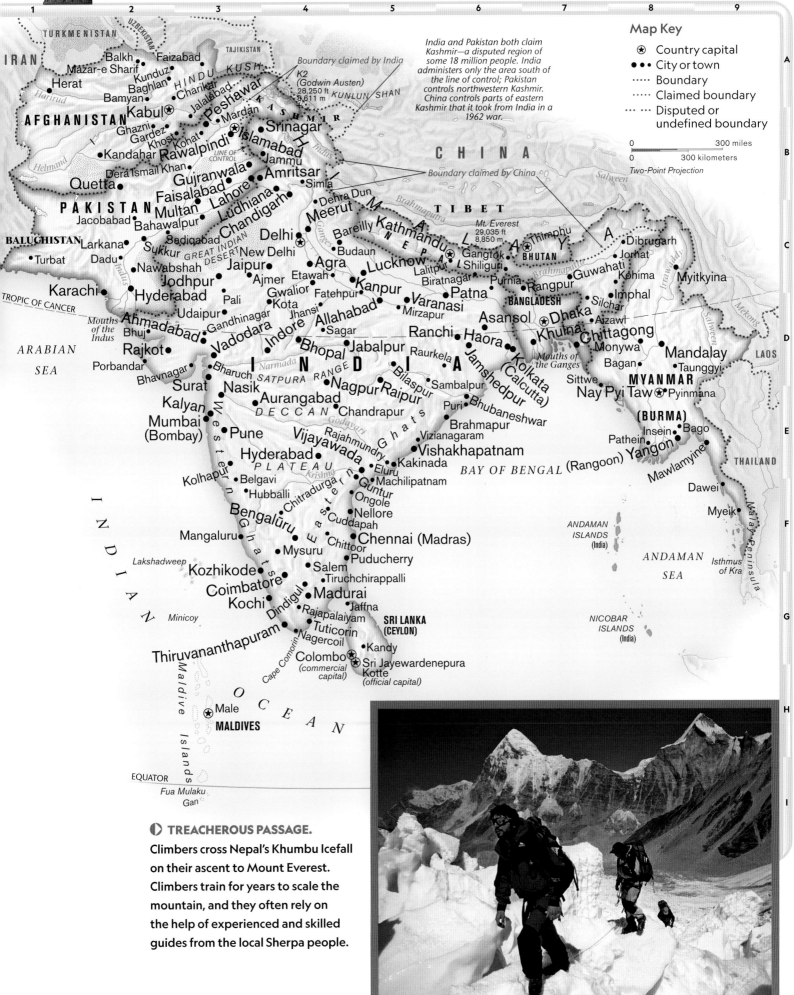

◖ **TREACHEROUS PASSAGE.**
Climbers cross Nepal's Khumbu Icefall on their ascent to Mount Everest. Climbers train for years to scale the mountain, and they often rely on the help of experienced and skilled guides from the local Sherpa people.

Southeastern Asia

THE BASICS

STATS

Largest country
Thailand 198,117 sq mi
(513,120 sq km)

Smallest country
Singapore 269 sq mi
(697 sq km)

Most populous country
Philippines 105,893,000

Least populous country
Brunei 451,000

Predominant languages
Filipino (based on Tagalog),
English, Vietnamese, Thai,
Khmer, Lao, French, Malay,
Bahasa Melayu, Mandarin

Predominant religions
Christianity, Buddhism, Islam

Highest GDP per capita
Singapore $93,900

Lowest GDP per capita
Cambodia $4,000

Highest life expectancy
Singapore 85 years

Lowest life expectancy
Laos 64 years

GEO WHIZ

The Philippines has one of the world's highest rates of deforestation. Studies estimate that from 2001 to 2019, the country lost three million acres (1.23 million ha) of tree cover, a 6.6 percent decrease since 2000.

Thailand means "land of the free." It is the only country in southeastern Asia never ruled by a colonial power.

The Plain of Jars, in northern Laos, takes its name from hundreds of huge stone urns spread across the ground. Archaeologists believe Bronze Age people made the jars and used them to hold the cremated remains of their dead.

The countries of southeastern Asia have long been influenced by neighboring giants India and China. The result is a mix of cultures, rich histories, violent conflicts, and future promise. Cambodia's spectacular 12th-century Angkor Wat provides a glimpse of former greatness. Colonial rule brought division and change, and struggles for independence took a heavy toll, as in Vietnam. Mainland countries are largely Buddhist, whereas peninsular Malaysia is mostly Muslim, and Christians dominate the Philippines. All but Laos have ocean access, with fisheries providing jobs and food for millions. Rivers like the Chao Phraya and the mighty Mekong provide transport and water-rich croplands dominated by rice growing. Tiny Singapore has gained global importance with its bustling port operations and high-tech focus.

SMILING BUDDHA.
A Buddhist monk admires a sculpture in Cambodia's Angkor temple complex. Built by the Khmer between 800 and 1200 C.E., the complex includes Buddhist and Hindu temples.

PRIMATES. Smaller than an adult human's hand, the Philippine tarsier is one of the world's smallest primates. Found on islands such as Bohol, the tarsier is active at night, hunting for insects.

SHIPPING HUB.
Huge container terminals, such as this one at Tanjong Pagar, make Singapore the world's busiest transshipment center, connected to 600 ports in 123 countries around the world.

◀ FLASHY RIDE. Colorful Philippine taxis, called jeepneys because of their origin as rebuilt World War II jeeps, are a common sight on the streets of Manila.

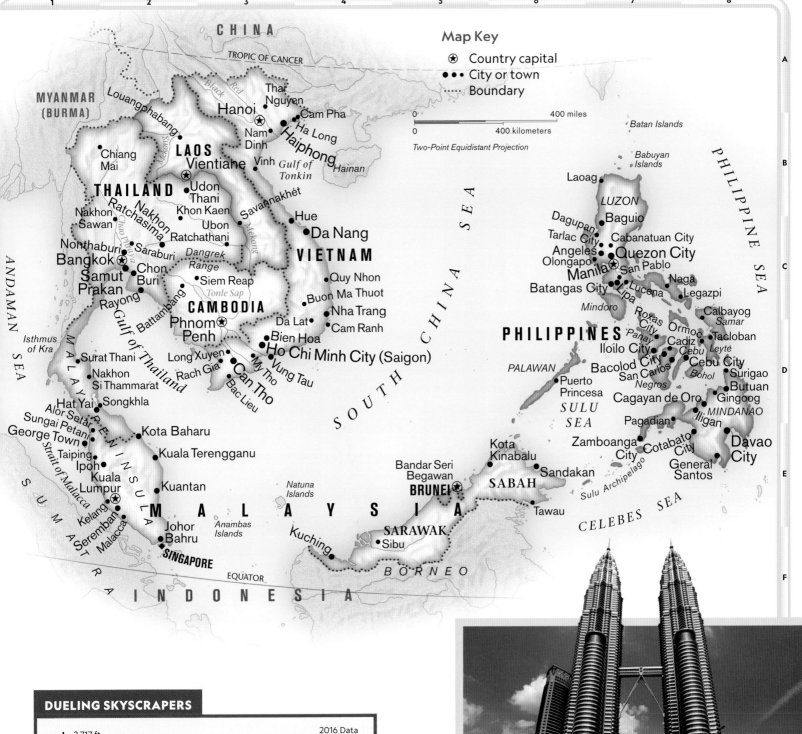

CHINA

TROPIC OF CANCER

Map Key
- ✪ Country capital
- ••• City or town
- ⋯⋯ Boundary

0 _____ 400 miles
0 _____ 400 kilometers
Two-Point Equidistant Projection

MYANMAR (BURMA)

Louangphabang
Black / Red
Thai Nguyen
Hanoi
Cam Pha
Ha Long
Nam Dinh
Haiphong
Hainan
Gulf of Tonkin

Chiang Mai
LAOS
Vientiane
Vinh

THAILAND
Udon Thani
Khon Kaen
Savannakhét

Nakhon Sawan
Ratchasima
Nakhon
Ratchathani
Ubon
Hue
Da Nang

VIETNAM

Nonthaburi
Saraburi
Dangrek Range
Mekong

Bangkok
Chon Buri
Siem Reap
Tonle Sap
Quy Nhon

Samut Prakan
Rayong
Battambang
CAMBODIA
Buon Ma Thuot
Nha Trang

Isthmus of Kra
Phnom Penh
Da Lat
Cam Ranh
Bien Hoa

Surat Thani
Long Xuyen
My Tho
Ho Chi Minh City (Saigon)
Vung Tau

Nakhon Si Thammarat
Rach Gia
Can Tho
Bac Lieu

SOUTH CHINA SEA

Hat Yai
Songkhla
Alor Setar
Sungai Petani
George Town
Kota Baharu
Taiping
Ipoh
Kuala Terengganu
Kuala Lumpur
Kuantan

Kelang
Seremban
Johor Bahru
MALAYSIA
Malacca
SINGAPORE

ANDAMAN SEA
Gulf of Thailand
MALAY PENINSULA
Strait of Malacca

EQUATOR
INDONESIA
SUMATRA

Natuna Islands
Anambas Islands
Kuching

Bandar Seri Begawan
BRUNEI
SARAWAK
Sibu
BORNEO

Batan Islands
Babuyan Islands

Laoag
LUZON
Dagupan
Baguio
Tarlac City
Cabanatuan City
Angeles
Quezon City
Olongapo
Manila
San Pablo
Batangas City
Lipa
Lucena
Naga
Legazpi
Mindoro
Roxas City
Panay
Calbayog
Samar

PHILIPPINES

Ormoc
Tacloban
Iloilo City
Cadiz
Leyte
Cebu
Bacolod City
Cebu City
San Carlos
Bohol
Surigao
Negros
Butuan
PALAWAN
Cagayan de Oro
Gingoog
Puerto Princesa
SULU SEA
Pagadian
Iligan
MINDANAO
Kota Kinabalu
Zamboanga City
Cotabato City
Davao City
Sandakan
SABAH
General Santos
Tawau
Sulu Archipelago
CELEBES SEA

PHILIPPINE SEA

DUELING SKYSCRAPERS

2016 Data

2,717 ft (828 m)
Burj Khalifa (Dubai, United Arab Emirates)

2073 ft (632 m)
Shanghai Tower (Shanghai, China)

1,972 ft (601 m)
Makkah Clock Royal Tower (Makkah/Mecca, Saudi Arabia)

1,965 ft (599 m)
Ping An International Finance Center (Shenzhen, China)

The world's four tallest buildings are in Asia. The 2,717-foot (828-m) Burj Khalifa, in the United Arab Emirates, was completed in 2010.

◒ STANDING TALL. The Petronas Twin Towers, the world's tallest twin towers, rise above Kuala Lumpur, Malaysia's capital.

THE BASICS

STATS

Largest country
Indonesia 735,358 sq mi
(1,904,569 sq km)

Smallest country
Timor-Leste 5,743 sq mi
(14,874 sq km)

Most populous country
Indonesia 262,787,000

Least populous country
Timor-Leste 1,322,000

Predominant languages
Indonesian, English, Dutch,
Javanese, Tetum, Portuguese

Predominant religions
Islam, Christianity

Highest GDP per capita
Indonesia $12,400

Lowest GDP per capita
Timor-Leste $5,400

Highest life expectancy
Indonesia 73 years

Lowest life expectancy
Timor-Leste 68 years

GEO WHIZ

In 2006, two species of sharks
that use their fins to "walk"
on coral reefs were discovered
off the northwestern coast of
Indonesia's Papua province.

When seen from the air,
Timor Island resembles a crocodile. According to local legend, a crocodile turned itself
into the island as a way of
saying thank-you to a boy
who saved its life.

Komodo dragons, the world's
heaviest lizard, live only on
Indonesia's Lesser Sunda
Islands. They eat all types
of prey.

Indonesia & Timor-Leste

Stretching more than 2,200
miles (3,520 km) from Sumatra
to New Guinea, Indonesia is
the world's largest island
nation and the fourth most
populous country. Most of its
262 million people live on the
volcanically active island of Java.
Indonesia shares rainforested
Borneo with Malaysia and Brunei. Most
Indonesians are of Malay ethnicity, though
there are large numbers
of Melanesians (see page
156), Chinese, and East Indians.
Arab traders brought Islam to the islands
in the 13th century, and today six out of
seven Indonesians are Muslim. Timor-Leste
gained independence from Indonesia in
2002. Timor-Leste and the
Philippines are Asia's only
mainly Catholic countries.

◉ **PROUD CITIZEN.**
A boy smiles broadly as
he waves the flag of Timor-
Leste (also known as East
Timor) in Díli, the capital city.

◑ **CITY ON THE MOVE.**
Skyscrapers and a busy freeway
are just one face of Jakarta,
Indonesia's national capital and
center of trade and industry. In
this city of more than 10 million
people, the modern and traditional, the rich and poor, live side
by side. Like the country, the city
has a very diverse population.

◖ **SPIRIT WORLD.** Masks, such as this one from Bali, Indonesia, were probably created originally for dance and storytelling rituals.

◗ **GREAT APE.** The Bornean orangutan is a critically endangered species found in the wild only on Borneo. Orangutans are the world's largest tree-living mammal. An adult male is pictured here.

3   4   5   6   7   8   9   10   11

PHILIPPINES

SOUTH CHINA SEA

BRUNEI

Natuna Islands

Sulu Archipelago

MALAYSIA

CELEBES SEA

Talaud Islands

PACIFIC OCEAN

BORNEO

Pontianak
Palangkaraya
Samarinda
Balikpapan
Banjarmasin

MOLUCCA SEA

Manado
Gorontalo

Morotai

Halmahera
Ternate

EQUATOR

Sorong

Biak

Jayapura

SULAWESI

Gulf of Tomini

Makassar Strait

Sula Islands

CERAM SEA

Batanme

Ceram

IRIAN JAYA

Maoke Mountains
+ Puncak Jaya
16,024 ft
4,884 m

PAPUA NEW GUINEA

INDONESIA

JAVA SEA

Parepare

Buru

Ambon

Buton

Tual

Aru Islands

Dolak

Merauke

NEW GUINEA

Tegal
Semarang
Madiun
Mojokerto
Surabaya
Pasuruan
Probolinggo
Pekalongan
Magelang
Surakarta
Yogyakarta
Kediri
Blitar
Malang
Jember

Makassar

BANDA SEA

Tukangbesi Islands

Tanimbar Islands

ARAFURA SEA

FLORES SEA

Bali
Lombok
Denpasar
Mataram
Sumbawa
Raba
Flores
Barat Daya Islands
Dili

Sumba

Kupang

TIMOR

TIMOR-LESTE
(EAST TIMOR)

TIMOR SEA

LESSER SUNDA ISLANDS

AUSTRALIA

Map Key
- ★ Country capital
- ••• City or town
- ····· Boundary

0 —————— 400 miles
0 —————— 400 kilometers

Two-Point Equidistant Projection

FOLLOWERS OF ISLAM

Country	Millions
Indonesia	204.8*
Pakistan	178.1
India	177.3
Bangladesh	148.6
Egypt	80.0
Nigeria	75.7
Iran	74.8
Turkey	74.7
Algeria	34.8
Morocco	32.4

*Figures are in millions, 2010 data

Islam's origins trace to southwestern Asia, but the religion has spread around the world. The country with the largest Muslim population is Indonesia.

◗ **GENETIC STOREHOUSE.** The rainforest in eastern Borneo's Kalimantan province is home to many rare species. Much of the forest has been lost as a result of activities such as logging and road building—a consequence of the spread of plantation agriculture, especially oil palm cultivation.

THE CONTINENT:
AFRICA

PHYSICAL			POLITICAL	
TOTAL AREA 11,608,000 sq mi (30,065,000 sq km)	**LOWEST POINT** Lake Assal, Djibouti -509 ft (-155 m)	**LARGEST LAKE** Lake Victoria 26,800 sq mi (69,500 sq km)	**POPULATION** 1,340,598,000	**LARGEST COUNTRY** Algeria 919,595 sq mi (2,381,741 sq km)
			LARGEST METROPOLITAN AREA Cairo, Egypt Pop. 20,901,000	
HIGHEST POINT Kilimanjaro, Tanzania 19,340 ft (5,895 m)	**LONGEST RIVER** Nile 4,160 mi (6,695 km)			**MOST DENSELY POPULATED COUNTRY** Mauritius 1,731 people per sq mi (669 per sq km)

AFRICA

Africa

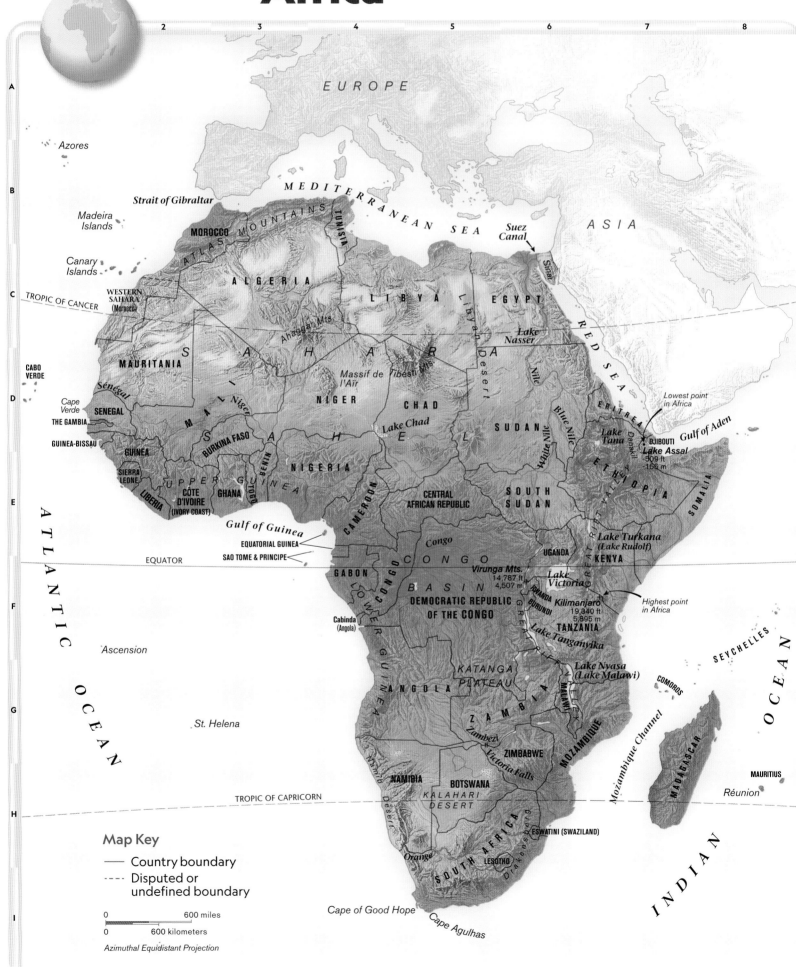

2   3   4   5   6   7   8

A

EUROPE

Azores

B   MEDITERRANEAN SEA

Strait of Gibraltar   ASIA

*Madeira
Islands*   *Suez
Canal*

MOROCCO   ATLAS MOUNTAINS   TUNISIA   Sinai

*Canary
Islands*   ALGERIA   LIBYA   EGYPT

C   TROPIC OF CANCER

WESTERN
SAHARA
(Morocco)   *Ahaggar Mts.*   *Lake
Nasser*   RED SEA

CABO
VERDE   S   A   H   A   R   A   *Libyan
Desert*

MAURITANIA   *Massif de
l'Aïr*   *Tibesti Mts.*   *Nile*   *Lowest point
in Africa*

Sénégal   M   *Niger*   NIGER   CHAD   ERITREA   *Gulf of Aden*

D   *Cape
Verde*   SENEGAL   A   *Lake Chad*   E   *Blue Nile*   *Lake
Tana*   DJIBOUTI   *Lake Assal*
-509 ft
-155 m

THE GAMBIA   L   S   L   SUDAN   *White Nile*

GUINEA-BISSAU   GUINEA   I   A   H   ETHIOPIA   SOMALIA

SIERRA
LEONE   BURKINA FASO   E   NIGERIA   CENTRAL
AFRICAN REPUBLIC   SOUTH
SUDAN

CÔTE
D'IVOIRE
(IVORY COAST)   UPPER GUINEA   BENIN   TOGO   GHANA   CAMEROON   *Lake Turkana
(Lake Rudolf)*

E   LIBERIA   *Gulf of Guinea*   *Congo*   UGANDA   KENYA

EQUATORIAL GUINEA   *Virunga Mts.
14,787 ft
4,507 m*   *Lake
Victoria*   GREAT RIFT VALLEY

SAO TOME & PRINCIPE   C   O   N   G   O   RWANDA
BURUNDI   *Kilimanjaro
19,340 ft
5,895 m*   *Highest point
in Africa*

EQUATOR   GABON   B   A   S   I   N

A   T   L   A   N   T   I   C   *Ascension*   LOWER GUINEA   DEMOCRATIC REPUBLIC
OF THE CONGO   GREAT RIFT VALLEY   TANZANIA

F   *Cabinda
(Angola)*   *Lake Tanganyika*   SEYCHELLES

O   C   E   A   N   *St. Helena*   KATANGA
PLATEAU   *Lake Nyasa
(Lake Malawi)*   COMOROS   I   N   D   I   A   N

ANGOLA   MALAWI

G   ZAMBIA   MOZAMBIQUE   *Mozambique Channel*   MADAGASCAR   O   C   E   A   N

Zambezi   ZIMBABWE   MAURITIUS

NAMIBIA   *Namib Desert*   BOTSWANA   *Victoria Falls*   *Réunion*

TROPIC OF CAPRICORN   KALAHARI
DESERT

H   ESWATINI (SWAZILAND)

Map Key

—— Country boundary

---- Disputed or
undefined boundary

SOUTH AFRICA   LESOTHO   *Drakensberg*

Orange

0 ——————— 600 miles

0 ——————— 600 kilometers

Azimuthal Equidistant Projection

I   *Cape of Good Hope*

Cape Agulhas

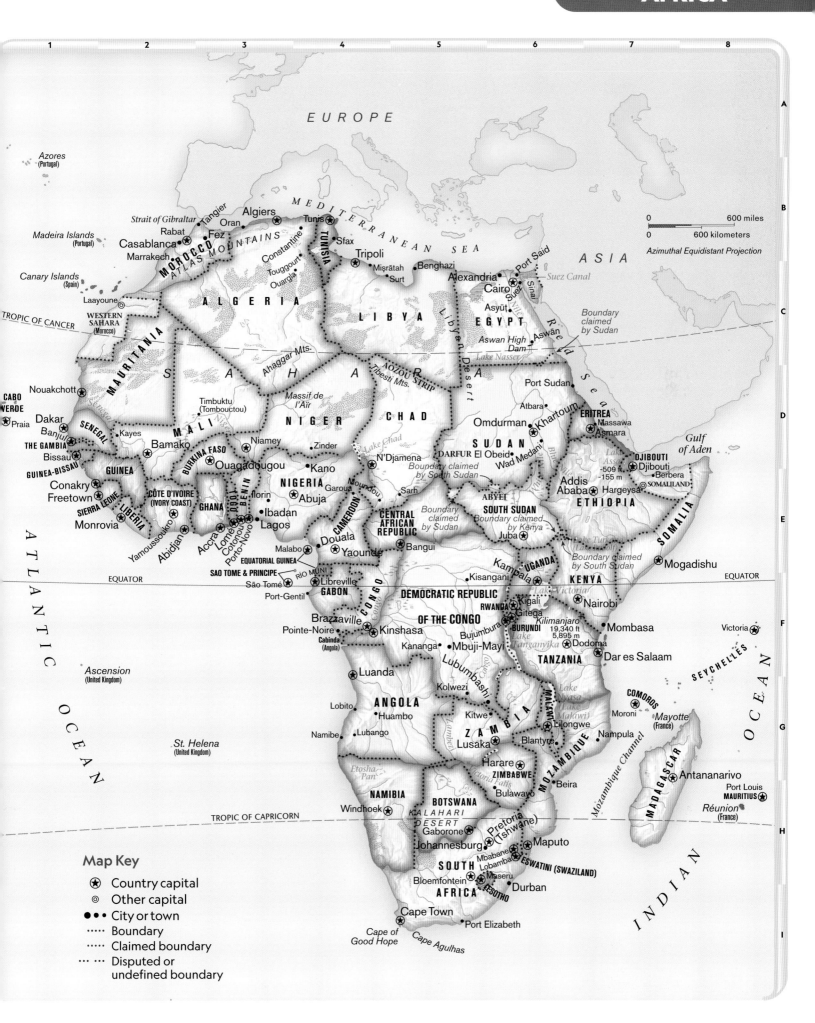

EUROPE

Azores
(Portugal)

Madeira Islands
(Portugal)

Canary Islands
(Spain)

MEDITERRANEAN SEA

Strait of Gibraltar
Tangier
Algiers
Tunis
TUNISIA
Sfax
Tripoli
Mişrātah
Benghazi
Port Said
Suez Canal
ASIA

Rabat
Oran
Fez
Casablanca
Constantine
Marrakech
MOROCCO
ATLAS MOUNTAINS
Touggourt
Ouargla
Surt
Alexandria
Cairo
Suez
Sinai

Laayoune
TROPIC OF CANCER
WESTERN SAHARA
(Morocco)
ALGERIA
LIBYA
EGYPT
Asyūt
Aswan High Dam
Aswān
Lake Nasser
Boundary claimed by Sudan

MAURITANIA
S A H A R A
Ahaggar Mts.
Tibesti Mts.
AOZOU STRIP
Massif de l'Aïr
Port Sudan

CABO VERDE
Praia
Nouakchott
Timbuktu
(Tombouctou)
NIGER
CHAD
Omdurman
Khartoum
Atbara
ERITREA
Massawa
Asmara

Dakar
Banjul
SENEGAL
Kayes
MALI
Bamako
Niamey
Zinder
N'Djamena
Lake Chad
SUDAN
DARFUR
El Obeid
Wad Medani
Gulf of Aden
DJIBOUTI
Djibouti

THE GAMBIA
Bissau
GUINEA-BISSAU
GUINEA
Conakry
Freetown
SIERRA LEONE
Monrovia
LIBERIA
BURKINA FASO
Ouagadougou
Kano
NIGERIA
Garoua
Moundou
Sarh
Boundary claimed by South Sudan
ABYEI
Boundary claimed by Sudan
SOUTH SUDAN
Addis Ababa
ETHIOPIA
Lake Assal
-509 ft
-155 m
Berbera
SOMALILAND
Hargeysa

Yamoussoukro
Abidjan
CÔTE D'IVOIRE
(IVORY COAST)
GHANA
Florin
Ibadan
Lagos
TOGO
BENIN
Abuja
Accra
Lomé
Cotonou
Porto-Novo
CAMEROON
Douala
Yaounde
Malabo
CENTRAL AFRICAN REPUBLIC
Bangui
Boundary claimed by Sudan
Juba
Boundary claimed by Kenya
Boundary claimed by South Sudan
SOMALIA
Mogadishu

EQUATOR
EQUATORIAL GUINEA
SAO TOME & PRINCIPE
São Tomé
RIO MUNI
Libreville
Port-Gentil
GABON
Brazzaville
Pointe-Noire
Cabinda
(Angola)
Kinshasa
CONGO
DEMOCRATIC REPUBLIC OF THE CONGO
Kisangani
Kampala
UGANDA
RWANDA
Kigali
Gitega
BURUNDI
Bujumbura
Lake Victoria
Lake Tanganyika
KENYA
Nairobi
Mombasa
Kilimanjaro
19,340 ft
5,895 m
Lake Turkana
(Lake Rudolf)
EQUATOR
Victoria
SEYCHELLES

Luanda
Kananga
Mbuji-Mayi
Dodoma
Dar es Salaam
TANZANIA

Ascension
(United Kingdom)
Lubumbashi
Kolwezi
Kitwe
Lake Nyasa
Lake Malawi
COMOROS
Moroni
Mayotte
(France)

St. Helena
(United Kingdom)
ANGOLA
Lobito
Huambo
ZAMBIA
Lilongwe
MALAWI
Nampula

Namibe
Lubango
Lusaka
Blantyre
MOZAMBIQUE

Harare
ZIMBABWE
Bulawayo
Beira
Mozambique Channel
MADAGASCAR
Antananarivo
Port Louis
MAURITIUS

Etosha Pan
Victoria Falls
TROPIC OF CAPRICORN
NAMIBIA
BOTSWANA
KALAHARI DESERT
Windhoek
Gaborone
Pretoria
(Tshwane)
Johannesburg
Maputo
Mbabane
Lobamba
ESWATINI (SWAZILAND)
Réunion
(France)

SOUTH AFRICA
Bloemfontein
Maseru
LESOTHO
Durban

ATLANTIC OCEAN
Cape Town
Cape of Good Hope
Cape Agulhas
Port Elizabeth

INDIAN OCEAN

0 — 600 miles
0 — 600 kilometers
Azimuthal Equidistant Projection

Map Key
⊛ Country capital
◎ Other capital
●●● City or town
····· Boundary
····· Claimed boundary
···· Disputed or undefined boundary

Africa

A COMPLEX GIANT

Africa spans nearly as far west to east as it does north to south. The Sahara—the world's largest hot desert—covers Africa's northern third, while to the south lie bands of grassland, tropical rainforest, and more desert. The East African Rift system marks where shifting tectonic plates are splitting off the continent's edge. Africa has a wealth of cultures, speaking some 1,600 languages—more than on any other continent. Though the continent is mostly rural, Africans increasingly migrate to booming cities like Lagos, Cairo, and Johannesburg. Despite rich natural resources—from oil and coal to gemstones and precious metals—and partly as a result of them, many countries in Africa have endured colonization, corruption, and disease.

COMMUNITY SERVICE. Volunteer efforts by youth happen in countries around the world. In Saad Zaghloul Square, Egyptian teens take a break from painting and other cleanup efforts to beautify the area.

CHARGE! Sensing danger, an African elephant charges. The world's largest land mammal, African elephants are at risk due to poaching and loss of habitat.

COLORFUL NEIGHBORHOOD. South Africa's Bo-Kaap once was known as the Malay Quarter because of its early settlers from Malaysia. Dating to the 18th century, this multicultural suburb overlooks Cape Town's city center.

AFRICAN SAVANNA. Zebras graze on the tall grasses of the Serengeti Plain, in eastern Africa. Each year some 200,000 zebras migrate through the Serengeti, following the seasonal rains.

CRYSTAL WATERS. A snorkeler swims in the clear blue waters off the Seychelles, one of Africa's island countries. Made up of 115 granite and coral islands, it lies about 1,000 miles (1,600 km) east of Kenya.

FREE RIDE. A woman in Kumasi, Ghana, goes about her day with her child wrapped snugly on her back in a Kente cloth carrier.

THE CONTINENT:
AFRICA

more about
Africa

◐ **WORSHIPPERS IN THE DESERT.** Muslim faithful gather before the Great Mosque in Mopti, Mali. An earthen structure typical of Muslim architecture in Africa's Sahel, the mosque was built between 1936 and 1943.

◑ **WINDOW ON THE PAST.** Traditional Egyptian sailing vessels called feluccas skim along the Nile River below the ruins at Qubbet al-Hawa. Tombs from ancient Egypt's sixth dynasty are carved into the hillside.

◐ **MODERN SKYLINE.** Established in 1899 as a railway supply depot, Nairobi, Kenya, is now one of Africa's most modern cities. In Maasai, an indigenous language, the name means "place of cold water."

THE CONTINENT:
AFRICA

◐ **POWER GRID.** In Uganda, about 40 percent of the rural population has access to the national electricity grid. In order to provide electricity to more rural residents, the country has supported renewable energy sources, such as solar, wind, and geothermal.

WHERE THE PICTURES ARE

Fort and freighter p. 136
Cooked snails p. 137
Muslims praying p. 134
Leptis Magna p. 137
Saad Zaghloul Square p. 132
Pyramids p. 137
Feluccas on the Nile pp. 134–135
Desert caravan p. 142
Sand dunes p. 136
Ngbaba players p. 143
Mountain gorilla p. 141
Shipping terminal p. 141
Dishes p. 138
Mother and child p. 133
Coffee berries p. 140
Solar panels p. 135
Nairobi skyline p. 134
Fody bird p. 135
Cocoa beans p. 138
Snorkeler p. 133
Bronze head from Benin p. 139
Whale sharks p. 140
Peanuts for export p. 138
Gold miners p. 135
Chokwe mask p. 143
Zebras p. 133
Elephant p. 132
Active volcano p. 142
Ring-tailed lemur p. 144
Cheetah p. 140
Bo-Kaap p. 132
Early man skull p. 145
Cape Town skyline p. 145
Victoria Falls p. 144

◐ **DIGGING FOR GOLD.** Miners dig a pit mine near the edge of the rainforest in Gabon. Oil and mineral extraction is an important part of the country's economy, but the practice exposes the fragile soil to erosion.

◐ **TROPICAL JEWEL.** A ruby red fody perches on a forest branch on Mahé Island in the Seychelles. Native to neighboring Madagascar, the fody eats seeds and insects.

THE CONTINENT:
AFRICA

Northern Africa

THE BASICS

STATS

Largest country
Algeria 919,595 sq mi
(2,381,741 sq km)

Smallest country
Tunisia 63,170 sq mi
(163,610 sq km)

Most populous country
Egypt 99,413,000

Least populous country
Libya 6,755,000

Predominant languages
Arabic, French,
indigenous languages

Predominant religions
Islam, indigenous beliefs

Highest GDP per capita
Algeria $15,200

Lowest GDP capita
Morocco $8,600

Highest life expectancy
Algeria, Libya, Morocco 77 years

Lowest life expectancy
Egypt 73 years

GEO WHIZ

Ibn Battuta, who was born in
Tangier, Morocco, in 1304, set
off on a pilgrimage to Mecca
that turned into a 29-year,
75,000-mile (120,700-km)
journey that took him from the
Middle East to India, China, the
East Indies, and back home.

Egypt's Aswan High Dam,
which forms Lake Nasser,
produces up to 10 billion
kilowatt hours of electricity
every year and provides water
for farms along the Nile in
years of drought.

Kairouan, Tunisia, is considered to be Islam's fourth
holiest city after Mecca,
Medina, and Jerusalem.

This region, which is made up of five countries, stretches from the Atlantic Ocean in the west to the Red Sea in the east. To the north the region is bounded by the Mediterranean Sea, while to the south lies the vast dry expanse of the Sahara. The world's longest river—the Nile— winds northward through Egypt, but most of the region is arid—meaning there is too little moisture to support trees or extensive vegeta-tion. Most of the region's population lives in coastal areas or in the fertile valley of the Nile River. In recent years, the region has experienced widespread instability as a result of tensions between conserva-tive Islamic groups and more liberal groups seeking modern-ization and democratic rule.

PORTUGAL

0 ____ 400 miles
0 ____ 400 kilometers
Albers Equal-Area Projection

(Spain) Ceuta
Strait of Gibraltar
Tangier

Madeira Islands
(Portugal)
Rabat Fez
Casablanca ⊛
Meknès
ATLANTIC
Safi **MOROCC**
OCEAN
Marrakech ● 13,665 ft
+4,165 m
Canary Islands
(Spain)
Agadir ● Jebel Toubkal ATLAS

*Western Sahara's sovereign status
is in dispute. It has been
administered by Morocco since
1979. Fighting between Morocco
and a Western Sahara
independence movement
called the Polisario Front ended
with a UN-brokered cease-fire in
1991, but no agreement on the
area's status has been reached.*

Guelmim
Tarfaya
Tindouf
Laayoune
Al Farciya
Erg Iguidi
**WESTERN
SAHARA**
(Morocco)

Ad Dakhla

Cap Barbas
Techla
Cap Blanc

MAURITANIA

S A

M

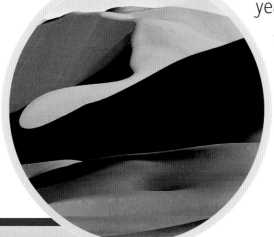

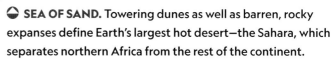

◯ **SEA OF SAND.** Towering dunes as well as barren, rocky expanses define Earth's largest hot desert—the Sahara, which separates northern Africa from the rest of the continent.

◑ **TRADING HARBOR.** In Algeria, historic meets modern with an ancient fort and a modern freighter. Over time, historic harbors have adapted to host larger shipping vessels to exchange more supplies and increase cash flow.

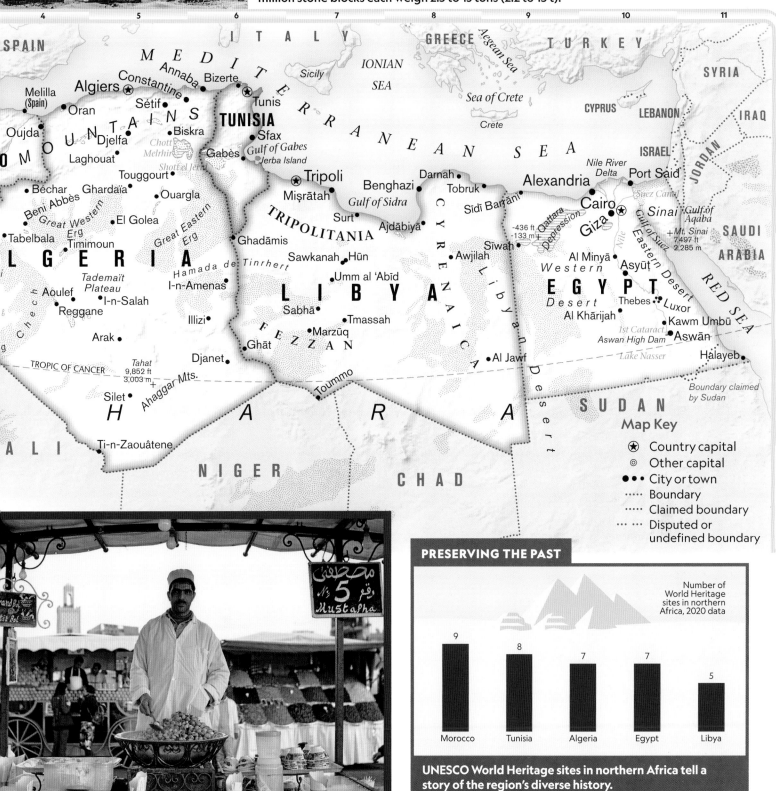

◑ MONUMENTAL ACHIEVEMENT. Pharaoh Khufu's Great Pyramid is the largest in Giza and towers some 481 feet (147 m). Its estimated 2.3 million stone blocks each weigh 2.5 to 15 tons (2.2 to 13 t).

THE CONTINENT:
AFRICA

SPAIN
ITALY
GREECE
TURKEY
SYRIA
CYPRUS
LEBANON
IRAQ
ISRAEL
JORDAN

MEDITERRANEAN SEA
Aegean Sea
IONIAN SEA
Sea of Crete
Crete
Sicily

Melilla (Spain)
Algiers
Annaba
Bizerte
Constantine
Sétif
Oran
Oujda
Tunis
TUNISIA
Biskra
Djelfa
Chott Melrhir
Laghouat
Sfax
Gabès
Gulf of Gabes
Jerba Island
Touggourt
Shott el Jerid
Béchar
Ghardaïa
Ouargla
Tripoli
Benghazi
Darnah
Tobruk
Alexandria
Nile River Delta
Port Said
Suez Canal
Beni Abbès
Great Western Erg
El Golea
Mişrātah
Gulf of Sidra
Surt
Sīdī Barrāni
Cairo
Giza
Sinai
Gulf of Aqaba
Tabelbala
Timimoun
Great Eastern Erg
Ghadāmis
Ajdābiyā
−436 ft −133 m
Qattara Depression
Sīwah
Mt. Sinai 7,497 ft 2,285 m
SAUDI ARABIA
Hamada de Tinrhert
Sawkanah
Hūn
Awjilah
Al Minyā
Asyūţ
Tademaït Plateau
I-n-Amenas
Umm al 'Abīd
Gulf of Suez
Eastern Desert
RED SEA
Aoulef
Reggane
I-n-Salah
Sabhā
Tmassah
Thebes
Luxor
Arak
Illizi
Marzūq
Al Khārijah
Kawm Umbū
Ghāt
FEZZAN
1st Cataract
Aswan High Dam
Aswān
TROPIC OF CANCER
Tahat 9,852 ft 3,003 m
Djanet
Al Jawf
Lake Nasser
Ḩalayeb
Silet
Ahaggar Mts.
Toummo
Boundary claimed by Sudan
Ti-n-Zaouâtene
SUDAN
NIGER
CHAD

ALGERIA
LIBYA
TRIPOLITANIA
CYRENAICA
Libyan Desert
EGYPT
Western Desert
SAHARA
MALI

Map Key

- ⊛ Country capital
- ◎ Other capital
- ••• City or town
- ⋯⋯ Boundary
- ⋯⋯ Claimed boundary
- ⋯⋯ Disputed or undefined boundary

● TASTY TREAT. Snails are a common snack served at roadside stalls, or souks, in Marrakech, Morocco. The seller above entices tourists and locals in Djemaa El Fna Square.

PRESERVING THE PAST

Number of World Heritage sites in northern Africa, 2020 data

Morocco	Tunisia	Algeria	Egypt	Libya
9	8	7	7	5

UNESCO World Heritage sites in northern Africa tell a story of the region's diverse history.

◑ COMPLEX CULTURE. Leptis Magna, a World Heritage site in Libya, was founded in the seventh century B.C.E. and became a major trade center. Following Roman and later Arab conquests, it fell into ruin.

THE CONTINENT: AFRICA

Western Africa

Stretching from Cabo Verde in the west (inset, opposite), Mauritania in the northwest, and the barren Sahara in the north, to Nigeria in the southeast, 16 countries make up western Africa. Three countries—Burkina Faso, Mali, and Niger—are landlocked, meaning they have no direct access to ocean trade. The remaining 13 have coastlines along the Atlantic Ocean or the Gulf of Guinea. Early kingdoms thrived in Mali, Ghana, and Benin, but European colonization disrupted traditional societies and economies, and left a legacy of political turmoil. Today, the countries are independent, but widespread use of French and English reflects the region's colonial past. Reliance on agriculture and falling global oil prices have left the region with a struggling economy.

THE BASICS

STATS

Largest country
Niger 489,191 sq miles
(1,267,000 sq km)

Smallest country
Cabo Verde 1,557 sq miles
(4,033 sq km)

Most populous country
Nigeria 203,453,000

Least populous country
Cabo Verde 568,000

Predominant languages
French, English, Portuguese, Arabic, Spanish, indigenous languages

Predominant religions
Islam, Christianity, indigenous beliefs

Highest GDP per capita
Cabo Verde $6,900

Lowest GDP per capita
Liberia $1,400

Highest life expectancy
Cabo Verde 72 years

Lowest life expectancy
Guinea-Biseau 51 years

GEO WHIZ

For more than 300 years, the House of Slaves on Senegal's Gorée Island served as a holding pen for enslaved people before they were sent to the Americas and elsewhere. Today, it is a museum and a memorial.

Nigeria is a major producer and exporter of oil. Port Harcourt, in the Niger River Delta, is the center of the country's oil industry.

⬯ **PREPARING DESSERT.** In Côte d'Ivoire a man holds roasted cacao beans in a bowl. The beans are processed to create chocolate. About 70 percent of the world's cacao comes from African countries.

⬯ **FULL OF COLOR.** Artistic ceramic plates brighten an outdoor marketplace in Kumasi, Ghana. This country has a long and rich cultural tradition of creating pottery for cooking and for serving food and water.

⬯ **WAITING FOR SHIPMENT.** Sacks of peanuts create an artificial mountain in Kano, Nigeria, where they wait for transport to Lagos and then export to world markets. Nigeria produces more than half of the region's peanut crop.

◑ **MASTER ARTISANS.** The ancient African kingdom of Benin produced outstanding bronze work. Each piece was created to honor the king.

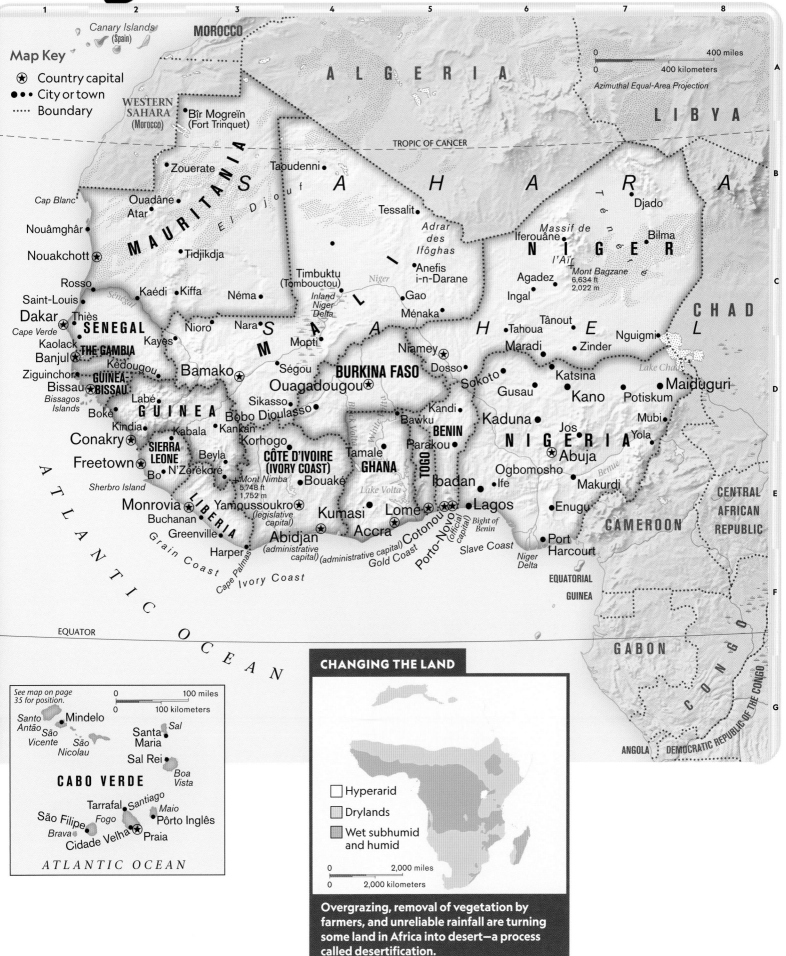

Map Key
★ Country capital
•••• City or town
•••• Boundary

0   400 miles
0   400 kilometers
Azimuthal Equal-Area Projection

MOROCCO

Canary Islands
(Spain)

WESTERN
SAHARA
(Morocco)

A L G E R I A

L I B Y A

• Bîr Mogreïn
(Fort Trinquet)

TROPIC OF CANCER

S   A   H   A   R   A

• Zouerate

• Taoudenni

El Djouf

• Djado

Cap Blanc

• Ouadâne
• Atar

• Tessalit

*Adrar
des
Ifôghas*

• Iferouâne

• Bilma

Massif de

N I G E R

Ténéré

Nouâmghâr •

• Tidjikdja

MAURITANIA

• Néma

• Timbuktu
(Tombouctou)

Niger

• Anefis
i-n-Darane

• Agadez

l'Aïr

*Mont Bagzane
6,634 ft
2,022 m*

Nouakchott ★

Rosso •

• Kaédi • Kiffa

*Inland
Niger
Delta*

• Gao

• Ingal

• Tânout

C H A D

Saint-Louis •

Sénégal

• Nioro

• Nara

M   A

• Mopti

• Ménaka

• Tahoua

• Zinder

• Nguigmi

Dakar ★
Cape Verde

SENEGAL

• Thiès

• Kayes

• Ségou

Niamey ★

Maradi •

Lake Chad

Kaolack •

THE GAMBIA

• Kédougou

Bamako ★

L   I

• Dosso

Sokoto •

Katsina •

• Maiduguri

Banjul ★

Ziguinchor •

GUINEA-
BISSAU

BURKINA FASO

Gusau •

Kano •

• Potiskum

Bissau ★

• Labé

Ouagadougou ★

• Sikasso

Kandi •

Kaduna •

• Mubi

*Bissagos
Islands*

• Boke

GUINEA

• Bobo Dioulasso

• Bawku

BENIN

• Yola

Kindia •

• Kabala

• Kankan

• Korhogo

Black Volta

Parakou •

N I G E R I A

Jos •

Conakry ★

SIERRA
LEONE

• Beyla

CÔTE D'IVOIRE
(IVORY COAST)

Tamale •

White Volta

TOGO

Ogbomosho •

• Abuja ★

Freetown •

• Bo • N'Zérékoré

GHANA

Ibadan •

• Ife

Makurdi •

Sherbro Island

*Mont Nimba
5,748 ft
1,752 m*

• Bouaké

Lake Volta

Lagos •

Enugu •

Benue

Monrovia ★

Yamoussoukro ★
*(legislative
capital)*

Kumasi •

Lomé ★

Port
Harcourt •

CENTRAL
AFRICAN
REPUBLIC

LIBERIA

Buchanan •

• Greenville

Abidjan •
*(administrative
capital)*

Accra ★

Cotonou •

Porto-Novo ★
*(official
capital)*

*Bight of
Benin*

CAMEROON

Grain Coast

Harper •

(administrative capital)
Gold Coast

Slave Coast

*Niger
Delta*

EQUATORIAL
GUINEA

Cape Palmas
Ivory Coast

A T L A N T I C   O C E A N

EQUATOR

GABON

CONGO

GUINEA-
BISSAU

DEMOCRATIC REPUBLIC OF THE CONGO

ANGOLA

*See map on page
35 for position.*

0   100 miles
0   100 kilometers

*Santo
Antão*

Mindelo •

*São
Vicente*

*São
Nicolau*

Santa
Maria •

Sal

• Sal Rei

*Boa
Vista*

CABO VERDE

• Tarrafal   • Santiago

São Filipe •

Fogo

Maio

• Pôrto Inglês

Brava

Cidade Velha •

★ Praia

A T L A N T I C   O C E A N

CHANGING THE LAND

☐ Hyperarid
☐ Drylands
☐ Wet subhumid
   and humid

0   2,000 miles
0   2,000 kilometers

Overgrazing, removal of vegetation by farmers, and unreliable rainfall are turning some land in Africa into desert—a process called desertification.

THE CONTINENT: AFRICA

THE BASICS

STATS

Largest country
Tanzania 365,754 sq miles
(947,300 sq km)

Smallest country
Djibouti 8,958 sq miles
(23,200 sq km)

Most populous country
Ethiopia 108,386,000

Least populous country
Djibouti 884,000

Predominant languages
French, Arabic, English,
Kiswahili, indigenous
languages

Predominant religions
Christianity, Islam,
indigenous beliefs

Highest GDP per capita
Djibouti, Kenya $3,500

Lowest GDP per capita
Somalia

Highest life expectancy
Djibouti 63 years

Lowest life expectancy
Somalia 52 years

GEO WHIZ

Mount Kilimanjaro is the
world's highest freestanding
mountain. It has three volcanic cones, two of which are
extinct while one is dormant.

In 2006, the 3.3-million-year-
old fossilized remains of a
child were found in northern
Ethiopia.

Eastern Africa

Eastern Africa's southern countries attract tourists to see big game—lions, elephants, giraffes, cape buffalo, zebras, wildebeests—that live on tropical grasslands called savannas. Some also come to the region to climb its towering volcanic mountains, such as Kilimanjaro and Mount Kenya. Along the western border lie Africa's Great Lakes, a part of the Rift Valley where tectonic forces are gradually separating eastern Africa from the rest of the continent. Religious and ethnic conflicts have plagued the region's northern countries for many years, leading to the political separation of Eritrea from Ethiopia. Civil unrest combined with drought has led to widespread famine, especially in Somalia.

SAFARI. With 23 national parks and 28 national reserves, ecotourism is a growing business in Kenya. In the Masai Mara National Reserve, visitors can observe cheetahs on the Serengeti.

FROM FIELD TO CUP. A worker on a coffee estate in Kenya holds freshly harvested coffee berries, which will soon be on their way to world markets. Coffee production was introduced to Kenya in 1900. Today, it directly or indirectly employs more than five million workers.

WHALE SHARKS. Off the coast of Tanzania near Mafia Island, tourists get up-close views of whale sharks. About the size of a school bus, whale sharks are the world's largest fish. They feed mostly on plankton.

SOURCE OF THE NILE

Nile River
DEMOCRATIC REPUBLIC OF THE CONGO
EQUATOR
UGANDA
Lake Victoria
KENYA
RWANDA
0   100 miles
0   100 kilometers
BURUNDI
TANZANIA

Lake Victoria is Africa's largest lake. It is also the second largest freshwater lake in the world and a primary source of the Nile River. Pollution and overfishing are endangering the lake's environment.

◑ **CRITICALLY ENDANGERED.** About half of Earth's roughly 1,000 wild mountain gorillas live in forests on the slopes of the Virunga Mountains. Poaching, habitat loss, and civil conflict threaten their survival.

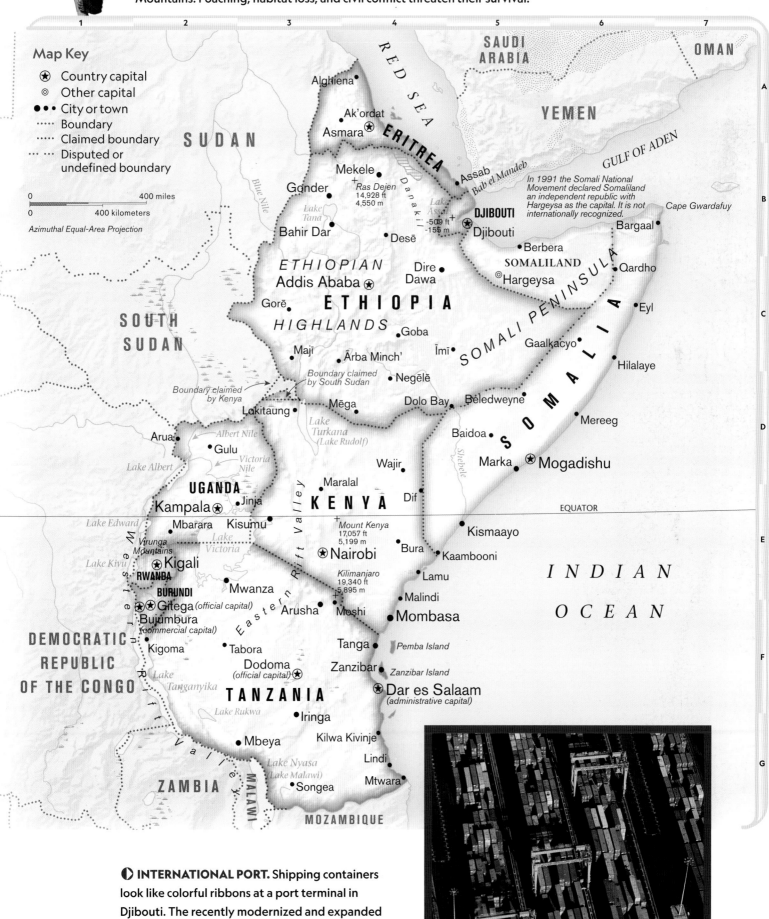

Map Key

★ Country capital
◎ Other capital
••• City or town
······ Boundary
······ Claimed boundary
······ Disputed or undefined boundary

0 ———— 400 miles
0 ———— 400 kilometers
Azimuthal Equal-Area Projection

SAUDI ARABIA

OMAN

YEMEN

RED SEA

GULF OF ADEN

SUDAN

Alghiena
Ak'ordat
Asmara ★ ERITREA
Mekele
Gonder + Ras Dejen 14,928 ft 4,550 m
Lake Tana
Bahir Dar Desē
Danakil
Assab
Bab el Mandeb
Lake Assal -509 ft -155 m
DJIBOUTI ★ Djibouti
Berbera
SOMALILAND
◎ Hargeysa
Cape Gwardafuy

In 1991 the Somali National Movement declared Somaliland an independent republic with Hargeysa as the capital. It is not internationally recognized.

Bargaal
Qardho

Blue Nile

ETHIOPIAN
Addis Ababa ★
Gorē
ETHIOPIA
HIGHLANDS
Dire Dawa
Goba
Eyl

SOUTH SUDAN

Majī
Arba Minch'
Īmī
Negēlē
Gaalkacyo
Hilalaye

SOMALI PENINSULA

Boundary claimed by South Sudan
Boundary claimed by Kenya
Lokitaung
Mēga
Dolo Bay
Beledweyne
SOMALIA

Arua
Albert Nile
Gulu
Lake Albert
Victoria Nile
Lake Turkana (Lake Rudolf)
Wajir
Baidoa
Marka ★ Mogadishu
Mereeg
Shebele

UGANDA
Kampala ★
Jinja
Maralal
KENYA
Dif
EQUATOR

Lake Edward
Mbarara Kisumu
Lake Victoria
+ Mount Kenya 17,057 ft 5,199 m
Kismaayo
Virunga Mountains
Lake Kivu
Kigali ★
RWANDA
★ Nairobi
Bura
Kaambooni
INDIAN OCEAN

BURUNDI
Mwanza
Kilimanjaro 19,340 ft 5,895 m
Lamu
★ ◎ Gitega (official capital)
Bujumbura (commercial capital)
Arusha Moshi
Malindi
Mombasa

DEMOCRATIC REPUBLIC OF THE CONGO

Kigoma
Tabora
Tanga
Pemba Island
Eastern Rift Valley
Dodoma (official capital) ★
Zanzibar
Zanzibar Island
Western
Lake Tanganyika
TANZANIA
★ Dar es Salaam (administrative capital)
Lake Rukwa
Iringa
Mbeya
Kilwa Kivinje
Lindi
Lake Nyasa (Lake Malawi)
Rift Valley
ZAMBIA
MALAWI
Songea
Mtwara
MOZAMBIQUE

◑ **INTERNATIONAL PORT.** Shipping containers look like colorful ribbons at a port terminal in Djibouti. The recently modernized and expanded port facility, with its deep natural harbor, is the economic mainstay of this small country in eastern Africa.

THE CONTINENT:
AFRICA

Central Africa

The Congo, a major commercial waterway of central Africa, flows through rainforests being cut for timber and palm oil plantations. This places a large area of Earth's biodiversity at risk. To the north, Lake Chad, a large, but shallow lake, fluctuates greatly in size due to high rates of evaporation, unreliable rainfall, and overuse by the 20 million people who live near its shores. Diamonds, copper, and chromium are mined in the Democratic Republic of the Congo (DRC) and the Central African Republic. Coffee is grown in the eastern highlands of the region, and livestock and cotton contribute to the economy of Chad. Religious and ethnic conflicts led to the separation of South Sudan from Sudan in 2011. Ongoing civil unrest and drought have led to widespread famine in South Sudan.

ACTIVE VOLCANO.
Mount Nyiragongo, in the
Virunga Mountains of the
DRC, contains one of the
world's largest lava lakes.

VANISHING FORESTS

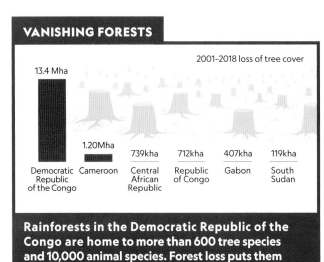

2001–2018 loss of tree cover

13.4 Mha	1.20Mha	739kha	712kha	407kha	119kha
Democratic Republic of the Congo	Cameroon	Central African Republic	Republic of Congo	Gabon	South Sudan

Rainforests in the Democratic Republic of the
Congo are home to more than 600 tree species
and 10,000 animal species. Forest loss puts them
at risk. Here, loss of tree cover is measured in millions
(M) or thousands (k) of hectares.

DESERT CARAVAN. Tuareg tribesmen lead
their camels across the desert in northern Chad.
The camels, loaded with trade goods such as salt,
are destined for distant market towns.

◑ **CELEBRATING A KING.** The Chokwe people of central Africa used masks such as this one to celebrate the inauguration of a new king.

ALGERIA

MALI

NIGER

ALGERIA

SAHARA

Aozou

AOZOU STRIP

Aozi

Tibesti Mts.

Emi Koussi
11,302 ft
3,445 m

Koro Toro

Mao

CHAD

SAHEL

Faya

Fada

Ennedi

Ounianga
Kébir

Biltine

Abéché

Ati

Lake Chad

N'Djamena

Am Timan

LIBYA

Libyan Desert

EGYPT

TROPIC OF CANCER

Boundary claimed
by Sudan

SAUDI
ARABIA

RED SEA

Lake Nubia
2nd Cataract

Wadi Halfa

Nubian

Desert

3rd
Cataract

Dongola

Nile

4th Cataract

Merowe

5th Cataract

Port Sudan

Tokar

Atbara

Khartoum
North

Omdurman

6th Cataract

Khartoum

SUDAN

ERITREA

YEMEN

DJIBOUTI

Jabal
Marrah
9,980 ft
3,042 m

El Fasher

El Obeid

Kosti

DARFUR

Nyala

En Nahud

Kadugli

Renk

Melut

Boundary claimed
by South Sudan

NIGERIA

Maroua

Garoua

Moundou

Mbé

Ngaoundéré

Sarh

Chari

Dar Rounga

Birao

Kafia Kingi

Ndélé

Gabras

ABYEI

Malakal

Leer

Raga

Wau

Rumbek

Boundary
claimed
by Sudan

SOUTH

SUDAN

ETHIOPIA

Bamenda

Garoua Boulaï

Bossangoa

Bouar

CENTRAL

AFRICAN REPUBLIC

Dobane

Obo

Mountain
Nile

Bor

Towot

Boundary claimed
by South Sudan

CAMEROON

Douala

Malabo

Bioko

EQUATORIAL
GUINEA

GULF OF
GUINEA

Principe

SAO TOME
AND PRINCIPE

São Tomé

Berbérati

Yaoundé

Ebolowa

Bata

RÍO MUNI

Oyem

Bambari

Bangui

Nola

Bangassou

Bondo

Gemena

Bumba

Isiro
(Paulis)

Vele

Congo

Maridi

Arua

Boundary claimed
by Kenya

Juba

Albert
Nile

Lake Albert

Bunia

SOMALIA

UGANDA

KENYA

São
Tomé

Libreville

GABON

Cap Lopez

Port-Gentil

Iguéla

Setté Cama

Mayumba

Pointe-
Noire

Tchibanga

Franceville

Makokou

Quésso

Mossaka

CONGO

Sanaga

Basankusu

Mbandaka

DEMOCRATIC

Kisangani

Boyoma Falls

Lake Edward

EQUATOR

Lake
Victoria

REPUBLIC

Inongo

Bandundu

OF THE CONGO

Kindu

Bukavu

Virunga
Mountains

Lake Kivu

RWANDA

BURUNDI

Western

ATLANTIC
OCEAN

ANGOLA

Boma

Brazzaville

Kinshasa

Kasai

Kwango

Mweka

Kananga

Kasongo

Mbuji-
Mayi

Kalemie

Congo

Lake
Tanganyika

TANZANIA

INDIAN
OCEAN

Kahemba

Kamina

Pweto

Lake Mweru

Rift

ANGOLA

Sandoa

KATANGA
PLATEAU

Kolwezi

Likasi

ZAMBIA

Valley

COMOROS

Lubumbashi

MOZAMBIQUE

MALAWI

Map Key

⊛ Country capital

• • • City or town

⋯⋯ Boundary

⋯⋯ Claimed boundary

⋯⋯ Disputed or
     undefined boundary

0 ——————— 400 miles
0 ——————— 400 kilometers

Azimuthal Equal-Area Projection

◑ **BACK IN THE GAME.**
Ngbaba (pronounced "g'baba") players use a long stick to hit a puck into the other team's pitch. A traditional Central African sport, ngbaba is returning after a pause due to regional conflict in the early 2000s.

THE CONTINENT:
AFRICA

Southern Africa

⊖ **NATURAL WONDER.** Victoria Falls, third largest waterfall in the world, is 5,500 feet (1,676 m) wide and 355 feet (108 m) high.

Ringed by uplands, the region's central basin holds the seasonally lush Okavango Delta and scorching Kalahari Desert. The mighty Zambezi thunders over Victoria Falls on its way to the Indian Ocean, where Madagascar is home to plants and animals found nowhere else in the world. Bantu and San are among the indigenous people who saw their hold on the land give way to Portuguese, Dutch, and British traders and colonists. The region offers a range of mineral resources and a variety of climates and soils that in some places yield bumper crops of grains, grapes, and citrus. Rich deposits of coal, diamonds, and gold have helped make South Africa the continent's economic powerhouse.

THE BASICS
STATS

Largest country
Angola 481,353 sq mi (1,246,700 sq km)

Smallest country
Seychelles 176 sq mi (455 sq km)

Most populous country
South Africa 55,380,000

Least populous country
Seychelles 95,000

Predominant languages
English, French, Portuguese, indigenous languages

Predominant religions
Christianity, Islam, indigenous beliefs

Highest GDP per capita
Seychelles $28,900

Lowest GDP per capita
Malawi $1,200

Highest life expectancy
Mauritius 76 years

Lowest life expectancy
Eswatini 52 years

GEO WHIZ

South Africa's Kruger National Park, one of the largest in Africa, covers about the same area as the country of Israel.

Great Zimbabwe National Monument has the largest ancient stone ruins in Africa south of the Sahara.

Treacherous crosscurrents off the northwest coast of Namibia have caused countless ships to wreck, earning the area the nickname Skeleton Coast.

◖ **STARING EYES.**
This ring-tailed lemur rests in the crook of a forest tree branch. The ring-tail, found only in Madagascar, spends time both on the ground and in trees. It eats fruits, leaves, insects, small birds, and even lizards.

GLITTERING GEMS

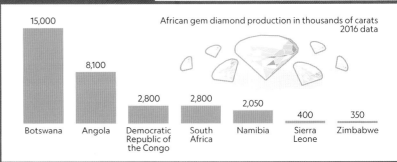

African gem diamond production in thousands of carats
2016 data

Botswana	Angola	Democratic Republic of the Congo	South Africa	Namibia	Sierra Leone	Zimbabwe
15,000	8,100	2,800	2,800	2,050	400	350

Diamonds are prized both for jewelry and for industrial uses. More than half of the world's diamond production comes from mines in Africa.

EARLY MAN. Dating back perhaps 70,000 years, this skull of "Broken Hill Man" was found in Zimbabwe.

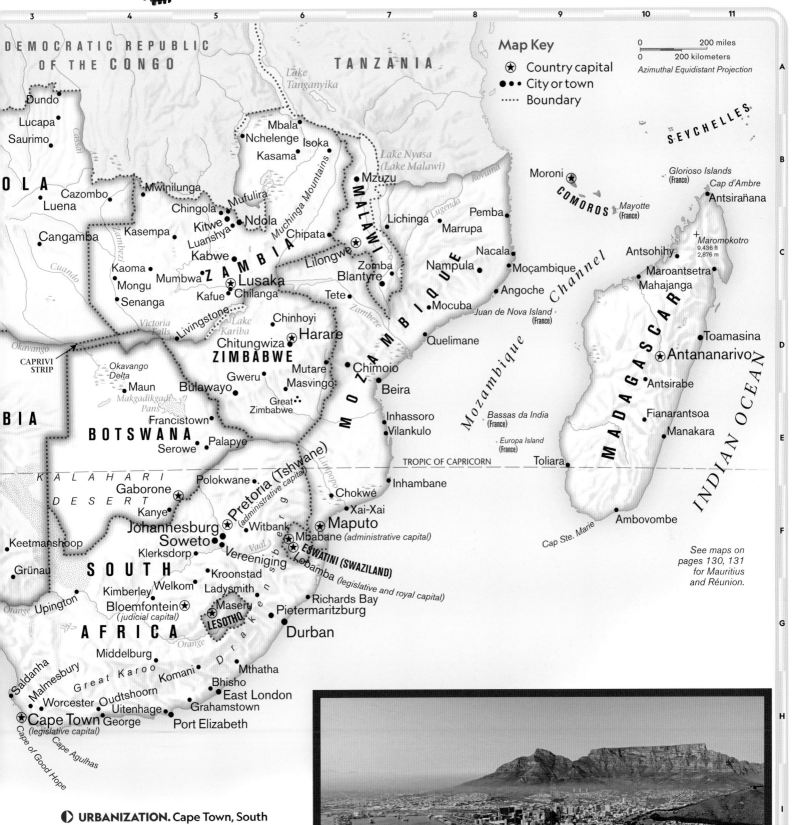

DEMOCRATIC REPUBLIC OF THE CONGO

TANZANIA

Lake Tanganyika

Lake Nyasa (Lake Malawi)

Map Key

⊛ Country capital
••• City or town
····· Boundary

0 ———— 200 miles
0 ———— 200 kilometers
Azimuthal Equidistant Projection

Dundo
Lucapa
Saurimo

Mbala
Nchelenge
Isoka
Kasama

Mzuzu

Moroni ⊛
COMOROS
Mayotte (France)

SEYCHELLES

Glorioso Islands (France)
Cap d'Ambre
Antsiranana

OLA
Cazombo
Luena
Cangamba

Mwinilunga
Mufulira
Chingola
Kitwe
Ndola
Luanshya
Kabwe
Kasempa

Zambezi

Lichinga
Marrupa
Pemba

Nacala
Nampula
Moçambique
Angoche

Maromokotro 9,436 ft 2,876 m
Antsohihy
Maroantsetra
Mahajanga

BIA

Kaoma
Mongu
Mumbwa
ZAMBIA
⊛ Lusaka
Senanga
Kafue
Chilanga

Lilongwe
MALAWI
Zomba
Blantyre

Chipata

Mocuba

Mozambique Channel

Cuando

Victoria Falls
Livingstone
Lake Kariba
Chinhoyi

Tete

Quelimane

Juan de Nova Island (France)

MADAGASCAR

Toamasina
⊛ Antananarivo
Antsirabe

Okavango
CAPRIVI STRIP

Okavango Delta
Maun
Makgadikgadi Pans

⊛ Harare
Chitungwiza
ZIMBABWE
Gweru
Bulawayo
Great Zimbabwe

Mutare
Masvingo
Chimoio

MOZAMBIQUE

Beira

Bassas da India (France)

Europa Island (France)

Fianarantsoa
Manakara

BIA

Francistown
BOTSWANA
Serowe
Palapye

Inhassoro
Vilankulo

TROPIC OF CAPRICORN

Toliara

Ambovombe

INDIAN OCEAN

KALAHARI DESERT

Polokwane

Gaborone
Kanye

Pretoria (Tshwane) (administrative capital)

Inhambane

Chokwé
Xai-Xai

Cap Ste. Marie

See maps on pages 130, 131 for Mauritius and Réunion.

Keetmanshoop

Johannesburg
Soweto
Klerksdorp
Vereeniging
Witbank

Maputo
Mbabane (administrative capital)
ESWATINI (SWAZILAND)
Lobamba (legislative and royal capital)

Grünau

Kroonstad
Welkom

SOUTH

Kimberley
Bloemfontein ⊛ (judicial capital)

Ladysmith
Masery
LESOTHO

Richards Bay
Pietermaritzburg

Upington
Orange

AFRICA

Orange

Durban

Saldanha
Malmesbury
Worcester
Oudtshoorn
Uitenhage
George

Middelburg
Komani
Bhisho
Grahamstown

Great Karoo

Mthatha
East London

⊛ Cape Town (legislative capital)
Cape Agulhas
Cape of Good Hope
Port Elizabeth

URBANIZATION. Cape Town, South Africa's second most populous metropolitan area and seat of the legislative capital, began as a Dutch supply station in 1652. Table Mountain rises in the background. Over several years, starting in 2015, dry winters created a water shortage that required residents and visitors to reduce consumption.

PHYSICAL

Area and population totals are for the independent countries in the region only.

HIGHEST POINT
Mount Wilhelm, Papua New Guinea
14,793 ft (4,509 m)

LONGEST RIVER
Murray-Darling, Australia
2,282 mi (3,672 km)

LARGEST LAKE
Lake Eyre, Australia
3,741 sq mi (9,690 sq km)

LAND AREA
3,297,000 sq mi
(8,538,000 sq km)

LOWEST POINT
Lake Eyre, Australia
-49 ft (-15 m)

POLITICAL

POPULATION
37,557,000

LARGEST METROPOLITAN AREA
Melbourne, Australia
Pop. 4,968,000

LARGEST COUNTRY
Australia
2,988,901 sq mi (7,741,220 sq km)

MOST DENSELY POPULATED COUNTRY
Nauru
1,250 people per sq mi (476 per sq km)

AUSTRALIA, NEW ZEALAND & OCEANIA

Australia, New Zealand & Oceania

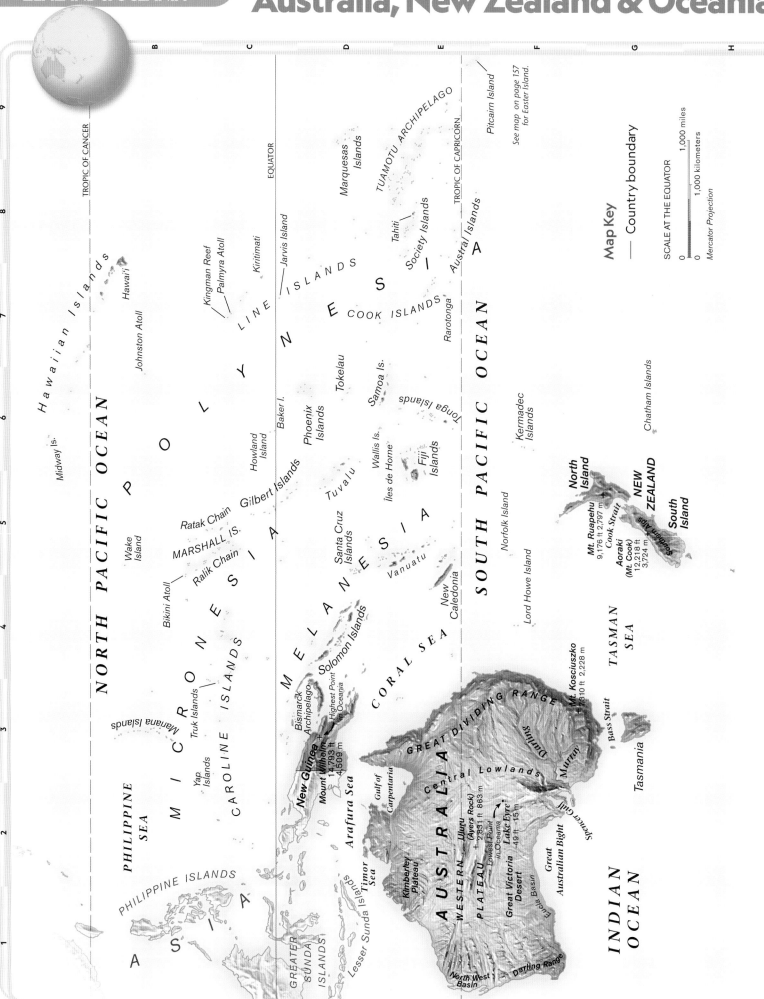

TROPIC OF CANCER

EQUATOR

TROPIC OF CAPRICORN

Pitcairn Island

See map on page 157
for Easter Island.

TUAMOTU ARCHIPELAGO

Marquesas
Islands

Tahiti
Society Islands

Austral Islands

P O L Y N E S I A

Kingman Reef
Palmyra Atoll

Kiritimati

Jarvis Island

LINE ISLANDS

COOK ISLANDS

Rarotonga

Hawaiian Islands

Hawai'i

Johnston Atoll

Midway Is.

NORTH PACIFIC OCEAN

Tokelau

Samoa Is.

Tonga Islands

Baker I.

Howland
Island

Phoenix
Islands

Wallis Is.

Îles de Horne

Fiji
Islands

Tuvalu

Santa Cruz
Islands

Kermadec
Islands

Norfolk Island

Lord Howe Island

SOUTH PACIFIC OCEAN

North
Island

NEW
ZEALAND

Cook Strait

Southern Alps

South
Island

Mt. Ruapehu
9,176 ft 2,797 m

Aoraki
(Mt. Cook)
12,218 ft
3,724 m

Chatham Islands

Wake
Island

Ratak Chain

Gilbert Islands

MARSHALL IS.

Ralik Chain

Bikini Atoll

M I C R O N E S I A

Yap
Islands

Truk Islands

Mariana Islands

CAROLINE ISLANDS

Vanuatu

New
Caledonia

M E L A N E S I A

Bismarck
Archipelago

Highest Point
in Oceania

Solomon Islands

CORAL SEA

TASMAN
SEA

Bass Strait

Tasmania

PHILIPPINE
SEA

PHILIPPINE ISLANDS

A S I A

GREATER
SUNDA
ISLANDS

Lesser Sunda Islands

Timor
Sea

New Guinea

Mount Wilhelm
14,793 ft
4,509 m

Arafura Sea

Gulf of
Carpentaria

Kimberley
Plateau

A U S T R A L I A

WESTERN

PLATEAU

Uluru
(Ayers Rock)
2,831 ft 863 m

Great Victoria
Desert

Eucla Basin

North West
Basin

Darling Range

Central Lowlands

Lake Eyre
Lowest Point
in Oceania
-49 ft -15 m

GREAT DIVIDING RANGE

Darling

Murray

Mt. Kosciuszko
7,310 ft 2,228 m

Great
Australian Bight

Spencer Gulf

INDIAN
OCEAN

Map Key

— Country boundary

SCALE AT THE EQUATOR

1,000 miles

1,000 kilometers

Mercator Projection

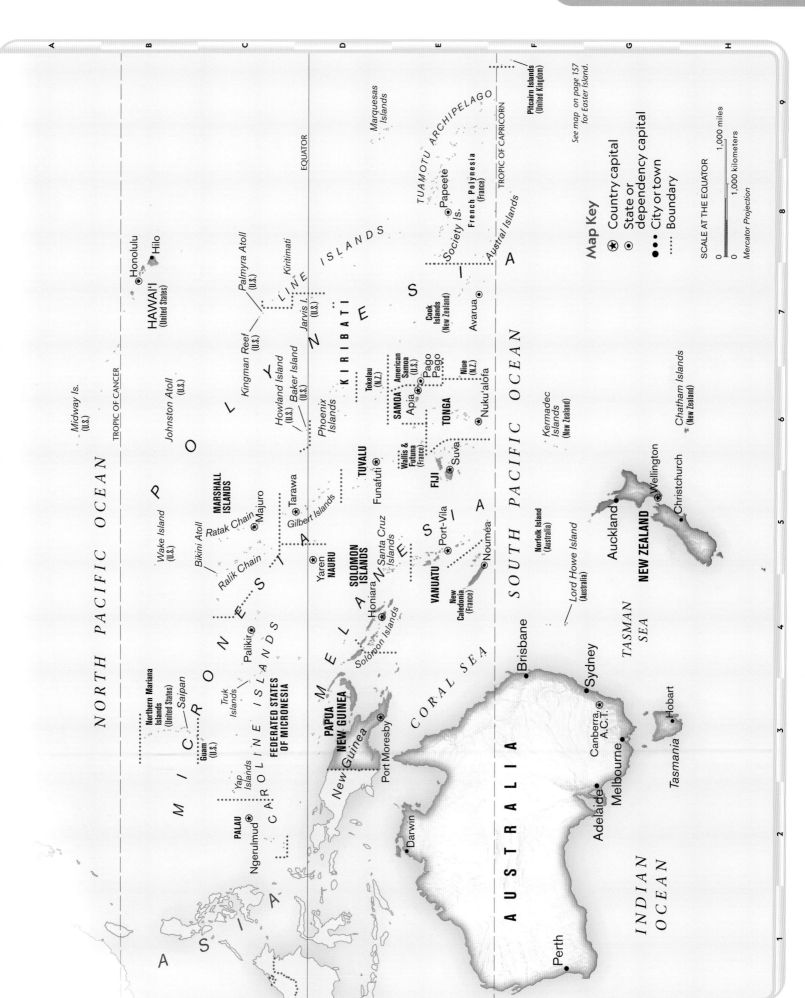

A B C D E F G H

9

8

7

6

5

4

3

2

1

NORTH PACIFIC OCEAN

SOUTH PACIFIC OCEAN

INDIAN OCEAN

CORAL SEA

TASMAN SEA

Marquesas Islands

TUAMOTU ARCHIPELAGO

Papeete
Society Is.
French Polynesia
(France)

Australs Islands

TROPIC OF CAPRICORN

Pitcairn Islands
(United Kingdom)

See map on page 157
for Easter Island.

EQUATOR

Palmyra Atoll
(U.S.)

Kiritimati

LINE ISLANDS

Jarvis I.
(U.S.)

Cook Islands
(New Zealand)
Avarua

POLYNESIA

Honolulu
Hilo
HAWAI'I
(United States)

Kingman Reef
(U.S.)

Howland Island
(U.S.)
Baker Island
(U.S.)

Phoenix Islands

KIRIBATI

Tokelau
(N.Z.)

American Samoa
(U.S.)
Pago Pago

Niue
(N.Z.)

TROPIC OF CANCER

Midway Is.
(U.S.)

Johnston Atoll
(U.S.)

SAMOA
Apia

TONGA
Nuku'alofa

Kermadec Islands
(New Zealand)

Chatham Islands
(New Zealand)

Wake Island
(U.S.)

MARSHALL ISLANDS

Ratak Chain

Bikini Atoll
Majuro

Tarawa

Gilbert Islands

TUVALU
Funafuti

Wallis & Futuna
(France)

FIJI
Suva

Wellington
Christchurch

Auckland
NEW ZEALAND

MICRONESIA

Ralik Chain

Yaren
NAURU

Santa Cruz Islands

Port-Vila

Nouméa

Norfolk Island
(Australia)

Lord Howe Island
(Australia)

CAROLINE ISLANDS

Palikir

SOLOMON ISLANDS

Honiara

MELANESIA

VANUATU

New Caledonia
(France)

Northern Mariana Islands
(United States)
Saipan

Truk Islands

FEDERATED STATES OF MICRONESIA

Solomon Islands

Guam
(U.S.)

Yap Islands

PALAU
Ngerulmud

PAPUA NEW GUINEA

New Guinea

Port Moresby

ASIA

Darwin

AUSTRALIA

Brisbane

Sydney

Canberra, A.C.T.
Melbourne
Hobart

Adelaide

Tasmania

Perth

Map Key
⊛ Country capital
⊙ State or dependency capital
• City or town
····· Boundary

SCALE AT THE EQUATOR
0   1,000 miles
0   1,000 kilometers
Mercator Projection

Australia,
New Zealand
& Oceania

WORLDS APART

⬯ **AUSTRALIAN TEDDY BEAR.**
Koalas, which are not bears at
all, are native to the eucalyptus
forests of eastern Australia.

This vast region includes Australia—the world's smallest continent—New Zealand, and a fleet of mostly tiny island worlds scattered across the Pacific Ocean. Apart from Australia, New Zealand, and Papua New Guinea, Oceania's other 11 independent countries cover about 25,000 square miles (65,000 sq km), an area only slightly larger than half of New Zealand's North Island. Twenty-one other island groups are dependencies of the United States, France, Australia, New Zealand, or the United Kingdom. Long isolation has allowed the growth of diverse marine communities, such as Australia's Great Barrier Reef, and the evolution of platypuses, kangaroos, kiwis, and other land animals that live nowhere else on the planet.

⬯ **ANCIENT VOYAGERS.** The Maoris are
believed to have sailed to New Zealand from
islands far to the northeast. *Tā moko,* the
unique Maori art of marking the skin, is a sacred
tradition, symbolizing a person's connection to
their family, tribe, and cultural identity.

PLACE OF LEGENDS. Once part of an ancient seabed, Uluṟu, also known as Ayers Rock, was exposed by erosion. This massive sandstone block is sacred to native Aboriginals. In 2017, the Uluṟu–Kata Tjuṯa National Park Board banned climbing on Uluṟu in an effort to promote respect for the sacred area.

TROPICAL HABITAT.
Brilliantly colored fish swim among branching corals in the warm waters of the Vatu-i-Ra Channel in the Fiji Islands. The waters around Fiji have some of the richest and most diverse fish populations in the world.

NATIVE COWBOYS.
Competition is fierce during a rodeo in Hope Vale, a community on Australia's Cape York Peninsula. Hope Vale is home to several Aboriginal clan groups.

THE REGION:
AUSTRALIA, NEW ZEALAND & OCEANIA

more about

Australia, New Zealand & Oceania

◐ **A WATER WORLD.** Located just seven degrees north of the Equator, the islands of the Republic of Palau were a United Nations Trust Territory until 1994, when they gained independence.

◐ **BIG JUMPER.** The red kangaroo, the largest living marsupial—an animal that carries its young in a pouch—is at home on the dry inland plains of Australia. It can cover 30 feet (9 m) in a single hop.

◐ **WOOLLY POPULATION.** Sheep outnumber people in Australia and New Zealand. Wool production is an important part of the economies of these two countries.

◐ **STILT HOUSES.** In Port Moresby, Papua New Guinea, people build stilt houses over the water in the Gulf of Papua. Stilt houses are used in this region to prevent homes from flooding and to keep out pests.

THE REGION:
AUSTRALIA, NEW ZEALAND & OCEANIA

WHERE THE PICTURES ARE

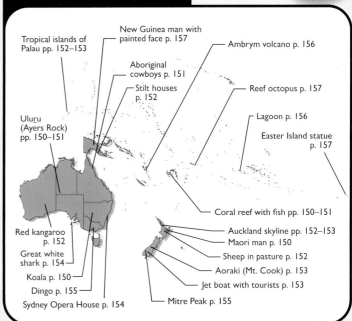

New Guinea man with painted face p. 157

Tropical islands of Palau pp. 152–153

Ambrym volcano p. 156

Aboriginal cowboys p. 151

Stilt houses p. 152

Reef octopus p. 157

Uluru (Ayers Rock) pp. 150–151

Lagoon p. 156

Easter Island statue p. 157

Red kangaroo p. 152

Coral reef with fish pp. 150–151

Great white shark p. 154

Auckland skyline pp. 152–153
Maori man p. 150

Koala p. 150

Sheep in pasture p. 152

Dingo p. 155

Aoraki (Mt. Cook) p. 153
Jet boat with tourists p. 153

Sydney Opera House p. 154

Mitre Peak p. 155

A WET RIDE. Tourists go for a wild ride in a jet boat on the roaring waters of New Zealand's Shotover River.

SNOWY PEAK. New Zealand's Aoraki (Mount Cook) rises above the clouds. Maori legend says that the peak is a frozen warrior surrounded by his brothers.

MODERN METROPOLIS. Modern buildings rise against a twilight sky in Auckland, on New Zealand's North Island. It is home to almost one-third of the country's population.

Australia & New Zealand

Most people in Australia live along the coast, far from the country's dry interior, known as the Outback. The most populous cities and the best croplands are in the southeast. This "Land Down Under" is increasingly linked by trade to Asia and to 4.5 million "neighbors" in New Zealand. Lying 1,200 miles (1,930 km) across the Tasman Sea, New Zealand is cooler, wetter, and more mountainous than Australia. Geologically active, it has ecosystems ranging from subtropical forests on North Island to snowy peaks on South Island. Both countries enjoy high standards of living and strong agricultural and mining outputs, including wool, wines, gold, coal, and iron ore.

◐ **SAILS AT SUNSET.** Reminiscent of a ship in full sail, the Sydney Opera House, in Sydney Harbor, has become a symbol of Australia that is recognized worldwide.

◐ **OCEAN TRAVELER.** Great white sharks inhabit the warm waters off the coast of southern Australia. These marine predators can grow up to 20 feet (6 m) in length.

◑ **DOG OF THE OUTBACK.** The dingo is a wild dog found throughout Australia except Tasmania. Unlike most domestic dogs, the dingo does not bark, although it howls.

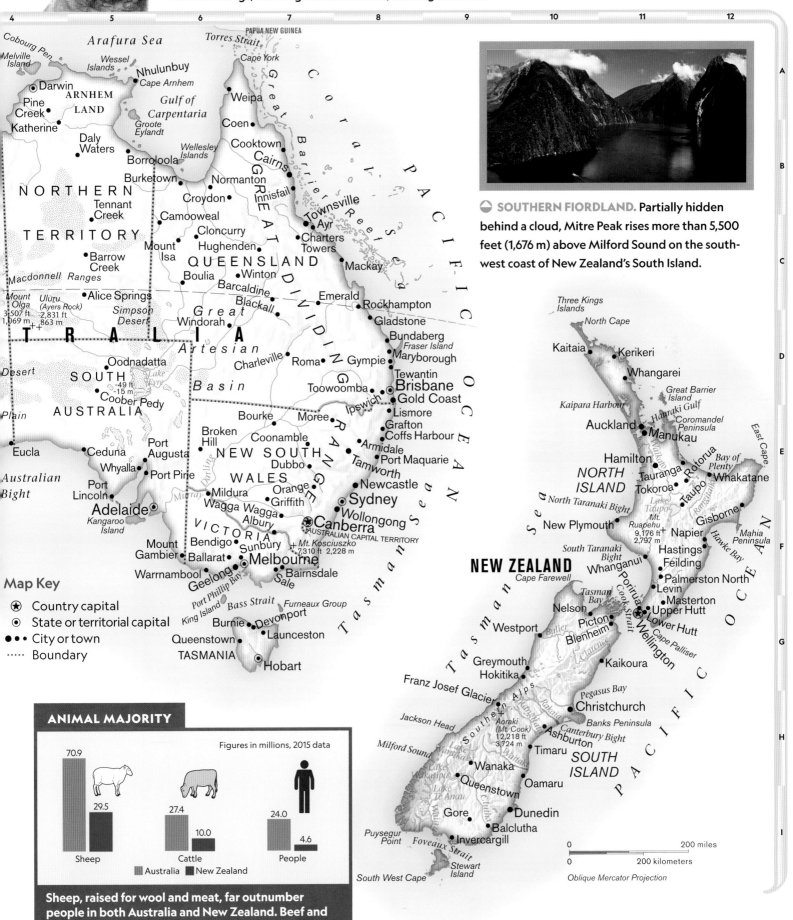

⬤ **SOUTHERN FIORDLAND.** Partially hidden behind a cloud, Mitre Peak rises more than 5,500 feet (1,676 m) above Milford Sound on the southwest coast of New Zealand's South Island.

Map Key

- ★ Country capital
- ◉ State or territorial capital
- ●●● City or town
- ⋯⋯ Boundary

ANIMAL MAJORITY

Figures in millions, 2015 data

	Sheep	Cattle	People
Australia	70.9	27.4	24.0
New Zealand	29.5	10.0	4.6

■ Australia ■ New Zealand

Sheep, raised for wool and meat, far outnumber people in both Australia and New Zealand. Beef and dairy cattle also surpass the human population.

Oblique Mercator Projection

0 — 200 miles
0 — 200 kilometers

THE REGION:
AUSTRALIA, NEW ZEALAND & OCEANIA

Oceania

THE BASICS

STATS

Largest country
Papua New Guinea
178,703 sq mi (462,840 sq km)

Smallest country
Nauru 8 sq mi (21 sq km)

Most populous country
Papua New Guinea 7,027,000

Least populous country
Nauru 10,000

Predominant languages
English, indigenous languages

Predominant religions
Christianity, indigenous beliefs

Highest GDP per capita
Palau $16,200

Lowest GDP per capita
Kiribati $2,000

Highest life expectancy
Tonga 76 years

Lowest life expectancy
Kiribati 66 years

GEO WHIZ

Five uninhabited islands in the Solomon group have disappeared due to rising sea levels caused by climate change, and the inhabited island of Nuatambu has lost more than 50 percent of its land area.

Most of the islands of Pacific countries are atolls, which are coral reefs encircling a lagoon.

Palau, Micronesia, offers diving opportunities to view historic shipwrecks and marine life.

◓ **TROPICAL PARADISE.**
A reef separates an area of seawater from the ocean, forming a quiet lagoon around the island of Bora Bora in the Society Islands of French Polynesia.

Although in its broadest sense Oceania includes Australia and New Zealand, more commonly it refers to some 25,000 islands that make up three large cultural regions in the Pacific Ocean. Melanesia, which extends from Papua New Guinea to Fiji, is closest to Australia. Micronesia lies mostly north of the Equator and includes Palau and the Federated States of Micronesia. New Zealand, Hawai'i, and Rapa Nui (Easter Island) mark the western, northern, and eastern limits of Polynesia, with Tahiti, Samoa, and Tonga near its heart. Oceania's people often face problems of limited living space and freshwater. Plantation agriculture, fishing, tourism, or mining form the economic base for most of the islands in this region.

◖ **LIVING EARTH.**
Ambrym volcano, in Vanuatu, is one of the most active volcanoes in Oceania. Ambrym continues to erupt regularly, adding to the island's black sand beaches.

◑ UNSOLVED MYSTERY. Carved from volcanic rock, the giant stone heads, called *moai*, on Rapa Nui (Easter Island) remain a mystery.

◑ PROBLEM-SOLVING. Octopuses live on coral reefs in the tropical waters of the South Pacific Ocean. They are one of the few solitary animals with high levels of problem-solving skills.

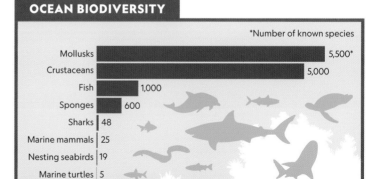

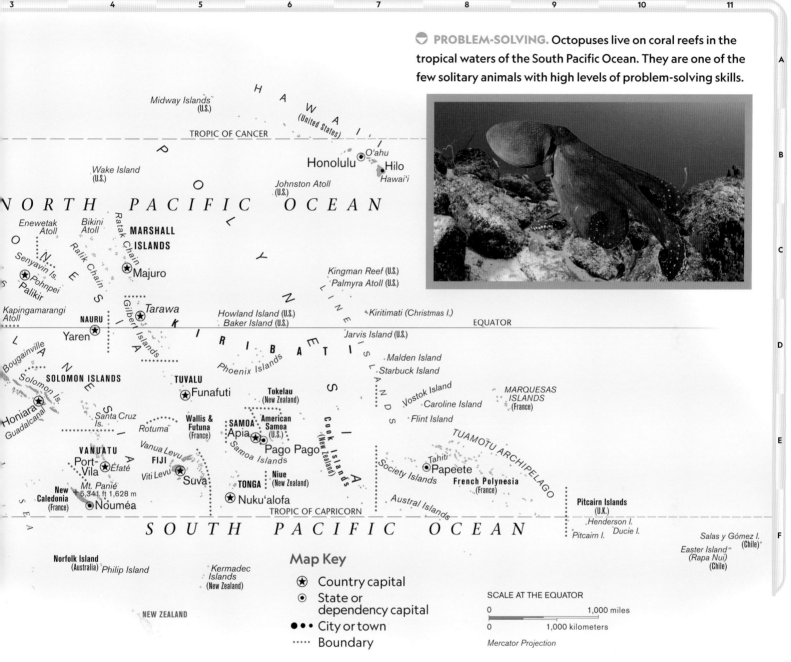

H
A
W
A
I
I
(United States)

Midway Islands
(U.S.)

TROPIC OF CANCER

O'ahu
Honolulu ⊙ Hilo
Hawai'i

Wake Island
(U.S.)

P
O
L
Y
N
E
S
I
A

Johnston Atoll
(U.S.)

NORTH PACIFIC OCEAN

Enewetak
Atoll

Bikini
Atoll

Senyavin Is.
★ Pohnpei
Palikir

M
I
C
R
O
N
E
S
I
A

Ralik Chain

Ratak Chain

MARSHALL
ISLANDS
★ Majuro

Kingman Reef (U.S.)
Palmyra Atoll (U.S.)

Kapingamarangi
Atoll

Gilbert Islands

Tarawa

NAURU
Yaren ★

Howland Island (U.S.)
Baker Island (U.S.)

★ Kiritimati (Christmas I.)

EQUATOR

Jarvis Island (U.S.)

L
I
N
E

I
S
L
A
N
D
S

Bougainville

K
I
R
I
B
A
T
I

Malden Island
Starbuck Island

M
E
L
A
N
E
S
I
A

Solomon Is.

SOLOMON ISLANDS

TUVALU
★ Funafuti

Vostok Island
Caroline Island

MARQUESAS
ISLANDS
(France)

Honiara ★
Guadalcanal

Santa Cruz
Is.

Phoenix Islands

Tokelau
(New Zealand)

Flint Island

Rotuma

Wallis &
Futuna
(France)

SAMOA
Apia ⊙

American
Samoa
(U.S.)

C
o
o
k

I
s
l
a
n
d
s
(New Zealand)

TUAMOTU ARCHIPELAGO

VANUATU

Vanua Levu

FIJI

Samoa Islands

Pago Pago

Society Islands

Tahiti
⊙ Papeete

Port-
Vila ★ Éfaté

Viti Levu
★ Suva

TONGA

Niue
(New Zealand)

French Polynesia
(France)

C
O
R
A
L

S
E
A

New
Caledonia
(France)
⊙ Nouméa

Mt. Panié
5,341 ft 1,628 m

★ Nuku'alofa

Austral Islands

Pitcairn Islands
(U.K.)

TROPIC OF CAPRICORN

Henderson I.
Pitcairn I.   Ducie I.

Salas y Gómez I.
(Chile)

SOUTH PACIFIC OCEAN

Easter Island
(Rapa Nui)
(Chile)

Norfolk Island
(Australia) Philip Island

Kermadec
Islands
(New Zealand)

Map Key

⊛ Country capital

⊙ State or
dependency capital

●●● City or town

····· Boundary

SCALE AT THE EQUATOR

0 ——————— 1,000 miles
0 ——————— 1,000 kilometers

Mercator Projection

NEW ZEALAND

◑ MELANESIAN CUSTOM. In the Huli culture of Papua New Guinea's Eastern Highlands, men adorn themselves with colorful paints, feathers, and grasses as they prepare to take part in festivals.

OCEAN BIODIVERSITY

*Number of known species

Mollusks	5,500*
Crustaceans	5,000
Fish	1,000
Sponges	600
Sharks	48
Marine mammals	25
Nesting seabirds	19
Marine turtles	5

The second longest double barrier reef in the world stretches 930 miles (1,500 km) along New Caledonia. The reef is habitat for a diversity of species—some still unclassified.

THE CONTINENT:
ANTARCTICA

PHYSICAL

LAND AREA	LOWEST POINT	AVERAGE PRECIPITATION
5,100,000 sq mi (13,209,000 sq km)	Byrd Glacier (depression) -9,416 ft (-2,870 m)	ON THE POLAR PLATEAU Less than 2 in (5 cm) per year
HIGHEST POINT	**COLDEST PLACE**	
Vinson Massif 16,067 ft (4,897 m)	Ridge A Annual average temperature -94°F (-70°C)	

POLITICAL

POPULATION	NUMBER OF INDEPENDENT COUNTRIES	NUMBER OF COUNTRIES OPERATING YEAR-ROUND RESEARCH STATIONS
There are no indigenous inhabitants, but there are scientists and other staff at both permanent and summer-only research stations.	0	21
	NUMBER OF COUNTRIES CLAIMING LAND	**NUMBER OF YEAR-ROUND RESEARCH STATIONS**
	7	40

ANTARCTICA

THE CONTINENT:
ANTARCTICA

ANTARCTICA
THE FROZEN SOUTH

Antarctica is the coldest, windiest, and even driest continent. Though its immense ice sheet holds more than 60 percent of Earth's freshwater, its interior averages less than two inches (5 cm) of precipitation per year. Hidden beneath the ice is a continent of valleys, mountains, and lakes, but less than 2 percent of the land actually breaks through the ice cover. Like a finger pointing north toward South America, the Antarctic Peninsula is the most visited region of the continent, but scientists occupy a total of more than 70 permanent and seasonal research stations throughout the continent, from which they study this frozen land.

🔵 FORMAL DRESS. Black-and-white gentoo penguins live in colonies year-round along the Antarctic Peninsula. These flightless birds dive to more than 300 feet (90 m) to catch fish and krill, their main food source.

⊙ **DRIFTING RESEARCH.** The U.S. Amundsen-Scott research station is located at the geographic South Pole. The station and the ice sheet on which it sits are drifting about 33 feet (10 m) each year.

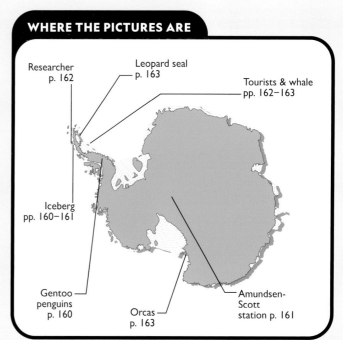

WHERE THE PICTURES ARE

Researcher
p. 162

Leopard seal
p. 163

Tourists & whale
pp. 162–163

Iceberg
pp. 160–161

Gentoo
penguins
p. 160

Orcas
p. 163

Amundsen-
Scott
station p. 161

⊙ **BLUE WONDER.** An iceberg drifts in the Lemaire Channel near the Antarctic Peninsula. The dense, compressed ice reflects only short wavelengths, giving the ice a blue tint.

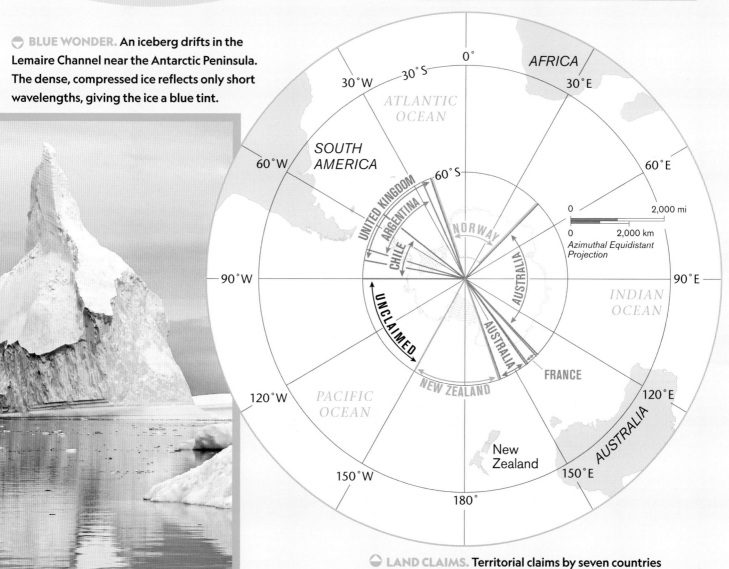

0°

AFRICA

30°W

30°S

30°E

*ATLANTIC
OCEAN*

SOUTH
AMERICA

60°W

60°S

60°E

UNITED KINGDOM

ARGENTINA

CHILE

NORWAY

AUSTRALIA

0   2,000 mi

0   2,000 km

*Azimuthal Equidistant
Projection*

90°W

90°E

*INDIAN
OCEAN*

UNCLAIMED

AUSTRALIA

FRANCE

NEW ZEALAND

120°W

*PACIFIC
OCEAN*

120°E

AUSTRALIA

New
Zealand

150°W

150°E

180°

⊙ **LAND CLAIMS.** Territorial claims by seven countries (shown above in color) are recognized by the Antarctic Treaty.

Antarctica

THE BASICS

Antarctica is the only continent that has no political boundaries and no economy or permanent population. Seven countries claim portions of the landmass (map, page 161), but according to the Antarctic Treaty, which preserves the continent for peaceful use and scientific study, no country rules.

GEO WHIZ

The Antarctic Convergence, an area where the waters of Earth's four oceans meet the cold Antarctic Circumpolar Current, is one of the planet's richest marine ecosystems.

Krill, a tiny shrimplike creature that thrives in Antarctic waters, is important in the Antarctic food chain. Whales, seals, and penguins are among the creatures that depend on it for survival.

The tiny wingless midge—less than one-quarter inch (6 mm) long—is Antarctica's largest land animal. This insect is able to survive high levels of salt, freezing temperatures, and ultraviolet radiation in the continent's extreme climate.

Mount Erebus, named for a British explorer's ship, is the world's southernmost active volcano.

◯ **NATURE STUDY.**

A researcher at Palmer Station examines penguin eggs attacked by skuas, birds that feed on these eggs.

Under the terms of the Antarctic Treaty, the region beyond 60° south latitude is set aside for peaceful scientific study and research. Antarctica was first visited by Europeans in 1821, but there has never been a permanent human population. Today, more than 4,000 scientists live at research stations during the southern summer (October to March), studying climate history preserved in the ice sheets that cover the continent and observing the effects of current climate change on plant and animal life. During the cold, dark southern winter, the research population drops to only a little more than 1,000. In addition to scientists, almost 55,000 tourists visit Antarctica during the southern summer, mainly along the Antarctic Peninsula, where they view wildlife such as seals, whales, penguins, and other birds.

1

South Orkney Islands

South Shetland Islands

Joinville Island

Palmer Station (United States)

Antarc

Bellingshausen Sea

DAY AND NIGHT

Average number of daylight hours per month, Palmer Station (64° 46'S; 64° 03'W), 2017 data

Month	Hours
JAN	19.42
FEB	15.78
MAR	12.51
APR	9.10
MAY	5.85
JUN	3.69
JUL	4.97
AUG	8.00
SEP	11.34
OCT	14.67
NOV	18.36
DEC	21.14

Because of its very high southern latitude, Antarctica experiences extreme fluctuations in the length of daylight hours. At the South Pole (90° S) there are months of total darkness.

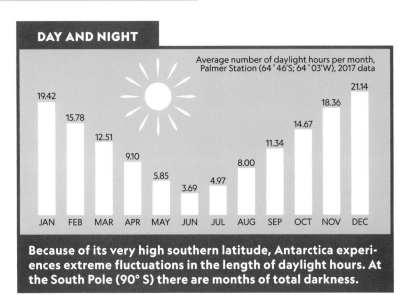

THE CONTINENT:
ANTARCTICA

◖ **STANDING GUARD.** Leopard seals' preferred food is penguins, but they also eat other species of seals.

ATLANTIC OCEAN

ANTARCTIC CIRCLE

Fimbul Ice Shelf

Cape Norvegia

Riiser-Larsen
Ice Shelf

Queen Maud Land

Riiser-Larsen
Peninsula

Lützow-Holm Bay

Enderby Land

INDIAN OCEAN

0 ——— 500 miles
0 ——— 500 kilometers
Azimuthal Equidistant Projection

Weddell
Sea

Coats Land

Larsen C iceberg
detached
July 12, 2017

Larsen
Ice Shelf

Mt. Jackson
10,446 ft 3,184 m

tic Peninsula

Filchner
Ice
Shelf

Berkner
Island

Cape Darnley

Amery
Ice Shelf

Alexander
Island

Ronne
Ice Shelf

Pensacola Mountains

Coldest place
in the world

RIDGE A

EAST

Prydz Bay

West
Ice Shelf

American
Highland

Transantarctic Mountains

POLAR
PLATEAU

ANTARCTICA

Vinson
Massif
16,067 ft
4,897 m

Ellsworth Mts.

Highest point
in Antarctica

South Pole
Amundsen-Scott Station
(United States)

Ellsworth Land

WEST

Vostok Station
(Russia)

Shackleton Ice Shelf

Thurston
Island

ANTARCTICA

Marie Byrd Land

Wilkes Land

Amundsen Sea

Getz Ice Shelf

Ross
Ice Shelf

Byrd
Glacier
-9,416 ft
-2,870 m

Lowest point
in Antarctica

Cape
Poinsett

Roosevelt
Island

PACIFIC
OCEAN

Ross
Sea

Mt. Erebus
12,448 ft
3,794 m

Ross I.

Cape Crozier

McMurdo Sound

Victoria Land

Porpoise Bay

Map Key

★ Pole

■ Research station

Mt. Minto
13,665 ft
4,165 m

Cape Adare

ANTARCTIC CIRCLE

★ South
Magnetic Pole

◖ **SOUTHERN EXPLORATION.** Adventurous tourists, riding in a Zodiac, get a close-up look at a humpback whale diving under the waters of the Weddell Sea. These motorized inflatable boats enable passengers to travel from their expedition ship, anchored in deep water, to the shores of the Antarctic Peninsula.

◖ **COLD SWIM.** A mother orca and her calf come up for air in the icy waters of McMurdo Sound. Orcas live in social groups called pods and work together to catch meals of fish, seals, or sea lions.

THE OCEANS

PHYSICAL

TOTAL SURFACE AREA	LARGEST OCEAN	GREATEST OCEAN DEPTH	TALLEST MOUNTAIN	LARGEST CORAL
139,434,000 sq mi (361,132,000 sq km)	Pacific 69,000,000 sq mi (178,800,000 sq km)	Challenger Deep, Pacific Ocean -36,037 ft (-10,984 m)	(SEAFLOOR TO SUMMIT) Mauna Kea, Hawai'i, U.S.A. 32,696 ft (9,966 m)	REEF ECOSYSTEM Great Barrier Reef, Australia 134,000 sq mi (348,300 sq km)
PERCENTAGE OF EARTH'S SURFACE 71%	SMALLEST OCEAN Arctic 5,600,000 sq mi (14,700,000 sq km)	LONGEST MOUNTAIN RANGE Mid-Ocean Ridge 37,000 mi (60,000 km)	GREATEST TIDAL RANGE Bay of Fundy, Canada's Atlantic Coast 53 ft (16 m)	

THE OCEANS

THE OCEANS

Investigating the Oceans

The map at right shows that more than 70 percent of Earth's surface is underwater, mainly covered by four great oceans. There is growing support for recognizing a fifth ocean, called the Southern Ocean, in the area from Antarctica to 60° S latitude. The oceans are really inter-connected bodies of water that together form one global ocean.

The ocean floor is as varied as the surface of the continents, but mapping the oceans is challenging. Past explorers cut their way through jungles of the Amazon and conquered the icy heights of the Himalaya, but explorers could not march across the floor of the Pacific Ocean, which in places descends to more than 36,000 feet (10,970 m) below the surface of the water.

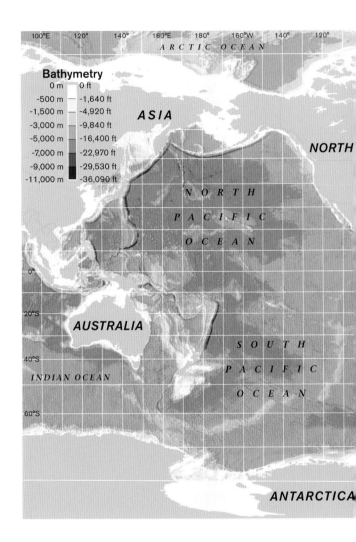

Bathymetry

0 m	0 ft
-500 m	-1,640 ft
-1,500 m	-4,920 ft
-3,000 m	-9,840 ft
-5,000 m	-16,400 ft
-7,000 m	-22,970 ft
-9,000 m	-29,530 ft
-11,000 m	-36,090 ft

ARCTIC OCEAN

ASIA

NORTH

NORTH PACIFIC OCEAN

AUSTRALIA

SOUTH PACIFIC OCEAN

INDIAN OCEAN

ANTARCTICA

🌐 **UNDERWATER LANDSCAPE.** The landscape of the ocean floor is varied and constantly changing. A continental edge that slopes gently beneath the water is called a continental shelf (1). Mountain ranges, called mid-ocean ridges (2), rise where ocean plates are spreading and magma flows out to create new land. Elsewhere, plates plunge into trenches (3) more than six miles (10 km) deep. In addition, magma, rising through vents called hot spots, pushes through ocean plates, creating seamounts (4) and volcanoes (5).

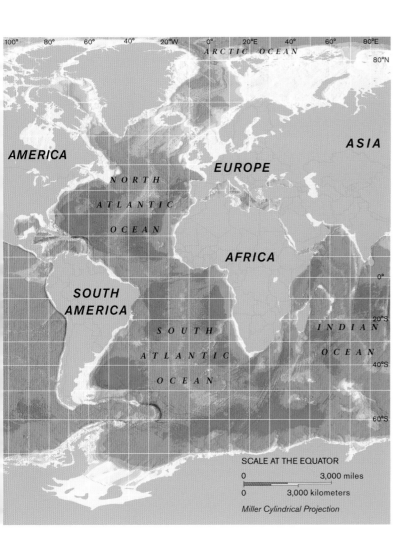

SCALE AT THE EQUATOR

0   3,000 miles

0   3,000 kilometers

Miller Cylindrical Projection

FROM OCEAN TO SATELLITE. In the 1990s, scientists developed the Argo Float to collect data from below the ocean surface. Argo Floats sink to a preset depth, often thousands of feet, where they gather data, such as temperature and salt content. At regular intervals, the floats rise to the surface (above) and transmit the data collected to a satellite. Then the cycle starts over again.

EYE ON THE OCEAN. Satellites orbiting high above Earth's surface record digital images of ocean colors, sea surface temperatures, and salinity levels. These can be used to identify and follow plant and animal activity as well as changes in the ocean environment.

SEEING WITH YOUR EARS.
Special instruments, such as this acoustic buoy, use sound waves bounced off the ocean floor to record variations in water temperature. This technique, called Acoustic Thermometry of Ocean Climate (ATOC), may someday help monitor long-term climate changes.

THE OCEANS

Pacific Ocean

🌐 **IN THE MIDST OF DANGER.**
A false-clown anemonefish swims among the tentacles of a sea anemone off the coast of the Philippines, in the western Pacific. This colorful fish is immune to the anemone's paralyzing sting.

THE BASICS

STATS

Surface area
69,000,000 sq mi
(178,800,000 sq km)

Percentage of Earth's water area
49.5%

Greatest depth
Challenger Deep
(in the Mariana Trench)
-36,037 ft (-10,984 m)

Tides
Highest: 30 ft (9 m)
near Korean peninsula
Lowest: 1 ft (0.3 m)
near Midway Islands

GEO WHIZ

The Pacific Ocean has more islands—tens of thousands of them—than any other ocean.

The ocean's name comes from the Latin *Mare Pacificum*, meaning "peaceful sea," but earthquakes and volcanic activity along the Ring of Fire generate powerful waves called tsunamis, which cause death and destruction when they slam ashore.

With the greatest area of tropical waters, the Pacific is also home to the largest number of coral reefs, including Earth's longest: Australia's Great Barrier Reef.

Only about 1,000 Hawaiian monk seals remain in the wild. Most live in protected waters of the Hawaiian archipelago.

The Pacific Ocean, largest of Earth's oceans, is more than 15 times larger than the United States and covers more than 30 percent of Earth's surface. The margins of the Pacific are often called the Ring of Fire because many active volcanoes and earthquakes occur where the ocean plate is moving under the edges of continental plates. The southwestern Pacific is dotted with many islands. Also in the western Pacific, Challenger Deep in the Mariana Trench plunges to 36,037 ft (10,984 m) below sea level. Most of the world's fish catch comes from the Pacific, and oil and gas reserves in the Pacific are an important energy source.

🌐 **CIRCLE OF LIFE.** Atolls, such as this one near Okinawa, Japan, are ocean landforms created by tiny marine animals called corals. These creatures live in warm tropical waters. The circular shapes of atolls often mark the coastlines of sunken volcanic islands.

SCALE AT THE EQUATOR

0 — 1,000 miles
0 — 1,000 kilometers
Mercator Projection

A S I A

Amur

Sea of Japan (East Sea)

Korea

Yellow Sea

East China Sea

Ryukyu Is.

Taiwan

Ryukyu Trench

Izu-Ogasawara Trench

Bonin Trench

Philippine Sea

Kyushu-Palau Ridge

Mariana Trench

West Mariana Basin

South China Sea

PHILIPPINE ISLANDS

Philippine Trench

Sulu Basin

Celebes Basin

Yap Trench

Palau Trench

West Caroline Basin

I N D O N E S I A

New Guinea

Banda Sea

Weber Basin

Continental Shelf

North Australian Basin

TROPIC OF CAPRICORN

A U S T R A L I A

South Australian Basin

I N D I A N
O C E A N

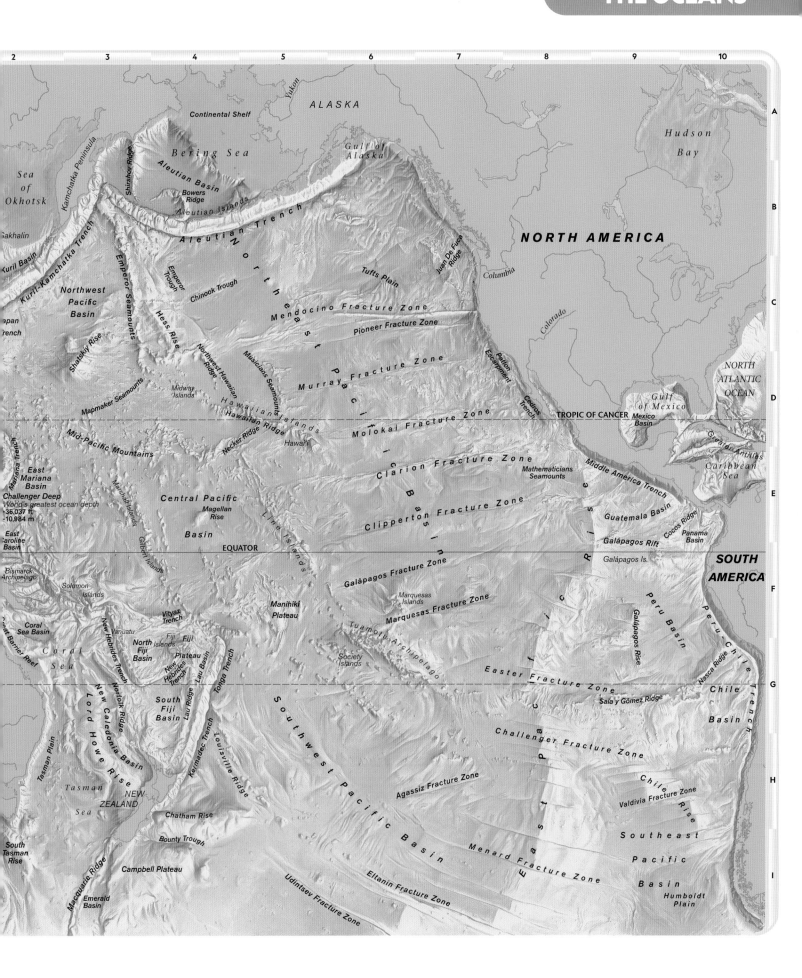

2   3   4   5   6   7   8   9   10

A   B   C   D   E   F   G   H   I

ALASKA

Continental Shelf

Yukon

Hudson Bay

Sea of Okhotsk

Bering Sea

Kamchatka Peninsula

Shirshov Ridge

Aleutian Basin

Bowers Ridge

Aleutian Islands

Gulf of Alaska

Sakhalin

Aleutian Trench

NORTH AMERICA

Kuril Basin

Kuril-Kamchatka Trench

Emperor Seamounts

Emperor Trough

Chinook Trough

North

Tufts Plain

Juan De Fuca Ridge

Columbia

Northwest Pacific Basin

Shatskiy Rise

Hess Rise

e

a

s

t

Mendocino Fracture Zone

Pioneer Fracture Zone

Colorado

Japan Trench

Northwest Hawaiian Ridge

Musicians Seamounts

Murray Fracture Zone

P

a

c

i

Patton Escarpment

NORTH ATLANTIC OCEAN

Mapmaker Seamounts

Midway Islands

Hawaiian Islands

Cedros Trench

TROPIC OF CANCER

Gulf of Mexico

Mexico Basin

Hawaiian Ridge

f

Necker Ridge

Molokai Fracture Zone

i

Mid-Pacific Mountains

Hawai'i

Clarion Fracture Zone

c

Mathematicians Seamounts

Middle America Trench

Greater Antilles

Caribbean Sea

Mariana Trench

East Mariana Basin

Marshall Islands

Central Pacific

Magellan Rise

B

a

s

i

Clipperton Fracture Zone

Guatemala Basin

Cocos Ridge

Panama Basin

Challenger Deep
World's greatest ocean depth
-36,037 ft
-10,984 m

Gilbert Islands

Basin

EQUATOR

Line Islands

n

Galápagos Rift

East Caroline Basin

Galápagos Fracture Zone

Galápagos Is.

SOUTH AMERICA

Bismarck Archipelago

Solomon Islands

Manihiki Plateau

Marquesas Islands

Marquesas Fracture Zone

Peru Basin

Coral Sea Basin

Vanuatu

Vityaz Trench

New Hebrides Trench

Fiji Islands

Fiji

Galápagos Rise

Great Barrier Reef

Coral Sea

North Fiji Basin

Fiji Plateau

New Hebrides Trench

Lau Basin

Tuamotu Archipelago

Society Islands

Peru-Chile Trench

Nasca Ridge

Lau Ridge

Tonga Trench

S

o

u

t

h

w

e

s

t

Easter Fracture Zone

Sala y Gómez Ridge

Chile Basin

New Caledonia Basin

Norfolk Ridge

South Fiji Basin

Kermadec Trench

Louisville Ridge

P

a

c

i

f

i

c

Challenger Fracture Zone

Tasman Plain

Lord Howe Rise

Tasman Sea

NEW ZEALAND

Chatham Rise

B

a

s

i

n

Agassiz Fracture Zone

E

a

s

t

P

a

c

i

f

i

c

Chile Rise

Valdivia Fracture Zone

Macquarie Ridge

Bounty Trough

Southeast Pacific Basin

South Tasman Rise

Emerald Basin

Campbell Plateau

Udintsev Fracture Zone

Eltanin Fracture Zone

Menard Fracture Zone

R

i

s

e

Humboldt Plain

Atlantic Ocean

THE BASICS

STATS

Surface area
35,400,000 sq mi
(91,700,000 sq km)

Percentage of Earth's water area
25.4%

Greatest depth
Puerto Rico Trench
-28,232 ft (-8,605 m)

Tides
Highest: 53 ft (16 m)
Bay of Fundy, Canada
Lowest: 1.5 ft (0.5 m)
Gulf of Mexico and
Mediterranean Sea

GEO WHIZ

The Atlantic Ocean gets its name from Greek mythology. "Atlantic" means "Sea of Atlas" in reference to the Greek god Atlas, who was forced to carry the weight of the heavens on his shoulders as a punishment.

The Atlantic Ocean is about half the size of the Pacific and is slowly growing. As molten rock from Earth's interior escapes where spreading occurs along the Mid-Atlantic Ridge, new ocean floor forms.

Each year, the amount of water that flows into the Atlantic Ocean from the Amazon River, in South America, is equal to 20 percent of Earth's available freshwater.

CAMOUFLAGE ON ICE. A young harp seal, called a pup, rests on the ice in Canada's Gulf of St. Lawrence. Pups are cared for by their mothers for only 12 days. After that, they must survive on their own.

Among Earth's great oceans, the Atlantic is second only to the Pacific in size. The floor of the Atlantic is split by the Mid-Atlantic Ridge, which is part of the Mid-Ocean Ridge—the longest mountain chain on Earth. The Atlantic poses many hazards to human activity. Tropical storms called hurricanes form in the warm tropical waters off the west coast of Africa and move across the ocean to bombard the islands of the Caribbean and coastal areas of North and Central America with damaging winds, waves, and rain in the late summer and fall. In the cold waters of the North Atlantic, sea ice and icebergs pose risks to shipping, especially during winter and spring.

The Atlantic has rich deposits of oil and natural gas, but drilling has raised concerns about pollution. In addition, the Atlantic has important marine fisheries, but overfishing has put some species at risk. Sea lanes between Europe and the Americas are among the most heavily trafficked in the world.

HIDDEN DANGER. Icebergs (right) are huge blocks of ice that break away, or calve, from the edges of glaciers. They pose a danger to ships because only about 10 percent of their bulk is visible above the waterline. A tragic disaster associated with an iceberg was the 1912 sinking of the R.M.S. *Titanic,* whose ghostly ruins lie below the waters of the North Atlantic Ocean (far right).

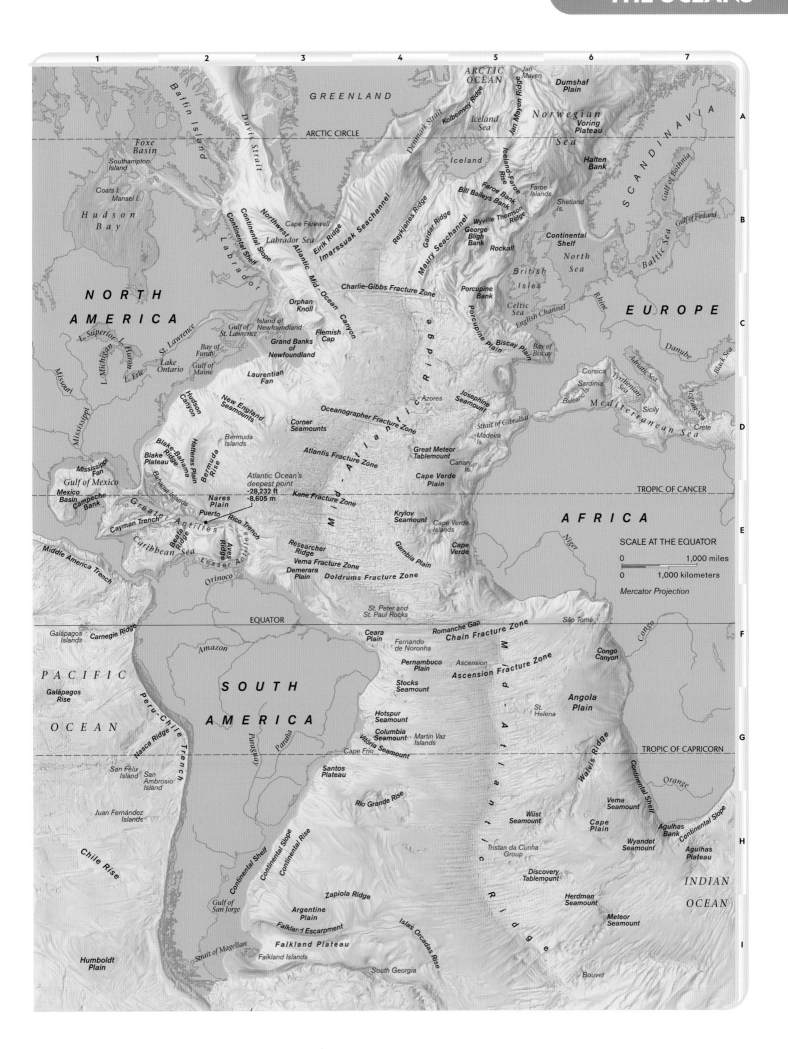

ARCTIC OCEAN
GREENLAND
Jan Mayen
Dumshaf Plain
Norwegian Sea
Voring Plateau
ARCTIC CIRCLE
Iceland Sea
Denmark Strait
Kolbeinsey Ridge
Iceland
Iceland-Faroe Rise
Halten Bank
SCANDINAVIA
Jan Mayen Ridge
Gulf of Bothnia
Foxe Basin
Southampton Island
Baffin Island
Davis Strait
Reykjanes Ridge
Gardar Ridge
Maury Seachannel
Bill Baileys Bank
Faroe Bank
Wyville Thomson Ridge
Faroe Islands
Shetland Is.
Gulf of Finland
Coats I.
Mansel I.
Continental Slope
Continental Shelf
Labrador Sea
Cape Farewell
Eirik Ridge
Atlantic Mid-Ocean Canyon
Imarssuak Seachannel
George Bligh Bank
Rockall
Continental Shelf
North Sea
Baltic Sea
Hudson Bay
Labrador
Charlie-Gibbs Fracture Zone
Porcupine Bank
British Isles
NORTH AMERICA
Orphan Knoll
Island of Newfoundland
Flemish Cap
Porcupine Plain
Celtic Sea
English Channel
Rhine
EUROPE
L. Superior
L. Huron
L. Michigan
St. Lawrence
Bay of Fundy
Gulf of Maine
Gulf of St. Lawrence
Grand Banks of Newfoundland
Biscay Plain
Bay of Biscay
Danube
Black Sea
Lake Ontario
L. Erie
Laurentian Fan
Mid-Atlantic Ridge
Azores
Josephine Seamount
Corsica
Sardinia
Tyrrhenian Sea
Adriatic Sea
Aegean Sea
Missouri
Hudson Canyon
New England Seamounts
Oceanographer Fracture Zone
Balearic Is.
Mediterranean Sea
Sicily
Crete
Corner Seamounts
Bermuda Islands
Atlantis Fracture Zone
Great Meteor Tablemount
Strait of Gibraltar
Madeira Is.
Blake-Bahama Ridge
Blake Plateau
Hatteras Plain
Bermuda Rise
Cape Verde Plain
Canary Is.
Mississippi
Mississippi Fan
Gulf of Mexico
Bahama Islands
Atlantic Ocean's deepest point -28,232 ft -8,605 m
Kane Fracture Zone
TROPIC OF CANCER
AFRICA
Mexico Basin
Campeche Bank
Nares Plain
Puerto Rico
Puerto Rico Trench
Krylov Seamount
Cape Verde Islands
SCALE AT THE EQUATOR
Cayman Trench
Greater Antilles
Beata Ridge
Aves Ridge
Lesser Antilles
Researcher Ridge
Gambia Plain
Cape Verde
0   1,000 miles
0   1,000 kilometers
Middle America Trench
Caribbean Sea
Vema Fracture Zone
Demerara Plain
Doldrums Fracture Zone
Niger
Mercator Projection
Orinoco
St. Peter and St. Paul Rocks
EQUATOR
Galápagos Islands
Carnegie Ridge
Amazon
Ceara Plain
Fernando de Noronha
Romanche Gap
Chain Fracture Zone
São Tomé
Congo
PACIFIC
Galápagos Rise
SOUTH AMERICA
Pernambuco Plain
Ascension
Ascension Fracture Zone
Congo Canyon
OCEAN
Stocks Seamount
Mid-Atlantic Ridge
Angola Plain
Paraguay
Paraná
Hotspur Seamount
Columbia Seamount
Vitória Seamount
Martin Vaz Islands
St. Helena
Peru-Chile Trench
Nasca Ridge
Cape Frio
TROPIC OF CAPRICORN
Santos Plateau
Walvis Ridge
Continental Shelf
Orange
San Félix Island
San Ambrosio Island
Rio Grande Rise
Vema Seamount
Juan Fernández Islands
Continental Shelf
Continental Slope
Continental Rise
Wüst Seamount
Cape Plain
Agulhas Bank
Continental Slope
Chile Rise
Wyandot Seamount
Agulhas Plateau
INDIAN OCEAN
Mid-Atlantic Ridge
Tristan da Cunha Group
Discovery Tablemount
Herdman Seamount
Zapiola Ridge
Gulf of San Jorge
Argentine Plain
Meteor Seamount
Falkland Escarpment
Islas Orcadas Rise
Strait of Magellan
Falkland Plateau
Humboldt Plain
Falkland Islands
South Georgia
Bouvet

THE OCEANS

Indian Ocean

THE BASICS

STATS

Surface area
29,400,000 sq mi
(76,200,000 sq km)

Percentage of Earth's water area
21%

Greatest depth
Java Trench
-23,376 ft (-7,125 m)

Tides
Highest: 36 ft (11 m)
Lowest: 2 ft (0.6 m)
Both along Australia's west coast

GEO WHIZ

Some of the world's largest breeding grounds for humpback whales are in the Indian Ocean and the Arabian Sea, and off the east coast of Africa.

The Bay of Bengal is sometimes called Cyclone Alley because of the large number of tropical storms that occur there each year between May and November.

Sailors from what is now Indonesia used seasonal winds called monsoons to reach Africa's east coast. They arrived on the continent long before Europeans did.

A December 2004 earthquake caused a tsunami that killed more than 225,000 people in countries bordering the Indian Ocean. Waves reached as high as 49 feet (15 m).

The Indian Ocean stretches from Africa's east coast to the southern coast of Asia and the western coast of Australia. It is the third largest of Earth's great oceans. Changing air pressure systems over its warm waters trigger South Asia's famous monsoon climate—a weather pattern in which winds reverse directions seasonally. The Bay of Bengal, an arm of the Indian Ocean, experiences devastating tropical storms. (They are called cyclones in this region, another word for hurricanes.) Islands along the eastern edge of the Indian Ocean plate experience earthquakes that sometimes cause destructive ocean waves called tsunamis.

The Arabian Sea, Persian Gulf, and Red Sea, extensions of the Indian Ocean, are important sources of oil and natural gas and account for nearly half of Earth's offshore oil production. Sea routes of the Indian Ocean connect the Middle East to the rest of the world, carrying vital energy resources on huge tanker ships.

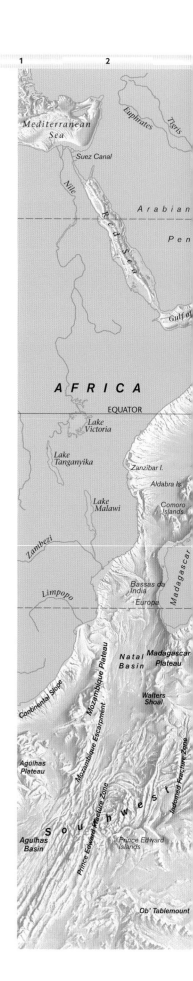

LIVING FOSSIL.
A coelacanth swims in the warm waters of the western Indian Ocean off the Comoro Islands. Once thought to have become extinct 66 million years ago along with the dinosaurs, a living coelacanth was discovered in 1938.

SCALE AT THE EQUATOR

0   1,000 miles
0   1,000 kilometers

Mercator Projection

Caspian
Sea

Persian Gulf

Gulf of Oman

Ra's al Hadd

Continental Shelf

Indus

ASIA

Brahmaputra

Ganges

Mekong

Salween

Irrawaddy

Yellow
Sea

Yangtze

Yellow
Sea

East
China
Sea

JAPAN

Japan
Trench

Izu-Ogasawara Trench

TROPIC OF CANCER

Taiwan

Continental Shelf

Ryukyu Islands

Ryukyu Trench

PACIFIC

OCEAN

Bonin Trench

nsula

INDIA

Hainan

South

China

Sea

Paracel
Islands

Macclesfield
Bank

Philippine Sea

Philippine Islands

Philippine

Benham
Seamount

Benham

Basin

Philippine Trench

West
Mariana
Basin

Mariana Trough

Aden

Socotra

Arabian
Sea

Arabian
Basin

Indus Fan

Continental Shelf

Bay of
Bengal

Ganges Fan

Andaman
Islands

Andaman
Basin

Gulf of Thailand

Sulu
Basin

Palawan Trough

World's greatest
ocean depth
-36,037 ft
-10,984 m

Mariana
Trench
Challenger
Deep

Yap Trench

Owen Fracture Zone

Carlsberg
Ridge

Chagos-Laccadive Plateau

Sri Lanka

Nicobar
Islands

Continental Shelf

Celebes
Basin

Palau Trench

Eauripik Rise

West
Caroline
Basin

East
Caroline
Basin

Somali

Basin

Coco-De-Mer
Seamounts

Maldive
Islands

Nikitin
Seamount

Ninetyeast Ridge

Sumatra

INDONESIA

Greater
Sunda Islands

Borneo

Banda Sea

Weber Deep

New
Guinea

Seychelles

Amirante
Isles

Mascarene Plateau

Chagos Trench

Diego
Garcia

Mid-Indian

Basin

Investigator Ridge

Java Sea

Java

Flores Sea

Lesser Sunda Islands

Arafura Sea

Farquhar
Group

Amirante Trench

Agalega
Islands

Saya de
Malha
Bank

Vema Trench

Christmas I.

Java Ridge

Java Trench

Indian Ocean's
deepest point
-23,376 ft
-7,125 m

Continental Shelf

Gulf
of
Carpentaria

Mascarene
Basin

Nazareth
Bank

Cargados
Carajos
Bank

Mascarene
Plain

Mauritius

Réunion

Rodrigues

Rodrigues
Fracture Zone

Egeria Fracture Zone

Mascarene Plateau

Mid-Indian Ridge

Osborn
Plateau

Wharton Basin

North
Australian
Basin

Exmouth Plateau

Mauritius
Trench

Madagascar
Basin

Atlantis II Fracture Zone

East Indiaman Ridge

Cuvier
Plateau

Perth
Basin

Naturaliste
Plateau

TROPIC OF CAPRICORN

AUSTRALIA

Broken Ridge

Diamantina Fracture Zone

Continental Shelf

Continental Slope

Great
Australian Bight

South Australian Basin

Indian Ridge

Amsterdam

St. Paul

Crozet
Basin

Crozet Plateau

Crozet
Islands

Kerguelen
Islands

Southeast Indian Ridge

Kerguelen
Plateau

South Tasman Rise

THE OCEANS

Arctic Ocean

The Arctic Ocean lies mostly north of the Arctic Circle, bounded by North America, Europe, and Asia. Unlike the other oceans, the Arctic is subject to persistent cold throughout the year. Also, because of its very high latitude, the Arctic experiences winters of perpetual night and summers of continual daylight. Except for coastal margins, the Arctic Ocean is covered by permanent drifting pack ice that averages almost 10 feet (3 m) in thickness. Most scientists are concerned that the polar ice may be melting due to climate change, putting at risk the habitat of polar bears and other arctic animals.

◑ **ARCTIC RESEARCH.** Scientists wearing cold weather survival suits prepare to measure salt content, nutrients, and plant and animal life in ice and meltwater. They also record data related to climate change, such as the shrinking of polar sea ice.

◑ **FREE RIDE.** A baby polar bear catches a ride as its mother crosses the frozen landscape of Canada's Arctic. Polar bear populations are showing signs of stress as sea ice shrinks.

0 — 200 miles
0 — 200 kilometers
Azimuthal Equidistant Projection

ARCTIC CIRCLE

SIBERIA

East Siberian Sea

New Siberian Is.

Chaun Bay

Wrangel Island

Chukchi Sea

Bering Strait

Kotzebue Sound

Point Barrow

Barrow Canyon

ALASKA

Yukon

Beaufort Slope

Beaufort Shelf

Beaufort Sea

Mackenzie Trough

Mackenzie

ARCTIC CIRCLE

FLAGS & FACTS

These flags and factoids represent the world's 195 independent countries—those with national governments that are recognized as having the highest legal authority over the land and people within their boundaries. Data are based on the CIA's 2020 *World Factbook*. The flags shown are national flags recognized by the United Nations. Area figures include land and inland water bodies. Languages are those most commonly spoken within a country or official languages, which are marked with an asterisk (*). Only the most commonly practiced religions are listed. All GDP per capita figures are in U.S. dollars and are adjusted to reflect purchasing power parity (PPP).

NORTH AMERICA

Antigua and Barbuda
Area: 171 sq mi
(443 sq km)
Population: 86,000
Percent urban: 24.6%
Capital: St. John's
Language: English*, Creole
Religion: Christianity
GDP per capita: $26,300
Life expectancy: 78 years

Bahamas, The
Area: 5,359 sq mi
(13,880 sq km)
Population: 333,000
Percent urban: 83%
Capital: Nassau
Language: English*, Creole
Religion: Christianity
GDP per capita: $31,200
Life expectancy: 73 years

Barbados
Area: 166 sq mi
(430 sq km)
Population: 293,000
Percent urban: 31.1%
Capital: Bridgetown
Language: English*, Bajan
Religion: Christianity
GDP per capita: $18,700
Life expectancy: 76 years

Belize
Area: 8,867 sq mi
(22,966 sq km)
Population: 386,000
Percent urban: 45.7%
Capital: Belmopan
Language: English*, Spanish, Creole, Maya
Religion: Christianity
GDP per capita: $8,300
Life expectancy: 69 years

Canada
Area: 3,855,101 sq mi
(9,984,670 sq km)
Population: 35,882,000
Percent urban: 81.4%
Capital: Ottawa
Language: English*, French*
Religion: Christianity
GDP per capita: $48,300
Life expectancy: 82 years

Costa Rica
Area: 19,730 sq mi
(51,100 sq km)
Population: 4,987,000
Percent urban: 79.3%
Capital: San José
Language: Spanish*, English
Religion: Christianity
GDP per capita: $16,900
Life expectancy: 79 years

Cuba
Area: 42,803 sq mi
(110,860 sq km)
Population: 11,116,000
Percent urban: 77%
Capital: Havana
Language: Spanish*
Religion: Christianity
GDP per capita: $12,300
Life expectancy: 79 years

Dominica
Area: 290 sq mi
(751 sq km)
Population: 74,000
Percent urban: 70.5%
Capital: Roseau
Languages: English*, Creole
Religion: Christianity
GDP per capita: $11,100
Life expectancy: 77 years

Dominican Republic
Area: 18,792 sq mi
(48,670 sq km)
Population: 10,299,000
Percent urban: 81.1%
Capital: Santo Domingo
Language: Spanish*
Religion: Christianity
GDP per capita: $16,900
Life expectancy: 78 years

El Salvador
Area: 8,124 sq mi
(21,041 sq km)
Population: 6,187,000
Percent urban: 72%
Capital: San Salvador
Language: Spanish*
Religion: Christianity
GDP per capita: $8,900
Life expectancy: 75 years

Grenada
Area: 133 sq mi
(344 sq km)
Population: 112,000
Percent urban: 36.3%
Capital: St. George's
Language: English*, Creole
Religion: Christianity
GDP per capita: $14,900
Life expectancy: 75 years

Guatemala
Area: 42,042 sq mi
(108,889 sq km)
Population: 16,581,000
Percent urban: 51.1%
Capital: Guatemala City
Language: Spanish*, indigenous languages
Religion: Christianity, indigenous beliefs
GDP per capita: $8,100
Life expectancy: 73 years

Haiti
Area: 10,714 sq mi
(27,750 sq km)
Population: 10,788,000
Percent urban: 55.3%
Capital: Port-au-Prince
Language: French*, Creole*
Religion: Christianity, indigenous beliefs
GDP per capita: $1,800
Life expectancy: 64 years

Honduras
Area: 43,278 sq mi
(112,090 sq km)
Population: 9,183,000
Percent urban: 57.1%
Capital: Tegucigalpa
Language: Spanish*, indigenous languages
Religion: Christianity
GDP per capita: $5,600
Life expectancy: 71 years

Jamaica
Area: 4,244 sq mi
(10,991 sq km)
Population: 2,812,000
Percent urban: 55.7%
Capital: Kingston
Language: English, Creole
Religion: Christianity
GDP per capita: $9,200
Life expectancy: 74 years

Mexico
Area: 758,449 sq mi
(1,964,375 sq km)
Population: 125,959,000
Percent urban: 80.2%
Capital: Mexico City
Language: Spanish
Religion: Christianity
GDP per capita: $19,900
Life expectancy: 76 years

Nicaragua
Area: 50,336 sq mi
(130,370 sq km)
Population: 6,085,000
Percent urban: 58.5%
Capital: Managua
Language: Spanish*
Religion: Christianity
GDP per capita: $5,800
Life expectancy: 74 years

Panama
Area: 29,120 sq mi
(75,420 sq km)
Population: 3,801,000
Percent urban: 67.7%
Capital: Panama City
Language: Spanish*, English
Religion: Christianity
GDP per capita: $25,400
Life expectancy: 79 years

St. Kitts and Nevis
Area: 101 sq mi
(261 sq km)
Population: 53,000
Percent urban: 30.8%
Capital: Basseterre
Language: English*
Religion: Christianity
GDP per capita: $26,800
Life expectancy: 76 years

St. Lucia
Area: 238 sq mi
(616 sq km)
Population: 166,000
Percent urban: 18.7%
Capital: Castries
Language: English*, Creole
Religion: Christianity
GDP per capita: $14,400
Life expectancy: 78 years

St. Vincent and the Grenadines
Area: 150 sq mi
(389 sq km)
Population: 102,000
Percent urban: 52.2%
Capital: Kingstown
Language: English*, Creole
Religion: Christianity
GDP per capita: $11,500
Life expectancy: 76 years

Trinidad and Tobago
Area: 1,980 sq mi
(5,128 sq km)
Population: 1,218,000
Percent urban: 53.2%
Capital: Port of Spain
Language: English, Creole,
Caribbean Hindustani
Religion: Christianity, Hinduism
GDP per capita: $31,400
Life expectancy: 73 years

SOUTH AMERICA

Argentina
Area: 1,073,518 sq mi
(2,780,400 sq km)
Population: 44,694,000
Percent urban: 91.9%
Capital: Buenos Aires
Language: Spanish*, English, Italian,
German, French
Religion: Christianity
GDP per capita: $20,900
Life expectancy: 77 years

Bolivia
Area: 424,164 sq mi
(1,098,581 sq km)
Population: 11,306,000
Percent urban: 69.4%
Capital: La Paz (administrative),
Sucre (constitutional)
Language: Spanish*, Quechua*,
Aymara*
Religion: Christianity
GDP per capita: $7,500
Life expectancy: 70 years

Brazil
Area: 3,287,611 sq mi
(8,514,877 sq km)
Population: 208,847,000
Percent urban: 86.6%
Capital: Brasília
Language: Portuguese*
Religion: Christianity
GDP per capita: $15,600
Life expectancy: 74 years

United States
Area: 3,796,741 sq mi
(9,833,517 sq km)
Population: 329,256,000
Percent urban: 82.3%
Capital: Washington, D.C.
Language: English, Spanish
Religion: Christianity
GDP per capita: $59,500
Life expectancy: 80 years

Colombia
Area: 439,735 sq mi
(1,138,910 sq km)
Population: 48,169,000
Percent urban: 80.8%
Capital: Bogotá
Language: Spanish*
Religion: Christianity
GDP per capita: $14,500
Life expectancy: 76 years

Ecuador
Area: 109,483 sq mi
(283,561 sq km)
Population: 16,499,000
Percent urban: 63.8%
Capital: Quito
Language: Spanish*, indigenous
languages
Religion: Christianity
GDP per capita: $11,500
Life expectancy: 77 years

Guyana
Area: 83,000 sq mi
(214,969 sq km)
Population: 741,000
Percent urban: 26.6%
Capital: Georgetown
Language: English*, Creole,
Amerindian languages, Caribbean
Hindustani
Religion: Christianity, Hinduism
GDP per capita: $8,200
Life expectancy: 69 years

Chile
Area: 291,932 sq mi
(756,102 sq km)
Population: 17,925,000
Percent urban: 87.6%
Capital: Santiago
Language: Spanish*, English
Religion: Christianity
GDP per capita: $24,500
Life expectancy: 79 years

Peru
Area: 496,224 sq mi
(1,285,216 sq km)
Population: 31,331,000
Percent urban: 77.9%
Capital: Lima
Language: Spanish*, Quechua*,
Aymara*
Religion: Christianity
GDP per capita: $13,300
Life expectancy: 74 years

Suriname
Area: 63,251 sq mi
(163,820 sq km)
Population: 598,000
Percent urban: 66.1%
Capital: Paramaribo
Language: Dutch*, English, Sranang
Tongo, Caribbean Hindustani,
Javanese
Religion: Christianity, Hinduism,
Islam
GDP per capita: $14,600
Life expectancy: 73 years

Uruguay
Area: 68,037 sq mi
(176,215 sq km)
Population: 3,369,000
Percent urban: 95.3%
Capital: Montevideo
Language: Spanish*
Religion: Christianity
GDP per capita: $22,400
Life expectancy: 77 years

Paraguay
Area: 157,048 sq mi
(406,752 sq km)
Population: 7,026,000
Percent urban: 61.6%
Capital: Asunción
Language: Spanish*, Guaraní*
Religion: Christianity
GDP per capita: $9,800
Life expectancy: 77 years

Venezuela
Area: 352,144 sq mi
(912,050 sq km)
Population: 31,689,000
Percent urban: 88.2%
Capital: Caracas
Language: Spanish*, indigenous
languages
Religion: Christianity
GDP per capita: $12,100
Life expectancy: 76 years

EUROPE

Albania
Area: 11,100 sq mi
(28,748 sq km)
Population: 3,057,000
Percent urban: 60.3%
Capital: Tirana
Language: Albanian*
Religion: Islam, Christianity
GDP per capita: $12,500
Life expectancy: 79 years

Andorra
Area: 181 sq mi
(468 sq km)
Population: 86,000
Percent urban: 88.1%
Capital: Andorra la Vella
Language: Catalan*, French,
Spanish, Portuguese
Religion: Christianity
GDP per capita: $49,900
Life expectancy: 83 years

Austria
Area: 32,383 sq mi
(83,871 sq km)
Population: 8,793,000
Percent urban: 58.3%
Capital: Vienna
Language: German*
Religion: Christianity
GDP per capita: $49,900
Life expectancy: 82 years

FLAGS & FACTS

Belarus
Area: 80,155 sq mi
(207,600 sq km)
Population: 9,528,000
Percent urban: 78.6%
Capital: Minsk
Language: Russian*, Belarusian*
Religion: Christianity
GDP per capita: $18,900
Life expectancy: 73 years

Belgium
Area: 11,787 sq mi
(30,528 sq km)
Population: 11,571,000
Percent urban: 98%
Capital: Brussels
Language: Dutch*, French*, German*
Religion: Christianity
GDP per capita: $46,600
Life expectancy: 81 years

Bosnia and Herzegovina
Area: 19,767 sq mi
(51,197 sq km)
Population: 3,850,000
Percent urban: 48.2%
Capital: Sarajevo
Language: Bosnian*, Serbian*,
Croatian*
Religion: Islam, Christianity
GDP per capita: $12,700
Life expectancy: 77 years

Bulgaria
Area: 42,811 sq mi
(110,879 sq km)
Population: 7,058,000
Percent urban: 75%
Capital: Sofia
Language: Bulgarian*
Religion: Christianity
GDP per capita: $21,700
Life expectancy: 75 years

Croatia
Area: 21,851 sq mi
(56,594 sq km)
Population: 4,270,000
Percent urban: 56.9%
Capital: Zagreb
Language: Croatian*
Religion: Christianity
GDP per capita: $24,400
Life expectancy: 76 years

Cyprus
Area: 3,572 sq mi
(9,251 sq km)
Population: 1,237,000
Percent urban: 66.8%
Capital: Nicosia
Language: Greek*, Turkish*
Religion: Christianity, Islam
GDP per capita: $37,000
Life expectancy: 79 years

Czechia (Czech Republic)
Area: 30,451 sq mi
(78,867 sq km)
Population: 10,686,000
Percent urban: 73.8%
Capital: Prague
Language: Czech*
Religion: Christianity
GDP per capita: $35,500
Life expectancy: 79 years

Denmark
Area: 16,639 sq mi
(43,094 sq km)
Population: 5,810,000
Percent urban: 87.9%
Capital: Copenhagen
Language: Danish, English
Religion: Christianity
GDP per capita: $49,900
Life expectancy: 80 years

Estonia
Area: 17,463 sq mi
(45,228 sq km)
Population: 1,244,000
Percent urban: 68.9%
Capital: Tallinn
Language: Estonian*, Russian
Religion: Christianity
GDP per capita: $31,800
Life expectancy: 77 years

Finland
Area: 130,558 sq mi
(338,145 sq km)
Population: 5,537,000
Percent urban: 85.4%
Capital: Helsinki
Language: Finnish*, Swedish*
Religion: Christianity
GDP per capita: $44,300
Life expectancy: 81 years

France
Area: 248,573 sq mi
(643,801 sq km)
Population: 67,364,000
Percent urban: 80.4%
Capital: Paris
Language: French*
Religion: Christianity
GDP per capita: $43,800
Life expectancy: 82 years

Germany
Area: 137,847 sq mi
(357,022 sq km)
Population: 80,458,000
Percent urban: 77.3%
Capital: Berlin
Language: German*
Religion: Christianity
GDP per capita: $50,400
Life expectancy: 81 years

Greece
Area: 50,949 sq mi
(131,957 sq km)
Population: 10,762,000
Percent urban: 79.1%
Capital: Athens
Language: Greek*
Religion: Christianity
GDP per capita: $27,700
Life expectancy: 81 years

Hungary
Area: 35,918 sq mi
(93,028 sq km)
Population: 9,826,000
Percent urban: 71.4%
Capital: Budapest
Language: Hungarian*, English,
German
Religion: Christianity
GDP per capita: $29,500
Life expectancy: 76 years

Iceland
Area: 39,769 sq mi
(103,000 sq km)
Population: 344,000
Percent urban: 93.8%
Capital: Reykjavík
Language: Icelandic, English,
Nordic languages
Religion: Christianity
GDP per capita: $51,800
Life expectancy: 83 years

Ireland (Éire)
Area: 27,133 sq mi
(70,273 sq km)
Population: 5,068,000
Percent urban: 63.2%
Capital: Dublin (Baile Átha Cliath)
Language: English*, Irish (Gaelic)*
Religion: Christianity
GDP per capita: $75,500
Life expectancy: 81 years

Italy
Area: 116,348 sq mi
(301,340 sq km)
Population: 62,247,000
Percent urban: 70.4%
Capital: Rome
Language: Italian*
Religion: Christianity
GDP per capita: $38,100
Life expectancy: 82 years

Kosovo
Area: 4,203 sq mi
(10,887 sq km)
Population: 1,908,000
Percent urban: 56.1%
Capital: Prishtinë
Language: Albanian*, Serbian*
Religion: Islam
GDP per capita: $10,500
Life expectancy: NA

Latvia
Area: 24,938 sq mi
(64,589 sq km)
Population: 1,924,000
Percent urban: 68.1%
Capital: Riga
Language: Latvian*, Russian
Religion: Christianity
GDP per capita: $27,600
Life expectancy: 75 years

Liechtenstein
Area: 62 sq mi
(160 sq km)
Population: 39,000
Percent urban: 14.3%
Capital: Vaduz
Language: German*
Religion: Christianity
GDP per capita: $139,100
Life expectancy: 82 years

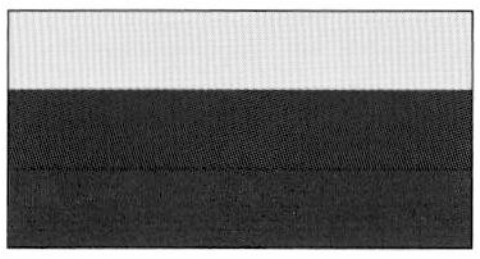

Lithuania
Area: 25,212 sq mi
(65,300 sq km)
Population: 2,793,000
Percent urban: 67.7%
Capital: Vilnius
Language: Lithuanian*
Religion: Christianity
GDP per capita: $32,300
Life expectancy: 75 years

Luxembourg
Area: 998 sq mi
(2,586 sq km)
Population: 606,000
Percent urban: 91%
Capital: Luxembourg
Language: Luxembourgish*, French*, German*, Portuguese
Religion: Christianity
GDP per capita: $104,000
Life expectancy: 82 years

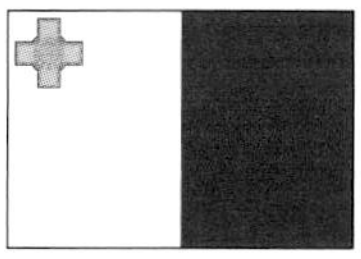

Malta
Area: 122 sq mi
(316 sq km)
Population: 449,000
Percent urban: 94.6%
Capital: Valletta
Language: Maltese*, English*
Religion: Christianity
GDP per capita: $42,000
Life expectancy: 81 years

Moldova
Area: 13,070 sq mi
(33,851 sq km)
Population: 3,438,000
Percent urban: 42.6%
Capital: Chisinau
Language: Moldovan*, Romanian*
Religion: Christianity
GDP per capita: $5,700
Life expectancy: 71 years

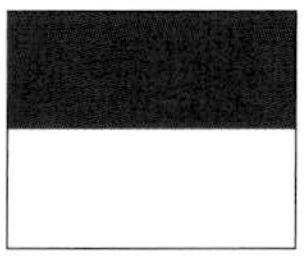

Monaco
Area: 1 sq mi
(2 sq km)
Population: 39,000
Percent urban: 100%
Capital: Monaco
Language: French*, English, Italian, Monegasque
Religion: Christianity
GDP per capita: $115,700
Life expectancy: 89 years

Montenegro
Area: 5,333 sq mi
(13,812 sq km)
Population: 614,000
Percent urban: 66.8%
Capital: Podgorica
Language: Montenegrin*, Serbian
Religion: Christianity, Islam
GDP per capita: $17,700
Life expectancy: NA

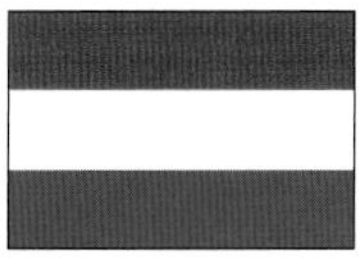

Netherlands
Area: 16,040 sq mi
(41,543 sq km)
Population: 17,151,000
Percent urban: 91.5%
Capital: Amsterdam (official), The Hague (administrative)
Language: Dutch*, Frisian
Religion: Christianity
GDP per capita: $53,600
Life expectancy: 81 years

North Macedonia
Area: 9,928 sq mi
(25,713 sq km)
Population: 2,119,000
Percent urban: 58%
Capital: Skopje
Language: Macedonian*, Albanian
Religion: Christianity, Islam
GDP per capita: $14,900
Life expectancy: 76 years

Norway
Area: 125,021 sq mi
(323,802 sq km)
Population: 5,372,000
Percent urban: 82.2%
Capital: Oslo
Language: Bokmal Norwegian*, Nynorsk Norwegian*
Religion: Christianity
GDP per capita: $71,800
Life expectancy: 82 years

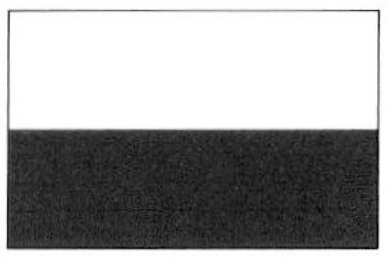

Poland
Area: 120,728 sq mi
(312,685 sq km)
Population: 38,421,000
Percent urban: 60.1%
Capital: Warsaw
Language: Polish*
Religion: Christianity
GDP per capita: $29,500
Life expectancy: 78 years

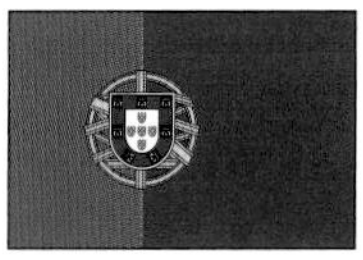

Portugal
Area: 35,556 sq mi
(92,090 sq km)
Population: 10,355,000
Percent urban: 65.2%
Capital: Lisbon
Language: Portuguese*, Mirandese*
Religion: Christianity
GDP per capita: $30,400
Life expectancy: 79 years

Romania
Area: 92,043 sq mi
(238,391 sq km)
Population: 21,457,000
Percent urban: 54%
Capital: Bucharest
Language: Romanian*
Religion: Christianity
GDP per capita: $24,500
Life expectancy: 75 years

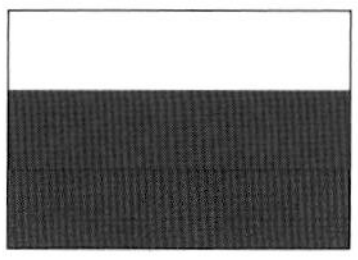

Russia
Area: 6,601,665 sq mi
(17,098,234 sq km)
Population: 144,478,000
Percent urban: 74.4%
Capital: Moscow
Language: Russian*
Religion: Christianity, Islam
GDP per capita: $27,800
Life expectancy: 71 years

San Marino
Area: 24 sq mi
(61 sq km)
Population: 34,000
Percent urban: 97.2%
Capital: San Marino
Language: Italian
Religion: Christianity
GDP per capita: $58,600
Life expectancy: 83 years

Serbia
Area: 29,913 sq mi
(77,474 sq km)
Population: 7,078,000
Percent urban: 56.1%
Capital: Belgrade
Language: Serbian*
Religion: Christianity
GDP per capita: $15,000
Life expectancy: 76 years

Slovakia
Area: 18,933 sq mi
(49,035 km)
Population: 5,445,000
Percent urban: 53.7%
Capital: Bratislava
Language: Slovak*
Religion: Christianity
GDP per capita: $33,000
Life expectancy: 77 years

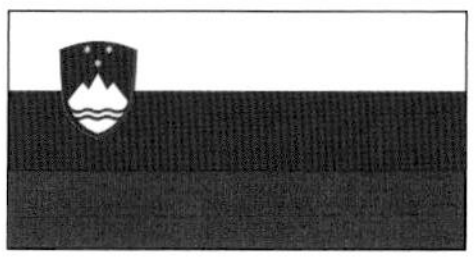

Slovenia
Area: 7,827 sq mi
(20,273 sq km)
Population: 2,102,000
Percent urban: 54.5%
Capital: Ljubljana
Language: Slovene*
Religion: Christianity
GDP per capita: $34,400
Life expectancy: 78 years

Spain
Area: 195,124 sq mi
(505,370 sq km)
Population: 49,331,000
Percent urban: 80.3%
Capital: Madrid
Language: Castilian Spanish*, Catalan, Galician, Basque
Religion: Christianity
GDP per capita: $38,300
Life expectancy: 82 years

Sweden
Area: 173,860 sq mi
(450,295 sq km)
Population: 10,041,000
Percent urban: 87.4%
Capital: Stockholm
Language: Swedish*
Religion: Christianity
GDP per capita: $51,500
Life expectancy: 82 years

Switzerland
Area: 15,937 sq mi
(41,277 sq km)
Population: 8,293,000
Percent urban: 73.8%
Capital: Bern
Language: German*, French*, Italian*, Romansch*
Religion: Christianity
GDP per capita: $61,400
Life expectancy: 83 years

FLAGS & FACTS

Ukraine
Area: 233,032 sq mi
(603,550 sq km)
Population: 43,952,000
Percent urban: 69.4%
Capital: Kyiv
Language: Ukrainian*, Russian
Religion: Christianity
GDP per capita: $8,700
Life expectancy: 72 years

United Kingdom
Area: 94,058 sq mi
(243,610 sq km)
Population: 65,105,000
Percent urban: 83.4%
Capital: London
Language: English, regional
languages
Religion: Christianity
GDP per capita: $44,100
Life expectancy: 81 years

Vatican City (Holy See)
Area: 0.17 sq mi
(0.44 sq km)
Population: 1,000
Percent urban: 100%
Capital: Vatican City
Language: Italian, Latin, French
Religion: Christianity
GDP per capita: NA
Life expectancy: NA

ASIA

Afghanistan
Area: 251,827 sq mi
(652,230 sq km)
Population: 34,941,000
Percent urban: 25.5%
Capital: Kabul
Language: Dari*, Pashto*, Uzbek
Religion: Islam
GDP per capita: $2,000
Life expectancy: 52 years

Armenia
Area: 11,484 sq mi
(29,743 sq km)
Population: 3,038,000
Percent urban: 63.1%
Capital: Yerevan
Language: Armenian*
Religion: Christianity
GDP per capita: $9,500
Life expectancy: 75 years

Azerbaijan
Area: 33,436 sq mi
(86,600 sq km)
Population: 10,047,000
Percent urban: 55.7%
Capital: Baku
Language: Azerbaijani (Azeri)*,
Russian
Religion: Islam
GDP per capita: $17,500
Life expectancy: 73 years

Bahrain
Area: 293 sq mi
(760 sq km)
Population: 1,443,000
Percent urban: 89.3%
Capital: Manama
Language: Arabic*, English, Farsi,
Urdu
Religion: Islam
GDP per capita: $48,500
Life expectancy: 79 years

Bangladesh
Area: 57,321 sq mi
(148,460 sq km)
Population: 159,453,000
Percent urban: 36.6%
Capital: Dhaka
Language: Bangla (Bengali)*
Religion: Islam, Hinduism
GDP per capita: $4,200
Life expectancy: 73 years

Bhutan
Area: 14,824 sq mi
(38,394 sq km)
Population: 766,000
Percent urban: 40.9%
Capital: Thimphu
Language: Dzongkha*, Sharchhopka,
Lhotshamkha
Religion: Buddhism, Hinduism
GDP per capita: $8,700
Life expectancy: 71 years

Brunei
Area: 2,226 sq mi
(5,765 sq km)
Population: 451,000
Percent urban: 77.6%
Capital: Bandar Seri Begawan
Language: Malay*, English, Chinese
Religion: Islam
GDP per capita: $78,200
Life expectancy: 77 years

Cambodia
Area: 69,898 sq mi
(181,035 sq km)
Population: 16,450,000
Percent urban: 23.4%
Capital: Phnom Penh
Language: Khmer*
Religion: Buddhism
GDP per capita: $4,000
Life expectancy: 65 years

China
Area: 3,705,405 sq mi
(9,596,960 sq km)
Population: 1,384,689,000
Percent urban: 59.2%
Capital: Beijing
Language: Standard Chinese or
Mandarin*, Yue or Cantonese, Wu,
Minbei, Minnan, Xiang, Gan, Hakka
dialects, numerous regionally
official languages
Religion: Folk religion, Buddhism,
Christianity
GDP per capita: $16,700
Life expectancy: 76 years

Georgia
Area: 26,911 sq mi
(69,700 sq km)
Population: 4,003,000
Percent urban: 58.6%
Capital: Tbilisi
Language: Georgian*
Religion: Christianity, Islam
GDP per capita: $10,700
Life expectancy: 76 years

India
Area: 1,269,219 sq mi
(3,287,263 sq km)
Population: 1,296,834,000
Percent urban: 34%
Capital: New Delhi
Language: Hindi*, English*, state
languages
Religion: Hinduism, Islam
GDP per capita: $7,200
Life expectancy: 69 years

Indonesia
Area: 735,358 sq mi
(1,904,569 sq km)
Population: 262,787,000
Percent urban: 55.3%
Capital: Jakarta
Language: Bahasa Indonesia*,
English, Dutch, Javanese, local
dialects
Religion: Islam, Christianity
GDP per capita: $12,400
Life expectancy: 73 years

Iran
Area: 636,371 sq mi
(1,648,195 sq km)
Population: 83,025,000
Percent urban: 74.9%
Capital: Tehran
Language: Persian (Farsi)*
Religion: Islam
GDP per capita: $20,200
Life expectancy: 74 years

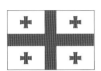

Iraq
Area: 169,235 sq mi
(438,317 sq km)
Population: 40,194,000
Percent urban: 70.5%
Capital: Baghdad
Language: Arabic*, Kurdish*
Religion: Islam
GDP per capita: $17,000
Life expectancy: 75 years

Israel
Area: 8,019 sq mi
(20,770 sq km)
Population: 8,425,000
Percent urban: 92.4%
Capital: Jerusalem
Language: Hebrew*, Arabic, English
Religion: Judaism, Islam
GDP per capita: $36,300
Life expectancy: 83 years

Japan
Area: 145,914 sq mi
(377,915 sq km)
Population: 126,168,000
Percent urban: 91.6%
Capital: Tokyo
Language: Japanese*
Religion: Shintoism, Buddhism
GDP per capita: $42,800
Life expectancy: 85 years

Jordan
Area: 34,495 sq mi
(89,342 sq km)
Population: 10,458,000
Percent urban: 91%
Capital: Amman
Language: Arabic*, English
Religion: Islam
GDP per capita: $12,500
Life expectancy: 75 years

Kazakhstan
Area: 1,052,089 sq mi
(2,724,900 sq km)
Population: 18,949,000
Percent urban: 57.4%
Capital: Nur-Sultan (Astana)
Language: Kazakh*, Russian*
Religion: Islam, Christianity
GDP per capita: $26,300
Life expectancy: 71 years

Kuwait
Area: 6,880 sq mi
(17,818 sq km)
Population: 4,438,000
Percent urban: 100%
Capital: Kuwait City
Language: Arabic*, English
Religion: Islam, Christianity
GDP per capita: $66,200
Life expectancy: 78 years

Kyrgyzstan
Area: 77,201 sq mi
(199,951 sq km)
Population: 5,849,000
Percent urban: 36.4%
Capital: Bishkek
Language: Kyrgyz*, Uzbek, Russian*
Religion: Islam, Christianity
GDP per capita: $3,700
Life expectancy: 71 years

Laos
Area: 91,429 sq mi
(236,800 sq km)
Population: 7,234,000
Percent urban: 35%
Capital: Vientiane
Language: Lao*, French, English,
indigenous languages
Religion: Buddhism
GDP per capita: $7,400
Life expectancy: 65 years

Lebanon
Area: 4,015 sq mi
(10,400 sq km)
Population: 6,100,000
Percent urban: 88.6%
Capital: Beirut
Language: Arabic*, French, English,
Armenian
Religion: Islam, Christianity
GDP per capita: $19,400
Life expectancy: 78 years

Malaysia
Area: 127,355 sq mi
(329,847 sq km)
Population: 31,810,000
Percent urban: 76%
Capital: Kuala Lumpur
Language: Bahasa Malaysia (Malay)*
Religion: Islam, Buddhism
GDP per capita: $29,000
Life expectancy: 75 years

Maldives
Area: 115 sq mi
(298 sq km)
Population: 392,000
Percent urban: 39.8%
Capital: Male
Language: Dhivehi*, English
Religion: Islam
GDP per capita: $19,100
Life expectancy: 76 years

Mongolia
Area: 603,908 sq mi
(1,564,116 sq km)
Population: 3,103,000
Percent urban: 68.4%
Capital: Ulaanbaatar
Language: Mongolian*
Religion: Buddhism
GDP per capita: $13,000
Life expectancy: 70 years

Myanmar (Burma)
Area: 261,228 sq mi
(676,578 sq km)
Population: 55,623,000
Percent urban: 30.6%
Capital: Nay Pyi Taw
Language: Burmese*
Religion: Buddhism, Christianity,
Islam
GDP per capita: $6,200
Life expectancy: 68 years

Nepal
Area: 56,827 sq mi
(147,181 sq km)
Population: 29,718,000
Percent urban: 19.7%
Capital: Kathmandu
Language: Nepali*, Maithali
Religion: Hinduism
GDP per capita: $2,700
Life expectancy: 71 years

North Korea
Area: 46,540 sq mi
(120,538 sq km)
Population: 25,381,000
Percent urban: 61.9%
Capital: Pyongyang
Language: Korean
Religion: Buddhism, Confucianism,
indigenous beliefs
GDP per capita: $1,700
Life expectancy: 71 years

Oman
Area: 119,499 sq mi
(309,500 sq km)
Population: 4,613,000
Percent urban: 84.5%
Capital: Muscat
Language: Arabic*, English
Religion: Islam
GDP per capita: $45,200
Life expectancy: 76 years

Pakistan
Area: 307,374 sq mi
(796,095 sq km)
Population: 207,863,000
Percent urban: 36.7%
Capital: Islamabad
Language: Urdu*, English*, Punjabi,
Sindhi, Saraiki
Religion: Islam
GDP per capita: $5,400
Life expectancy: 68 years

Philippines
Area: 115,831 sq mi
(300,000 sq km)
Population: 105,893,000
Percent urban: 46.9%
Capital: Manila
Language: Filipino (Tagalog)*,
English*
Religion: Christianity
GDP per capita: $8,300
Life expectancy: 69 years

Qatar
Area: 4,473 sq mi
(11,586 sq km)
Population: 2,364,000
Percent urban: 99.1%
Capital: Doha
Language: Arabic*, English
Religion: Islam, Christianity,
Hinduism
GDP per capita: $124,500
Life expectancy: 79 years

Saudi Arabia
Area: 830,000 sq mi
(2,149,690 sq km)
Population: 33,091,000
Percent urban: 83.8%
Capital: Riyadh
Language: Arabic*
Religion: Islam
GDP per capita: $54,800
Life expectancy: 76 years

Singapore
Area: 269 sq mi
(697 sq km)
Population: 5,996,000
Percent urban: 100%
Capital: Singapore
Language: English*, Mandarin*,
Malay*, Tamil*
Religion: Buddhism, Christianity,
Islam, Taosim
GDP per capita: $93,900
Life expectancy: 85 years

South Korea
Area: 38,502 sq mi
(99,720 sq km)
Population: 51,418,000
Percent urban: 81.5%
Capital: Seoul
Language: Korean, English
Religion: Christianity, Buddhism
GDP per capita: $39,400
Life expectancy: 83 years

Sri Lanka
Area: 25,332 sq mi
(65,610 sq km)
Population: 22,577,000
Percent urban: 18.5%
Capital: Colombo (commercial),
Sri Jayewardenepura Kotta (official)
Language: Sinhala*, Tamil*, English
Religion: Buddhism, Hinduism,
Islam, Christianity
GDP per capita: $12,800
Life expectancy: 77 years

Syria
Area: 71,498 sq mi
(185,180 sq km)
Population: 19,454,000
Percent urban: 54.2%
Capital: Damascus
Language: Arabic*, Kurdish,
Armenian, Aramaic, Circassian,
French
Religion: Islam, Christianity
GDP per capita: $2,900
Life expectancy: 75 years

FLAGS & FACTS

Tajikistan
Area: 55,637 sq mi
(144,100 sq km)
Population: 8,605,000
Percent urban: 27.1%
Capital: Dushanbe
Language: Tajik*, Uzbek
Religion: Islam
GDP per capita: $3,200
Life expectancy: 68 years

Thailand
Area: 198,117 sq mi
(513,120 sq km)
Population: 68,616,000
Percent urban: 49.9%
Capital: Bangkok
Language: Thai*, English
Religion: Buddhism
GDP per capita: $17,900
Life expectancy: 75 years

Timor-Leste (East Timor)
Area: 5,743 sq mi
(14,874 sq km)
Population: 1,322,000
Percent urban: 30.6%
Capital: Díli
Language: Tetun*, Portuguese*,
Indonesian, English
Religion: Christianity
GDP per capita: $5,400
Life expectancy: 68 years

Turkey
Area: 302,535 sq mi
(783,562 sq km)
Population: 81,257,000
Percent urban: 75.1%
Capital: Ankara
Language: Turkish*, Kurdish
Religion: Islam
GDP per capita: $26,900
Life expectancy: 75 years

Turkmenistan
Area: 188,456 sq mi
(488,100 sq km)
Population: 5,411,000
Percent urban: 51.6%
Capital: Ashgabat
Language: Turkmen*, Russian
Religion: Islam, Christianity
GDP per capita: $18,100
Life expectancy: 70 years

United Arab Emirates
Area: 32,278 sq mi
(83,600 sq km)
Population: 9,701,000
Percent urban: 86.5%
Capital: Abu Dhabi
Language: Arabic*, Persian, English,
Hindi, Urdu
Religion: Islam
GDP per capita: $67,700
Life expectancy: 78 years

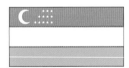

Uzbekistan
Area: 172,742 sq mi
(447,400 sq km)
Population: 30,024,000
Percent urban: 50.5%
Capital: Tashkent
Language: Uzbek*, Russian
Religion: Islam, Christianity
GDP per capita: $6,900
Life expectancy: 74 years

Vietnam
Area: 127,881 sq mi
(331,210 sq km)
Population: 97,040,000
Percent urban: 35.9%
Capital: Hanoi
Language: Vietnamese*, English
Religion: Buddhism, Christianity
GDP per capita: $6,900
Life expectancy: 74 years

Yemen
Area: 203,850 sq mi
(527,968 sq km)
Population: 28,667,000
Percent urban: 36.6%
Capital: Sanaa
Language: Arabic*
Religion: Islam
GDP per capita: $1,300
Life expectancy: 66 years

AFRICA

Algeria
Area: 919,595 sq mi
(2,381,741 sq km)
Population: 41,657,000
Percent urban: 72.6%
Capital: Algiers
Language: Arabic*, Berber*, French
Religion: Islam
GDP per capita: $15,200
Life expectancy: 77 years

Angola
Area: 481,353 sq mi
(1,246,700 sq km)
Population: 30,356,000
Percent urban: 65.5%
Capital: Luanda
Language: Portuguese*, Umbundu
Religion: Christianity
GDP per capita: $6,800
Life expectancy: 60 years

Benin
Area: 43,483 sq mi
(112,622 sq km)
Population: 11,341,000
Percent urban: 47.3%
Capital: Porto-Novo (official),
Cotonou (administrative)
Language: French*, Fon, Yoruba
Religion: Christianity, Islam,
indigenous beliefs
GDP per capita: $2,300
Life expectancy: 62 years

Botswana
Area: 224,607 sq mi
(581,730 sq km)
Population: 2,249,000
Percent urban: 69.4%
Capital: Gaborone
Language: English*, Setswana
Religion: Christianity
GDP per capita: $17,800
Life expectancy: 63 years

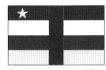

Burkina Faso
Area: 105,869 sq mi
(274,200 sq km)
Population: 19,743,000
Percent urban: 29.4%
Capital: Ouagadougou
Language: French*, indigenous
languages
Religion: Islam, Christianity
GDP per capita: $1,900
Life expectancy: 56 years

Burundi
Area: 10,745 sq mi
(27,830 sq km)
Population: 11,845,000
Percent urban: 13%
Capital: Bujumbura (commercial),
Gitega (official)
Language: Kirundi*, French*,
English*
Religion: Christianity
GDP per capita: $700
Life expectancy: 61 years

Cabo Verde
Area: 1,557 sq mi
(4,033 sq km)
Population: 568,000
Percent urban: 65.7%
Capital: Praia
Language: Portuguese*, Creole
Religion: Christianity
GDP per capita: $6,900
Life expectancy: 72 years

Cameroon
Area: 183,568 sq mi
(475,440 sq km)
Population: 25,641,000
Percent urban: 56.4%
Capital: Yaoundé
Language: English*, French*,
indigenous languages
Religion: Christianity, Islam
GDP per capita: $3,700
Life expectancy: 59 years

Central African Republic
Area: 240,535 sq mi
(622,984 sq km)
Population: 5,745,000
Percent urban: 41.4%
Capital: Bangui
Language: French*, Sangho,
indigenous languages
Religion: Christianity, indigenous
beliefs, Islam
GDP per capita: $700
Life expectancy: 53 years

Chad
Area: 495,755 sq mi
(1,284,000 sq km)
Population: 15,833,000
Percent urban: 23.1%
Capital: N'Djamena
Language: French*, Arabic*,
indigenous languages
Religion: Islam, Christianity
GDP per capita: $2,300
Life expectancy: 51 years

Comoros
Area: 863 sq mi
(2,235 sq km)
Population: 821,000
Percent urban: 29%
Capital: Moroni
Language: Arabic*, French*,
Shikomoro*
Religion: Islam
GDP per capita: $1,600
Life expectancy: 65 years

Congo
Area: 132,047 sq mi
(342,000 sq km)
Population: 5,062,000
Percent urban: 66.9%
Capital: Brazzaville
Language: French*, Lingala,
Monokutuba, other indigenous
languages
Religion: Christianity
GDP per capita: $6,600
Life expectancy: 60 years

**Congo, Democratic
Republic of the**
Area: 905,354 sq mi
(2,344,858 sq km)
Population: 85,281,000
Percent urban: 44.5%
Capital: Kinshasa
Language: French*, Lingala, other
indigenous languages
Religion: Christianity
GDP per capita: $800
Life expectancy: 58 years

Côte d'Ivoire (Ivory Coast)
Area: 124,504 sq mi
(322,463 sq km)
Population: 26,261,000
Percent urban: 50.8%
Capitals: Abidjan (administrative),
Yamoussoukro (legislative)
Language: French*, Dioula, other
indigenous languages
Religion: Islam, Christianity
GDP per capita: $3,900
Life expectancy: 59 years

Djibouti
Area: 8,958 sq mi
(23,200 sq km)
Population: 884,000
Percent urban: 77.8%
Capital: Djibouti
Language: French*, Arabic*, Somali,
Afar
Religion: Islam
GDP per capita: $3,600
Life expectancy: 64 years

Egypt
Area: 386,662 sq mi
(1,001,450 sq km)
Population: 99,413,000
Percent urban: 42.7%
Capital: Cairo
Language: Arabic*, English, French
Religion: Islam, Christianity
GDP per capita: $12,700
Life expectancy: 73 years

Equatorial Guinea
Area: 10,831 sq mi
(28,051 sq km)
Population: 797,000
Percent urban: 72.1%
Capital: Malabo
Language: Spanish*, French*,
Portuguese*, indigenous languages
Religion: Christianity, indigenous
beliefs
GDP per capita: $36,000
Life expectancy: 65 years

Eritrea
Area: 45,406 sq mi
(117,600 sq km)
Population: 5,971,000
Percent urban: 40.1%
Capital: Asmara
Language: Tigrinya*, Arabic*,
English*, indigenous languages
Religion: Islam, Christianity
GDP per capita: $1,600
Life expectancy: 65 years

Eswatini (Swaziland)
Area: 6,704 sq mi
(17,364 sq km)
Population: 1,087,000
Percent urban: 23.8%
Capital: Mbabane (administrative),
Lobamba (legislative and royal)
Language: English*, siSwati*
Religion: Christianity
GDP per capita: $9,900
Life expectancy: 52 years

Ethiopia
Area: 426,372 sq mi
(1,104,300 sq km)
Population: 108,386,000
Percent urban: 20.8%
Capital: Addis Ababa
Language: Amharic*, Oromo, Somali,
Tigrinya, Afar
Religion: Christianity, Islam
GDP per capita: $2,200
Life expectancy: 63 years

Gabon
Area: 103,347 sq mi
(267,667 sq km)
Population: 2,119,000
Percent urban: 89.4%
Capital: Libreville
Language: French*, indigenous
languages
Religion: Christianity
GDP per capita: $19,200
Life expectancy: 52 years

Gambia, The
Area: 4,363 sq mi
(11,300 sq km)
Population: 2,093,000
Percent urban: 61.3%
Capital: Banjul
Language: English*, indigenous
languages
Religion: Islam
GDP per capita: $1,700
Life expectancy: 65 years

Ghana
Area: 92,098 sq mi
(238,533 sq km)
Population: 28,102,000
Percent urban: 56.1%
Capital: Accra
Language: English*, Assanta, Ewe,
Fante
Religion: Christianity, Islam
GDP per capita: $4,700
Life expectancy: 67 years

Guinea
Area: 94,926 sq mi
(245,857 sq km)
Population: 11,855,000
Percent urban: 36.1%
Capital: Conakry
Language: French*, indigenous
languages
Religion: Islam
GDP per capita: $2,000
Life expectancy: 61 years

Guinea-Bissau
Area: 13,948 sq mi
(36,125 sq km)
Population: 1,833,000
Percent urban: 43.4%
Capital: Bissau
Language: Portuguese*, Creole,
Pular, Mandingo
Religion: Islam, Christianity,
indigenous beliefs
GDP per capita: $1,800
Life expectancy: 51 years

Kenya
Area: 224,081 sq mi
(580,367 sq km)
Population: 48,398,000
Percent urban: 27%
Capital: Nairobi
Language: English*, Kiswahili*,
indigenous languages
Religion: Christianity, Islam
GDP per capita: $3,500
Life expectancy: 64 years

Lesotho
Area: 11,720 sq mi
(30,355 sq km)
Population: 1,962,000
Percent urban: 28.2%
Capital: Maseru
Language: Sesotho*, English*, Zulu,
Xhosa
Religion: Christianity, indigenous
beliefs
GDP per capita: $3,600
Life expectancy: 53 years

Liberia
Area: 43,000 sq mi
(111,369 sq km)
Population: 4,810,000
Percent urban: 51.2%
Capital: Monrovia
Language: English*, indigenous
languages
Religion: Christianity, Islam
GDP per capita: $1,400
Life expectancy: 63 years

Libya
Area: 679,362 sq mi
(1,759,540 sq km)
Population: 6,755,000
Percent urban: 80.1%
Capital: Tripoli
Language: Arabic*, Italian, English,
Berber
Religion: Islam
GDP per capita: $10,000
Life expectancy: 77 years

Madagascar
Area: 226,658 sq mi
(587,041 sq km)
Population: 25,684,000
Percent urban: 37.2%
Capital: Antananarivo
Language: French*, Malagasy*,
English
Religion: Christianity, indigenous
beliefs, Islam
GDP per capita: $1,600
Life expectancy: 66 years

Malawi
Area: 45,747 sq mi
(118,484 sq km)
Population: 19,843,000
Percent urban: 16.9%
Capital: Lilongwe
Language: English*, Chichewa, other
indigenous languages
Religion: Christianity, Islam
GDP per capita: $1,200
Life expectancy: 62 years

FLAGS & FACTS

Mali
Area: 478,841 sq mi
(1,240,192 sq km)
Population: 18,430,000
Percent urban: 42.4%
Capital: Bamako
Language: French*, Bambara, other
indigenous languages
Religion: Islam
GDP per capita: $2,200
Life expectancy: 60 years

Mauritania
Area: 397,955 sq mi
(1,030,700 sq km)
Population: 3,840,000
Percent urban: 53.7%
Capital: Nouakchott
Language: Arabic*, indigenous
languages
Religion: Islam
GDP per capita: $4,400
Life expectancy: 63 years

Mauritius
Area: 788 sq mi
(2,040 sq km)
Population: 1,364,000
Percent urban: 40.8%
Capital: Port Louis
Language: Creole, English*
Religion: Hinduism, Christianity,
Islam
GDP per capita: $21,600
Life expectancy: 76 years

Morocco
Area: 172,414 sq mi
(446,550 sq km)
Population: 34,314,000
Percent urban: 62.5%
Capital: Rabat
Language: Arabic*, Tamazight*,
French
Religion: Islam
GDP per capita: $8,600
Life expectancy: 77 years

Mozambique
Area: 308,642 sq mi
(799,380 sq km)
Population: 27,234,000
Percent urban: 36%
Capital: Maputo
Language: Portuguese*, Emakhuwa,
Xichangana, other indigenous
languages
Religion: Christianity, Islam
GDP per capita: $1,200
Life expectancy: 54 years

Namibia
Area: 318,261 sq mi
(824,292 sq km)
Population: 2,533,000
Percent urban: 50%
Capital: Windhoek
Language: English*, indigenous
languages, Afrikaans
Religion: Christianity, indigenous
beliefs
GDP per capita: $11,300
Life expectancy: 64 years

Niger
Area: 489,191 sq mi
(1,267,000 sq km)
Population: 19,866,000
Percent urban: 16.4%
Capital: Niamey
Language: French*, indigenous
languages
Religion: Islam
GDP per capita: $1,200
Life expectancy: 56 years

Nigeria
Area: 356,669 sq mi
(923,768 sq km)
Population: 203,453,000
Percent urban: 50.3%
Capital: Abuja
Language: English*, indigenous
languages
Religion: Islam, Christianity,
indigenous beliefs
GDP per capita: $5,900
Life expectancy: 54 years

Rwanda
Area: 10,169 sq mi
(26,338 sq km)
Population: 12,187,000
Percent urban: 17.2%
Capital: Kigali
Language: Kinyarwanda*, French*,
English*, Kiswahili
Religion: Christianity
GDP per capita: $2,100
Life expectancy: 64 years

Sao Tome and Principe
Area: 372 sq mi
(964 sq km)
Population: 204,000
Percent urban: 72.8%
Capital: São Tomé
Language: Portuguese*, Forro
Religion: Christianity
GDP per capita: $3,200
Life expectancy: 65 years

Senegal
Area: 75,955 sq mi
(196,722 sq km)
Population: 15,021,000
Percent urban: 47.2%
Capital: Dakar
Language: French*, Wolof, other
indigenous languages
Religion: Islam
GDP per capita: $2,700
Life expectancy: 62 years

Seychelles
Area: 176 sq mi
(455 sq km)
Population: 95,000
Percent urban: 56.7%
Capital: Victoria
Language: Creole*, English*, French*
Religion: Christianity
GDP per capita: $28,900
Life expectancy: 75 years

Sierra Leone
Area: 27,699 sq mi
(71,740 sq km)
Population: 6,312,000
Percent urban: 42.1%
Capital: Freetown
Language: English*, Mende, Temne,
Krio
Religion: Islam, Christianity
GDP per capita: $1,600
Life expectancy: 59 years

Somalia
Area: 246,201 sq mi
(637,657 sq km)
Population: 11,259,000
Percent urban: 45%
Capital: Mogadishu
Language: Somali*, Arabic*, Italian,
English
Religion: Islam
GDP per capita: NA
Life expectancy: 53 years

South Africa
Area: 470,693 sq mi
(1,219,090 sq km)
Population: 55,380,000
Percent urban: 66.4%
Capital: Pretoria (Tshwane)
(administrative), Cape Town
(legislative), Bloemfontein (judicial)
Language: IsiZulu*, IsiXhosa*, other
indigenous languages*, Afrikaans*,
English*
Religion: Christianity
GDP per capita: $13,500
Life expectancy: 64 years

South Sudan
Area: 248,777 sq mi
(644,329 sq km)
Population: 10,205,000
Percent urban: 19.6%
Capital: Juba
Language: English*, Arabic,
indigenous languages
Religion: Animism, Christianity
GDP per capita: $1,500
Life expectancy: NA

Sudan
Area: 718,723 sq mi
(1,861,484 sq km)
Population: 43,121,000
Percent urban: 34.6%
Capital: Khartoum
Language: Arabic*, English*
Religion: Islam
GDP per capita: $4,600
Life expectancy: 64 years

Tanzania
Area: 365,754 sq mi
(947,300 sq km)
Population: 55,451,000
Percent urban: 33.8%
Capital: Dar es Salaam
(administrative), Dodoma (official)
Language: Kiswahili*, English*,
indigenous languages
Religion: Christianity, Islam
GDP per capita: $3,200
Life expectancy: 63 years

Togo
Area: 21,925 sq mi
(56,785 sq km)
Population: 8,176,000
Percent urban: 23.1%
Capital: Lomé
Language: French*, Ewe, Mina,
Kabye, Dagomba
Religion: Indigenous beliefs,
Christianity, Islam
GDP per capita: $5,600
Life expectancy: 76 years

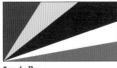

Tunisia
Area: 63,170 sq mi
(163,610 sq km)
Population: 11,516,000
Percent urban: 68.9%
Capital: Tunis
Language: Arabic*, French, Berber
Religion: Islam
GDP per capita: $11,800
Life expectancy: 76 years

Uganda
Area: 93,065 sq mi
(241,038 sq km)
Population: 40,854,000
Percent urban: 23.8%
Capital: Kampala
Language: English*, Swahili*, Ganda
(Luganda)
Religion: Christianity, Islam
GDP per capita: $2,400
Life expectancy: 56 years

Zambia
Area: 290,587 sq mi
(752,618 sq km)
Population: 16,445,000
Percent urban: 43.5%
Capital: Lusaka
Language: English*, Bemba, Nyanja,
Tonga, other indigenous languages
Religion: Christianity
GDP per capita: $4,000
Life expectancy: 53 years

Zimbabwe
Area: 150,872 sq mi
(390,757 sq km)
Population: 14,030,000
Percent urban: 32.2%
Capital: Harare
Language: Shona*, Ndebele*, English*,
indigenous languages*
Religion: Christianity, indigenous
beliefs
GDP per capita: $2,300
Life expectancy: 60 years

AUSTRALIA,
NEW ZEALAND & OCEANIA

Australia
Area: 2,988,901 sq mi
(7,741,220 sq km)
Population: 23,470,000
Percent urban: 86%
Capital: Canberra, A.C.T.
Language: English
Religion: Christianity
GDP per capita: $50,300
Life expectancy: 82 years

Fiji
Area: 7,056 sq mi
(18,274 sq km)
Population: 927,000
Percent urban: 56.2%
Capital: Suva
Language: English*, Fijian*, Hindi
Religion: Christianity, Hinduism
GDP per capita: $9,800
Life expectancy: 73 years

Kiribati
Area: 313 sq mi
(811 sq km)
Population: 109,000
Percent urban: 54.1%
Capital: Tarawa
Language: English*, I-Kiribati
Religion: Christianity
GDP per capita: $2,000
Life expectancy: 67 years

Marshall Islands
Area: 70 sq mi
(181 sq km)
Population: 76,000
Percent urban: 77%
Capital: Majuro
Language: Marshallese*, English*
Religion: Christianity
GDP per capita: $3,400
Life expectancy: 73 years

Micronesia, Federated States of
Area: 271 sq mi
(702 sq km)
Population: 104,000
Percent urban: 22.7%
Capital: Palikir
Language: English*, indigenous
languages
Religion: Christianity
GDP per capita: $3,400
Life expectancy: 73 years

Nauru
Area: 8 sq mi
(21 sq km)
Population: 10,000
Percent urban: 100%
Capital: Yaren
Language: Nauruan*, English
Religion: Christianity
GDP per capita: $12,200
Life expectancy: 67 years

New Zealand
Area: 103,799 sq mi
(268,838 sq km)
Population: 4,546,000
Percent urban: 86.5%
Capital: Wellington
Language: English*, Maori*
Religion: Christianity
GDP per capita: $38,900
Life expectancy: 81 years

Palau
Area: 177 sq mi
(459 sq km)
Population: 22,000
Percent urban: 79.9%
Capital: Ngerulmud
Language: Palauan*, English*,
Filipino
Religion: Christianity
GDP per capita: $16,200
Life expectancy: 73 years

Papua New Guinea
Area: 178,703 sq mi
(462,840 sq km)
Population: 7,027,000
Percent urban: 13.2%
Capital: Port Moresby
Language: Tok Pisin*, English*, Hiri
Motu*, other indigenous languages
Religion: Christianity
GDP per capita: $3,700
Life expectancy: 67 years

Samoa
Area: 1,093 sq mi
(2,831 sq km)
Population: 201,000
Percent urban: 18.2%
Capital: Apia
Language: Samoan*, English*
Religion: Christianity
GDP per capita: $5,700
Life expectancy: 74 years

Solomon Islands
Area: 11,157 sq mi
(28,896 sq km)
Population: 660,000
Percent urban: 23.7%
Capital: Honiara
Language: English*, Melanesian
pidgin, indigenous languages
Religion: Christianity
GDP per capita: $2,200
Life expectancy: 76 years

Tonga
Area: 288 sq mi
(747 sq km)
Population: 106,000
Percent urban: 23.1%
Capital: Nuku'alofa
Language: Tongan*, English*
Religion: Christianity
GDP per capita: $5,600
Life expectancy: 76 years

Tuvalu
Area: 10 sq mi
(26 sq km)
Population: 11,000
Percent urban: 62.4%
Capital: Funafuti
Language: Tuvaluan*, English*,
Samoan, Kiribati
Religion: Christianity
GDP per capita: $3,800
Life expectancy: 67 years

Vanuatu
Area: 4,706 sq mi
(12,189 sq km)
Population: 283,000
Percent urban: 25.3%
Capital: Port Vila
Language: Bislama*, English*,
French*, indigenous languages
Religion: Christianity
GDP per capita: $2,700
Life expectancy: 74 years

Glossary

acid rain precipitation containing acid droplets resulting from the mixture of moisture in the air with carbon dioxide, nitrogen oxide, sulfur dioxide, and hydrocarbons released by factories and motor vehicles

archipelago group or chain of islands

atheist person or group that does not believe in any deity

basin area of land that is lower at the center than at the rim

bathymetry measurement of depth at various places in the ocean or other body of water

bay body of water, usually smaller than a gulf, that is partially surrounded by land

biomass total volume of organic material in a certain area or ecosystem that can be used as a renewable energy source (a biofuel)

border area along each side of the boundary that separates one country from another

boundary most commonly, a line that has been established by people to mark the limit of one political unit, such as a country or state, and the beginning of another. Geographical features such as mountains sometimes act as boundaries.

caloric supply measure of the amount of food available to a particular person, household, or community

canal human-made waterway that is used by ships or to carry water for irrigation

canyon deep, narrow valley that has steep sides

carat unit of weight for precious stones equal to 200 milligrams

cliff very steep rock face, usually along a coast or on the side of a mountain

climate change change in typical climate patterns, including temperature or precipitation; may result from natural cycles or from human activities such as use of fossil fuels

continent one of the seven main land-masses on Earth's surface

continental climate interior areas found only in the Northern Hemisphere north of mild climate regions; summer to winter temperature extremes

country territory with a government that is the highest legal authority over the land and people within its boundaries

Creole language formed from a mixture of different languages, such as French and an indigenous language

delta lowland formed by silt, sand, and gravel deposited by a river at its mouth

desert hot or cold region that receives 10 inches (25 cm) or less of rain or other forms of precipitation a year

desertification spread of desertlike conditions in semiarid regions that is the result of human pressures, such as overgrazing, removal of natural vegetation, and cultivation of land, as well as climatic changes

divide elevated boundary line separating river systems from which rivers flow in different directions

dry climate areas experiencing low annual precipitation and day to night temperature extremes

earthquake sudden movement or shaking of Earth's crust, often resulting in damage on the surface

elevation distance above sea level, usually measured in feet or meters

escarpment cliff that separates two nearly flat land areas that lie at different elevations

fault break in Earth's crust along which movement up, down, or sideways occurs

fjord/fiord long narrow coastal inlet associated with past glaciation, as in Norway and Chile

fork place where a river splits into two smaller streams

geographic pole 90° N or 90° S latitude; location of the ends of Earth's axis

glacier large, slow-moving mass of ice

greenhouse gases gases, such as carbon dioxide and methane, that contribute to atmospheric warming

gross domestic product (GDP) per capita total value of goods and services produced by a country's economy in a year divided by the country's total population. Figures in this atlas are in U.S. dollars and based on **purchasing power parity (PPP),** an economic calculation for comparing the value of different currencies that takes into account the cost of living in each country.

gulf portion of the ocean that cuts into the land; usually larger than a bay

harbor body of water, sheltered by natural or artificial barriers, that is deep enough for ships

hemisphere half a sphere. Earth can be divided into Northern and Southern Hemispheres, or Eastern and Western Hemispheres.

highland climate areas associated with mountains where elevation is the main factor in determining temperature and precipitation

highlands an elevated area or the more mountainous region of a country

hybrid car a car that is powered by gasoline and electricity

ice cap thick layer of ice and snow covering less than 19,300 square miles (50,000 sq km)

ice sheet thick layer of ice and snow covering more than 19,300 square miles (50,000 sq km)

indigenous naturally occurring in a particular area or region, as with people, languages, or religions

inlet narrow opening in the land that is filled with water flowing from an ocean, a lake, or a river

island landmass, smaller than a continent, that is completely surrounded by water

lagoon shallow body of water that is open to the sea but also protected from it by a reef or sandbar

lake body of water that is surrounded by land. Large lakes are sometimes called seas.

landform physical feature shaped by tectonic activity, weathering, and erosion. Earth's four major kinds are plains, mountains, plateaus, and hills.

landmass large area of Earth's crust that lies above sea level, such as a continent

large-scale map map, such as a street map, that shows a small area in great detail

Latin America cultural region generally considered to include Mexico, Central America, South America, and the West Indies. Spanish and Portuguese are the principal languages.

latitude measurement in degrees north or south of 0° (Equator) to 90°

leeward side away from or sheltered from the wind

life expectancy average number of years a person can expect to live

lingua franca language not native to the local population that is used as a common or commercial language

longitude measurement in degrees east or west from 0° (prime meridian) to 180°

magma molten rock in Earth's mantle

magnetic pole point at which the axis of Earth's magnetic field intersects Earth's surface. Compass needles align with Earth's magnetic field so that one end points to the north magnetic pole, the other to the south magnetic pole.

mesa eroded plateau, broader than it is high, found in arid or semiarid regions

metropolitan area a city and its surrounding suburbs or communities

Middle East term commonly used for the countries of southwestern Asia, but which can also include northern Africa from Morocco to Egypt

molten liquefied by heat; melted

mountain landform, higher than a hill, that rises at least 1,000 feet (300 m) above the surrounding land and is wider at its base than at its top, or peak. A series of mountains is called a range.

nation people who share a common culture or sense of history. It is often used as another word for "country," although people within a country may be of many cultures.

ocean the large body of salt water that surrounds the continents and covers more than two-thirds of Earth's surface

pack ice large blocks of ice that form on the surface of the sea, pushed together by wind and currents

peninsula extension of land that is surrounded by water on three sides

pidgin simplified form of speech that allows speakers of different languages to communicate

plain large area of relatively flat land that is often covered with grasses

plantation agriculture type of commercial agriculture specializing in one or two crops, such as coffee or bananas

plate tectonics theory that Earth's crust is broken into large sections, or plates, that slowly move over the mantle (diagram, p. 17)

plateau relatively flat area, larger than a mesa, that rises above the surrounding landscape

poaching illegal killing or taking of animals from their natural habitats

polar climate area north of the Arctic Circle and south of the Antarctic Circle where temperatures remain cold year-round and precipitation is low

population density in a country, the average number of people living on each square mile or square kilometer of land (calculated by dividing population by land area)

Prairie Provinces popular name for the Canadian provinces of Manitoba, Saskatchewan, and Alberta

prime meridian imaginary line that runs through Greenwich, England, and is accepted as the line of 0° longitude

projection process of representing the round Earth on a flat surface, such as a map

Glossary

rain shadow dry region on the leeward side of a mountain range

reef offshore ridge made of coral, rocks, or sand. A reef that lies parallel to a coastline and is separated from it by a lagoon is called a barrier reef.

renewable resources resources that are replenished naturally, but the supply of which can be endangered by overuse and pollution

revolution movement of Earth in its orbit around the sun (365 days/1 year)

rotation movement of Earth on its axis (24 hours/1 day)

rural relating to an area outside a city and its surrounding suburbs with low population density and an agricultural economy

Sahel semiarid grassland in Africa along the Sahara's southern border

savanna tropical grassland with scattered trees

scale on a map, a means of explaining the relationship between distances on the map and actual distances on Earth's surface

sea ocean or a partially enclosed body of salt water that is connected to the ocean. Completely enclosed bodies of salt water, such as the Dead Sea, are really lakes.

sea level average surface level of Earth's oceans from which the height of land areas can be measured

Silk Road ancient trade route stretching from China to the Mediterranean

slot canyon very narrow, deep canyon formed by water and wind erosion

small-scale map map, such as a country map, that shows a large area without much detail

sound long, broad inlet of the ocean that lies parallel to the coast and often separates an island and the mainland

Soviet Union shortened name for the Union of Soviet Socialist Republics (U.S.S.R.), a former Communist republic (1920–1991) in eastern Europe and northern and central Asia, made up of 15 republics, of which Russia was the largest

staple chief food of a people's diet

steppe Slavic word referring to relatively flat, mostly treeless temperate grasslands that stretch across much of the central parts of Europe and Asia

strait narrow passage of water that connects two larger bodies of water

Sunbelt U.S. region made up of southern and western states that are experiencing major population in-migration and economic growth

territory land that is under the jurisdiction of a country but is not a state or a province

topography features, such as mountains and valleys, that are evident on Earth's surface

tornado violently rotating column of air associated with thunderstorms

transshipment movement of goods or containers to one location before moving on, often by a different form of transportation, to a final destination

tributary stream that flows into a larger river

tropical cyclone large weather system that forms over warm tropical water. With sustained winds of at least 74 miles an hour (119 km/h), it is called a hurricane in the Atlantic Ocean and eastern Pacific; a cyclone in the Bay of Bengal, Indian Ocean, and South Pacific, and a typhoon in the western Pacific.

tropics region lying within $23^1/2°$ north and south of the Equator that experiences warm temperatures year-round

tsunami very large ocean wave caused by an earthquake or other powerful underwater disturbance, such as a volcanic eruption

urban relating to a city and its densely populated surrounding area with a non-agricultural economy

valley long depression, usually created by a river, that is bordered by higher land

virgin forest forest made up of trees that have never been cut down by humans

volcano opening in Earth's crust through which molten rock erupts. A volcano that has not erupted in the past 10,000 years but is expected to erupt again is said to be dormant.

wat Buddhist monastery or temple in southeastern Asia

windward side or direction that faces the wind

Geo Facts & Figures

PLANET EARTH

Mass:
   6,584,800,000,000,000,000,000 tons
   (5,973,600,000,000,000,000,000
   metric tons)
Distance around the Equator: 24,901 mi
   (40,075 km)
Area: 196,940,000 sq mi
   (510,072,000 sq km)
Land area: 57,506,000 sq mi
   (148,940,000 sq km)
Water area: 139,434,000 sq mi
   (361,132,000 sq km))

The Continents
Asia: 17,208,000 sq mi
   (44,570,000 sq km)
Africa: 11,608,000 sq mi
   (30,065,000 sq km)
North America: 9,449,000 sq mi
   (24,474,000 sq km)
South America: 6,880,000 sq mi
   (17,819,000 sq km)
Antarctica: 5,100,000 sq mi
   (13,209,000 sq km)
Europe: 3,841,000 sq mi
   (9,947,000 sq km)
Australia: 2,970,000 sq mi
   (7,692,000 sq km)

Highest Mountain on Each Continent
Everest, Asia: 29,035 ft (8,850 m)
Cerro Aconcagua, South America:
   22,831 ft (6,959 m)
Denali (Mt. McKinley), North America:
   20,310 ft (6,190 m)
Kilimanjaro, Africa: 19,340 ft
   (5,895 m)
El'brus, Europe: 18,510 ft (5,642 m)
Vinson Massif, Antarctica: 16,067 ft
   (4,897 m)
Kosciuszko, Australia: 7,310 ft
   (2,228 m)

Lowest Point on Each Continent
Byrd Glacier (depression), Antarctica:
   −9,416 ft (−2,870 m)
Dead Sea, Asia: −1,424 ft (−434 m)
Lake Assal, Africa: −509 ft (−155 m)
Laguna del Carbón, South America:
   −344 ft (−105 m)
Death Valley, North America:
   −282 ft (−86 m)
Caspian Sea, Europe: −92 ft (−28 m)
Lake Eyre, Australia: −49 ft (−15 m)

Longest Rivers
Nile, Africa: 4,160 mi (6,695 km)
Amazon, South America: 4,150 mi
   (6,679 km)
Yangtze (Chang), Asia: 3,880 mi
   (6,244 km)
Mississippi-Missouri, North America:
   3,710 mi (5,971 km)
Yenisey-Angara, Asia: 3,610 mi
   (5,810 km)
Yellow (Huang), Asia: 3,590 mi (5,778 km)
Ob-Irtysh, Asia: 3,430 mi (5,520 km)
Amur, Asia: 3,420 mi (5,504 km)
Lena, Asia: 3,200 mi (5,150 km)
Congo, Africa: 3,180 mi (5,118 km)

Largest Islands
Greenland: 836,000 sq mi
   (2,166,000 sq km)
New Guinea: 306,000 sq mi
   (792,500 sq km)
Borneo: 280,100 sq mi (725,500 sq km)
Madagascar: 226,600 sq mi
   (587,000 sq km)
Baffin: 196,000 sq mi (507,500 sq km)
Sumatra: 165,000 sq mi
   (427,300 sq km)
Honshu: 87,800 sq mi (227,400 sq km)
Great Britain: 84,200 sq mi
   (218,100 sq km)
Victoria: 83,900 sq mi (217,300 sq km)
Ellesmere: 75,800 sq mi
   (196,200 sq km)

Oceans
Pacific: 69,000,000 sq mi
   (178,800,000 sq km)
Atlantic: 35,400,000 sq mi
   (91,700,000 sq km)
Indian: 29,400,000 sq mi
   (76,200,000 sq km)
Arctic: 5,600,000 sq mi
   (14,700,000 sq km)

Largest Seas (by area)
Coral: 1,615,500 sq mi
   (4,184,000 sq km)
South China: 1,388,400 sq mi
   (3,596,000 sq km)
Caribbean: 1,094,200 sq mi
   (2,834,000 sq km)
Bering: 973,000 sq mi
   (2,520,000 sq km)
Mediterranean: 953,300 sq mi
   (2,469,000 sq km)
Okhotsk: 627,400 sq mi
   (1,625,000 sq km)
Gulf of Mexico: 591,500 sq mi
   (1,532,000 sq km)
Norwegian: 550,200 sq mi
   (1,425,000 sq km)
Greenland: 447,100 sq mi
   (1,158,000 sq km)
Japan (East Sea): 389,200 sq mi
   (1,008,000 sq km)

Largest Lakes (by area)
Caspian Sea, Europe-Asia: 143,200 sq mi
   (371,000 sq km)
Superior, North America: 31,700 sq mi
   (82,100 sq km)
Victoria, Africa: 26,800 sq mi
   (69,500 sq km)
Huron, North America: 23,000 sq mi
   (59,600 sq km)
Michigan, North America: 22,300 sq mi
   (57,800 sq km)
Tanganyika, Africa: 12,600 sq mi
   (32,600 sq km)
Baikal, Asia: 12,200 sq mi
   (31,500 sq km)

Geo Facts & Figures

Largest Lakes (cont'd)

Great Bear, North America: 12,100 sq mi
 (31,300 sq km)
Malawi (Nyasa), Africa: 11,200 sq mi
 (28,900 sq km)
Great Slave, North America: 11,000 sq mi
 (28,600 sq km)

GEOGRAPHIC EXTREMES

Highest Mountain
Everest, China/Nepal:
 29,035 ft (8,850 m)

Deepest Point in the Ocean
Challenger Deep, Mariana Trench, Pacific:
 -36,037 ft (-10,984 m)

Hottest Place
Dalol, Danakil Depression, Ethiopia:
 annual average temperature 93°F
 (34°C)

Coldest Place
Ridge A, Antarctica:
 annual average temperature -94°F
 (-70°C)

Wettest Place
Mawsynram, Meghalaya, India: annual
 average rainfall 467 in (1,187 cm)

Driest Place
Arica, Atacama Desert, Chile: barely
 measurable rainfall

Largest Hot Desert
Sahara, Africa: 3,475,000 sq mi
 (9,000,000 sq km)

Largest Cold Desert
Antarctica: 5,100,000 sq mi
 (13,209,000 sq km)

PEOPLE

Most Populous Continent
Asia   4,641,055,000

Least Populous Continent
Antarctica   no permanent population
Australia   23,470,000

Population Density by Continent (highest to lowest)

Continent	Density
Asia	269.7 people/sq mi
	104.1 people/sq km
Europe	194.6 people/sq mi
	75.2 people/sq km
Africa	115.5 people/sq mi
	44.6 people/sq km
North America	62.7 people/sq mi
	24.2 people/sq km
South America	62.6 people/sq mi
	24.2 people/sq km
Australia	7.9 people/sq mi
	3.0 people/sq km

Most Populous Country
China   1,384,689,000

Least Populous Country
Vatican City   1,000

Most Densely Populated Countries

Monaco	39,000.0 people/sq mi
	(19,500.0 people/sq km)
Singapore	22,280.6 people/sq mi
	(8,602.6 people/sq km)
Vatican City	5,886.3 people/sq mi
	(2,272.7 people/sq km)
Bahrain	4,917.6 people/sq mi
	(1,898.7 people/sq km)
Malta	3,680.1 people/sq mi
	(1,420.9 people/sq km)
Maldives	3,407.0 people/sq mi
	(1,315.4 people/sq km)
Bangladesh	2,781.8 people/sq mi
	(1,074.0 people/sq km)
Barbados	1,764.8 people/sq mi
	(681.4 people/sq km)
Mauritius	1,731.7 people/sq mi
	(668.6 people/sq km)
Lebanon	1,519.1 people/sq mi
	(586.5 people/sq km)

Least Densely Populated Countries

Mongolia	5.1 people/sq mi
	(2.0 people/sq km)
Australia	7.9 people/sq mi
	(3.0 people/sq km)
Namibia	8.0 people/sq mi
	(3.1 people/sq km)
Iceland	8.7 people/sq mi
	(3.3 people/sq km)
Guyana	8.9 people/sq mi
	(3.4 people/sq km)
Canada	9.3 people/sq mi
	(3.6 people/sq km)
Suriname	9.5 people/sq mi
	(3.7 people/sq km)
Mauritania	9.6 people/sq mi
	(3.7 people/sq km)
Libya	9.9 people/sq mi
	(3.8 people/sq km)

Most Populous Metropolitan Areas

Tokyo, Japan	37,468,000
Delhi, India	30,291,000
Shanghai, China	27,058,000
São Paulo, Brazil	22,043,000
Mexico City, Mexico	21,782,000
Dhaka, Bangladesh	21,006,000
Cairo, Egypt	20,901,000
Beijing, China	20,463,000
Mumbai (Bombay), India	20,411,000
Osaka, Japan	19,165,000

Countries With the Highest Population Growth Rate

Syria	4.25%
Niger	3.66%
Angola	3.43%
Benin	3.40%
Uganda	3.34%
Malawi	3.30%
Chad	3.18%
Democratic Republic of the Congo	3.18%
Mali	2.95%
Zambia	2.89%

Countries With the Lowest Population Growth Rate

Lebanon	-6.68%
Lithuania	-1.13%
Latvia	-1.12%
Moldova	-1.08%
Bulgaria	-0.65%
Estonia	-0.65%
Federated States of Micronesia	-0.6%
Croatia	-0.5%
Serbia	-0.47%
Romania	-0.37%

Countries With the Highest Life Expectancy

Monaco	89 years
Japan	85 years
Singapore	85 years
Andorra	83 years
Iceland	83 years
Israel	83 years
San Marino	83 years
South Korea	83 years
Switzerland	83 years
Australia	82 years
Austria	82 years
Canada	82 years
France	82 years
Italy	82 years
Liechtenstein	82 years
Luxembourg	82 years
Norway	82 years
Spain	82 years

Countries With the Lowest Life Expectancy

Chad	51 years
Guinea-Bissau	51 years
Afghanistan	52 years
Eswatini (Swaziland)	52 years
Gabon	52 years
Central African Republic	53 years
Lesotho	53 years
Somalia	53 years
Zambia	53 years
Mozambique	54 years
Nigeria	54 years

Countries With the Highest Percent Urban Population

Kuwait	100%
Monaco	100%
Nauru	100%
Singapore	100%
Vatican City	100%
Qatar	99.1%
Belgium	98%
San Marino	97.2%
Uruguay	95.3%
Malta	94.6%

Countries With the Lowest Percent Urban Population

Burundi	13%
Papua New Guinea	13.2%
Liechtenstein	14.3%
Niger	16.4%
Malawi	16.9%
Rwanda	17.2%
Samoa	18.2%
Sri Lanka	18.5%
St. Lucia	18.7%
South Sudan	19.6%

Countries With the Highest Gross Domestic Product per Person (PPP)

Liechtenstein	$139,100
Qatar	$124,500
Monaco	$115,700
Luxembourg	$104,000
Singapore	$93,900
Brunei	$78,200
Ireland	$75,500
Norway	$71,800
United Arab Emirates	$67,700
Kuwait	$66,200

Countries With the Lowest Gross Domestic Product per Person (PPP)

Burundi	$700
Central African Republic	$700
Democratic Republic of the Congo	$800
Malawi	$1,200
Mozambique	$1,200
Niger	$1,200
Yemen	$1,300
Liberia	$1,400
South Sudan	$1,500
Comoros	$1,600
Eritrea	$1,600
Madagascar	$1,600
Sierra Leone	$1,600

BACK OF THE BOOK

Geo Facts & Figures

With an adult's help, check out these websites for more information about various topics discussed in this atlas.

Antarctica
www.coolantarctica.com

Biomes
www.blueplanetbiomes.org

Climate change
climate.nasa.gov

Climates
www.worldclimate.com

Countries of the world (statistics)
www.cia.gov/library/publications/resources/the-world-factbook

Endangered species
www.iucnredlist.org

Extreme facts about the world
www.extremescience.com

Flags of the world
www.crwflags.com/fotw/flags

Languages: "Say Hello"
www.ipl.org/div/hello

Mapping the world
www.google.com/earth

National anthems
www.nationalanthems.info

Natural disasters
Earthquakes:
earthquake.usgs.gov/earthquakes
Hurricanes: www.nhc.noaa.gov
Tsunamis: www.tsunami.noaa.gov
Volcanoes:
volcanoes.usgs.gov/index.html

Population
Population clock:
www.census.gov/popclock
World population: www.prb.org/2020-world-population-data-sheet

Religions of the world
www.adherents.com

Solar system
solarsystem.nasa.gov/planets

Time
Time around the world:
www.worldtimeserver.com
Time zones: worldtimezone.com

Weather around the world
weather.com

World Heritage sites
whc.unesco.org/en/list

ABBREVIATIONS

°E	degrees East	L.	Lake	N.Z.	New Zealand
°N	degrees North	LA.	Louisiana	OKLA.	Oklahoma
°S	degrees South	LIECH.	Liechtenstein	OREG.	Oregon
°W	degrees West	LUX.	Luxembourg	P.E.I.	Prince Edward Island
°C	degrees Celsius	m	meters	p.	page
°F	degrees Fahrenheit	MASS.	Massachusetts	pp.	pages
AFGHAN.	Afghanistan	MD.	Maryland	PA.	Pennsylvania
ALA.	Alabama	ME.	Maine	Pen.	Peninsula
ARK.	Arkansas	mi	miles	R.I.	Rhode Island
B.&H.	Bosnia and Herzegovina	MICH.	Michigan	Rep.	Republic
BELG.	Belgium	MINN.	Minnesota	S	South
COLO.	Colorado	MISS.	Mississippi	S. DAK.	South Dakota
CONN.	Connecticut	MO.	Missouri	S.C.	South Carolina
D.C.	District of Columbia	MONT.	Montana	sq km	square kilometers
DEL.	Delaware	MONT.	Montenegro	sq mi	square miles
DEM.	Democratic	Mt.	Mount, Mountain	St., Ste.	Saint, Sainte
E	East	Mts.	Mountains	Str.	Strait
FLA.	Florida	N	North	SWITZ.	Switzerland
ft	feet	N. DAK.	North Dakota	TENN.	Tennessee
GA.	Georgia	N. MEX.	New Mexico	U.A.E.	United Arab Emirates
GDP	Gross Domestic Product	N.B.	New Brunswick	U.K.	United Kingdom
I.	Island	N.C.	North Carolina	U.S./U.S.A.	United States
ILL.	Illinois	N.H.	New Hampshire	VA.	Virginia
IND.	Indiana	N.J.	New Jersey	VT.	Vermont
Is.	Islands	N.P.	National Park	W	West
KANS.	Kansas	N.Y.	New York	W. VA.	West Virginia
km	kilometers	NEBR.	Nebraska	WASH.	Washington
KY.	Kentucky	NETH.	Netherlands	WIS.	Wisconsin
KYRG.	Kyrgyzstan	NEV.	Nevada	WYO.	Wyoming

Metric Conversions

CONVERSION TO METRIC MEASURES

SYMBOL	WHEN YOU KNOW	MULTIPLY BY	TO FIND	SYMBOL
		LENGTH		
in	inches	2.54	centimeters	cm
ft	feet	0.30	meters	m
yd	yards	0.91	meters	m
mi	miles	1.61	kilometers	km
		AREA		
in²	square inches	6.45	square centimeters	cm²
ft²	square feet	0.09	square meters	m²
yd²	square yards	0.84	square meters	m²
mi²	square miles	2.59	square kilometers	km²
--	acres	0.40	hectares	ha
		MASS		
oz	ounces	28.35	grams	g
lb	pounds	0.45	kilograms	kg
--	short tons	0.91	metric tons	t
		VOLUME		
in³	cubic inches	16.39	milliliters	mL
liq oz	liquid ounces	29.57	milliliters	mL
pt	pints	0.47	liters	L
qt	quarts	0.95	liters	L
gal	gallons	3.79	liters	L
ft³	cubic feet	0.03	cubic meters	m³
yd³	cubic yards	0.76	cubic meters	m³
		TEMPERATURE		
°F	degrees Fahrenheit	5/9 after subtracting 32	degrees Celsius (centigrade)	°C

CONVERSION FROM METRIC MEASURES

SYMBOL	WHEN YOU KNOW	MULTIPLY BY	TO FIND	SYMBOL
		LENGTH		
cm	centimeters	0.39	inches	in
m	meters	3.28	feet	ft
m	meters	1.09	yards	yd
km	kilometers	0.62	miles	mi
		AREA		
cm²	square centimeters	0.16	square inches	in²
m²	square meters	10.76	square feet	ft²
m²	square meters	1.20	square yards	yd²
km²	square kilometers	0.39	square miles	mi²
ha	hectares	2.47	acres	--
		MASS		
g	grams	0.04	ounces	oz
kg	kilograms	2.20	pounds	lb
t	metric tons	1.10	short tons	--
		VOLUME		
mL	milliliters	0.06	cubic inches	in³
mL	milliliters	0.03	liquid ounces	liq oz
L	liters	2.11	pints	pt
L	liters	1.06	quarts	qt
L	liters	0.26	gallons	gal
m³	cubic meters	35.31	cubic feet	ft³
m³	cubic meters	1.31	cubic yards	yd³
		TEMPERATURE		
°C	degrees Celsius (centigrade)	9/5 then add 32	degrees Fahrenheit	°F

Index

Map references are in boldface (**58**) type. Letters and numbers following in lightface (D12) locate the place-names using the map grid. (Refer to page 7 for more details.)

1st Cataract — Arkansas

Bioko — Central Russian Upland

Delhi — Fraser Plateau

Happy Valley — Juiz de Fora

Lake Region – Marcus Island

Namsos — Oodaaq Island

BACK OF THE BOOK

BACK OF THE BOOK

Solimões — Tibet, Plateau of

BACK OF THE BOOK

Vladikavkaz — Arabian Sea

Arafura Sea — Galápagos Fracture Zone

Galápagos Rift — North Australian Basin